BEYOND OVERSIGHT

Developing Grassroots Nonprofit Boards for Community and Institutional Change

David P. Moxley

NASW PRESS

National Association of Social Workers
Washington, DC

James J. Kelly, PhD, ACSW, LCSW, President
Elizabeth J. Clark, PhD, ACSW, MPH, Executive Director

Cheryl Y. Bradley, *Publisher*
Lisa M. O'Hearn, *Managing Editor*
John Cassels, *Project Manager and Staff Editor*
Dac Nelson, *Copyeditor*
Lori J. Holtzinger, *Proofreader and Indexer*

Cover by Larnish & Associates
Interior design by Electronic Quill
Printed and bound by Victor Graphics

Library of Congress Cataloging-in-Publication Data

Moxley, David (David P.)
Beyond oversight: developing grassroots nonprofit boards for community and institutional change / David P. Moxley.
    p. cm.
  Includes bibliographical references and index.
  ISBN 978-0-87101-401-6
  1. Nonprofit organizations—Management. 2. Social work administration. 3. Associations, institutions, etc.—Management. I. Title.
  HD62.6.M687 2010
  658.4'22—dc22

2010045344

Printed in the United States of America

CONTENTS

To Norbu of the Europa generation.
May the obelisk guide you to the source.

About the Author

David P. Moxley, PhD, DPA, is a member of the faculty of the Anne and Henry Zarrow School of Social Work at the University of Oklahoma, Norman, and teaches in the school's graduate concentration on administration and community practice. Focusing on the development of social work practice in community health, particularly in the integration of health and social services, he serves as the Oklahoma Healthcare Authority Medicaid endowed professor and professor of social work. Moxley came to the University of Oklahoma from Wayne State University in Detroit, where, for over 20 years, he served on the faculty of the School of Social Work. With considerable experience in action research, Moxley combines inquiry with technical assistance to grassroots community service organizations—entities that have global significance, are emerging rapidly given the numerous challenges societies face in the provision of social and human services, and form the backbone of social innovation worldwide. His work cuts across multiple fields of human services and social welfare, including serious mental illness, developmental disabilities, youth services, and aging. The common thread is innovation in community support of people who can benefit from enhanced support in the face of multiple life challenges, which often involve serious health concerns.

Penetration to the meaning of a thing or process as distinct from the ability to describe it exactly involves a participation by the knower in the known.

—Owen Barfield, "The Rediscovery of Meaning,"
Saturday Evening Post, January 7, 1961

The question is: What kind of person, institution, or community will result from following a particular course of conduct or from adopting a given rule or policy? This focuses attention on the internal relevance of what we do; and it allows the conclusion that consequences for character will have priority, in many important cases, over consequences for particular ends such as winning a game or managing an enterprise.

—Philip Selznick, *The Moral Commonwealth:
Social Theory and the Promise of Community*, 1992

THE CONCEPT OF BOARD DEVELOPMENT

Two Board Members at Lunch

Sally (the board chair): What do you think we should do in the next year to develop the board of the agency?

Sam (the recruitment chair): Recruit a few more members who will work harder than the ones we have.

Sally: Don't you think board development is something more than just getting new members?

Sam: No.

Purpose and Focus of the Book

This book is intended for those people who are interested in boards of community service organizations. It is for those people who believe that board development is more than the recruitment of new members—that it involves something more, such as the development of vision and focus. I write this book for those individuals who have undertaken leadership roles in community service organizations and agencies. Most often nonprofit, these organizations form voluntarily to address some of the most pressing needs society faces. Those issues come in many different forms and reflect various sectors of society, including ecology and animal rights, human rights, economic and community development, and health and human services, to name a few.

Throughout the United States, hundreds and hundreds of small experiments are occurring in which citizens from many different backgrounds come together into voluntary nonprofit organizations. These organizations seek to advance the public good and public interest in a range of areas like the arts, community service, and social service (Clifton & Dahms, 1993; Hamilton & Tragert, 1998). They push forward new ideas about justice and equity (Horton, 1998) and about the provision of social utilities like the education of children and youths (Meier, 1995) and health care (Salamon & Anheier, 1996).

Despite a cynicism that has shrouded U.S. social welfare for a number of decades (Champagne & Harpham, 1984; Perlmuter, 1984), these organizations—often described as "grassroots" agencies—are experimenting with potential solutions to vexing social problems. Sometimes with the support of foundations, the public sector, and corporations—other times through their own means and devices—these agencies often offer innovative responses and solutions. They are energized by strong commitments to making an impact on some kind of community problem, or fulfilling some kind of human need (Turnbull, 1995).

This book focuses on the boards of these organizations because these structures are so fundamental to the success of community and social service agencies as they try new ways of advancing quality of life, the support of people who face serious social problems, and the development of community (Rifkin, 1995). A community service board exists to govern an agency, typically a nonprofit one. It offers agency management and staff members both policy leadership and policy development to guide the direction of the organization in its service or community activities.

Through my own research on board structures—as well as my direct experience with boards as a consultant, a member, and as a consumer of board decisions and actions during my service as an agency administrator—I have personally experienced the importance of board performance.

In these various roles with boards, I discovered that many of them have become preoccupied with a narrowly defined function, typically focusing on accountability and trusteeship (Miller, 1988). I do not want to present as unimportant the monitoring of executive performance, fiscal performance, and the fulfillment of the expectations of external funders, but these activities receive their share of attention in a number of other books and monographs on the governing boards of nonprofit and voluntary agencies. Indeed, as privatization, contractual arrangements, or purchase of service arrangements have become basic tools of social policy, many board members see their role as holding the agency accountable for its performance in an environment in which the voluntary organization is an extension of the public or private sectors.

The lines between private and public are increasingly blurred in the United States as all levels of government remove themselves from the direct provision of services and transfer these service functions to the voluntary sector (Bozeman, 1987), and now more recently to an emerging for-profit sector. The business model that is now so in vogue in human and social services has gained ascendancy (Osborne & Gaebler, 1992). Boards based on trusteeship—that is, those that conceive of their role as ensuring the "proper" running and accountability of the agency—may very well be the most prominent type of governance structure (Gummer, 1990).

Board Development as Stewardship

But this book is not merely about trusteeship. It focuses on board development as an expression of stewardship. Many voluntary and nonprofit community and social service agencies emerge out of social action (Bettencourt, 1996). They are often tied to a social movement and become one concrete expression of this movement (Silberberg, 1997).

The members of the boards of these agencies often come together because they are dissatisfied or disaffected. They may be disaffected and alarmed by how people coping with HIV/AIDS drift into poverty and become isolated in their communities. They may be alarmed and angered by the mistreatment of women. They may be concerned about supporting gay and lesbian citizens who face a cruel and disparaging society. They may be indignant about the discrimination and stigma experienced by people with serious mental illness as they cope with inhospitable and isolating communities. Or they may address the economic state of the community (Henton, Melville, & Walesh, 1997). These board members, especially early in the development of their agencies, may be people who have actually experienced firsthand the insults and deprivations experienced by the people the agency has chosen to represent and for whom they wish to advocate (Bettencourt, 1996; Hick & McNutt, 2002). Their experiences with the "problem" the agency seeks to address are primary—based on first-person experience—rather than secondary like those possessed by professionals and lay advocates (Ezell, 2001; Schneider & Lester, 2001; D. Smith, 1997).

The call of trusteeship does not typically bring these kinds of people into board structures. The desire to steward an agency toward more effective and relevant solutions to the social problem that has served as the organizing impulse of the agency may be a salient if not principal motivating force for board membership. Trusteeship becomes salient when boards must confront the reality of financial viability: They find that they need to secure funds to advance their cause from state and federal sources, from private federated sources like the United Way, or from foundation and corporate sources. Trusteeship may also become important when the agency is confronted with formalizing and growing. But growth and development are two different things. "Growth" involves the expansion of size and mass. *"Development" involves the creation of increasingly sophisticated and competent structures to achieve a desired end state* (Ackoff, 1991; Gawthrop, 1984).

The stewards are often far ahead of the trustees. It is not unusual for boards of community service agencies to adopt a vanguard role (Hasenfeld, 1983; Kramer, 1981). They undertake on their own the organization and delivery of services and community supports to populations whose needs are not legitimized and consequently not addressed by those institutions responsible for identifying needs and problems and planning and financing solutions (Garr, 1995). Witness the vanguard role in action in such diverse areas as mental retardation, autism, domestic violence, HIV/AIDS, serious mental illness, homelessness, and epilepsy in which advocates created systems of support and service—often innovative ones—well before the funders were willing to recognize that a need or problem existed. Those boards incorporating stewardship perhaps are the ones willing to engage in vigorous resource development. They establish bold visions, assert the human rights of the people who bear the negative effects of serious social problems, and create networks among and between people to sponsor responses to these negative effects (Chait, Holland, & Taylor, 1996). Stewardship can involve the emotional side of social action—board membership can demand a sort of empathic engagement and emotional awareness of the issue at hand combined with an intellectual rigor demanding a full understanding of the dimensions of the given social issue.

Trusteeship expresses the contractual and the business aspects of the agency whereas stewardship expresses spirit, compassion, and commitment. Perhaps trusteeship is the more rational face of the board whereas stewardship is the more irrational or affective face. But without stewardship, the board will likely lack the energy it requires to create the "good" it seeks to produce on behalf of a community, a population, or a group of people (Block, 1993).

Concept of Board Development

For me, as author, stewardship and development go hand in hand. By *development* I mean the intentional and purposeful enhancement and improvement of board resources, structure, and performance over time. The "developing board" is a structure that becomes very conscious of what it is trying to do, why it is trying to do it, and how it wants to do it. By virtue of this kind of clarity, informed by well thought out means and ends, the board of the community service organization can begin to identify the strengths and assets it needs to make it robust, resilient, and effective. These challenges must be met using all of the resources of the board to make the agency effective. My hypothesis is this: *A strong board, a developing board, creates a strong and developing agency.* The strong board is purposeful both in its establishment of vision for the agency it seeks to steward, and in the development of its own resources that it needs to undertake this stewardship successfully. The board has a vitality that is created through a conscious commitment to its own development (Zander, 1993).

Relevant Audiences

Board development is critical because the work of community agencies is critical. This simple observation establishes the relevant audiences of this book. It is intended for those board members who see themselves developing as stewards of the agencies they govern. It is intended for those executives and agency admin-istrators who see the need for the development of vital and energetic boards. It is intended for agency staff members who are involved in board committees and other structures. And it is intended for those students who want to learn about how boards can develop with an eye toward their own involvement in a board of a community and social service agency. Those readers who are more interested in the trustee function of the board can look elsewhere for very fine and relevant materi-als, such as the work by Carver and Carver (1997).

Boards committed to their development may want to incorporate this book into their own continuing education and knowledge-building endeavors. The book can be useful in the orientation process that helps board members, advisory com-mittee members, and staff members gain an understanding of board development as a process and outcome. It can offer board members an understanding of how to proceed with their own board development plan and it offers strategies to the board on how to implement board development through (1) strengthening internal pro-cesses and structures, (2) linking to the agency, and (3) linking to the community. Thus, the book stands as an "on-the-shelf" resource. It can be referenced to gain an understanding of a specific board development need or to address this need (for example, formulation of vision). It can be used as an action guide to create a board development plan, and as a continuing education resource to orient board mem-bers and to help them to become informed about board development.

Organization of the Book

The book is organized into six principal sections. It comprises 18 chapters in addi-tion to the Prologue and Epilogue. Section 1 places board development into the context of a changing policy environment and identifies the properties of the devel-oping board. This section underscores the vital role served by community and social service organizations in a social policy context that increasingly constrains human services at a time when there is considerable need for innovation in grassroots, community-based service organizations. Section 2 examines the development of the board as a complex system, including its institutional, functional, performance, and lifespan dimensions.

Section 3 examines the development of board identity and presents the two principal questions that a board must answer to develop in a viable manner. Section 4 devotes four chapters to the support of board development involving the board development mission, the board development committee, the leadership of board members, and the interface between the agency and the board. The three chap-ters of section 5 examine the development of board members, whereas section 6 examines board development as a cycle that incorporates self-evaluation, the board development retreat, and the board development plan.

At the end of each chapter, I offer some questions to prompt further thinking, and perhaps to provoke discussion and debate among board members. I recommend their use as exercises useful in extending the thinking of board members about their roles and functions within community and social service agencies.

My hope is that this volume serves as a relevant resource to the boards of community and social service agencies. Many of these agencies are involved in heroic work that is quite demanding and trying at times. We need to reflect, now more than ever, on how important these organizations are to the realization of strong communities and to compassionate responses to human need. We need to reflect, now more than ever, on how essential high-performing boards are to the realization of effectiveness and vitality on the part of these agencies. Although boards will most likely continue to be in the background of the day-to-day work of these agencies, the contributions they make to effectiveness, innovation, and high performance cannot and should not be overlooked. Board development is essential to agency performance and must be an objective of those structures that can influence development the most: that is, the boards that steward community and social service agencies.

Questions for Board Discussion

1. Is board development important to your agency or organization? What reasons support the need to engage in board development? Why is it important to the success of the agency or organization?
2. What external forces are operating on the agency that make board development relevant at this time? Describe these forces and characterize how they influence the agency. Why are they significant to board development?
3. What are the current functions of your board? Is the board satisfied or dissatisfied with these functions? Should they change in light of the external forces operating on the agency?
4. Characterize the stewardship of the board. What activities undertaken by your board indicate that it engages in the stewardship of the agency?
5. What is the board's vision of its role? How does it want to develop to better achieve this role on behalf of the agency?

AN OVERVIEW OF BOARD DEVELOPMENT

This section introduces and frames board development as a fundamental responsibility of the boards of community service organizations. Board development is presented as a process in which community service boards foster the viability of the agencies they govern by strengthening their own functioning and performance in an intentional manner.

Thus, the process of board development is both thoughtful and intentional, requiring the community service board to reflect on its strengths and needs and to undertake activities that lead to furthering the performance of this vital organizational system. Chapter 1 underscores the imperative of board development addressing the numerous external and internal factors that create the need for this form of organizational improvement and change. In addition, the imperative of board development also comes from the motivation of board members themselves who actualize their commitment to community service through the strengthening and development of the board system. Chapter 1 also presents board development as a quality of the board as an exemplary system. Board development lies beyond "typical" or "routine" board practice in a region labeled by contemporary organizational theorists as "high performance" (Hanna, 1988; Nelson & Burns, 1984). The high-performance board is very concerned with its own development because it holds high expectations of community service, and of the agency that is chartered to realize these expectations (Chait, Holland, & Taylor, 1993).

Chapter 2 summarizes the conditions of high performance. Five properties of board development are offered as essential to the achievement of high performance:

1. energy to devote to board development (Ackoff, 1991),
2. a rich vision of community service that infuses board development with relevance (Kiefer & Senge, 1984),
3. a strong set of beliefs within the board that inform the substance of community service (Kiefer & Senge, 1984),
4. a commitment to continuous improvement (Kennedy, 1991), and
5. a commitment to continuous or progressive learning (Kline & Saunders, 1993).

These properties offer a set of basic qualities that frame and propel board development as a fundamental responsibility of the community service board.

The rationale offered within chapters 1 and 2 reminds us that board development is not elusive, but is very real to those boards that are staking out great expectations in the diverse areas of community service represented among nonprofit, public, and quasipublic organizations. Board development is or can be a basic strategy by which community service boards achieve higher levels of performance.

▪ 1 ▪

Imperative of Board Development
in Community Service

A Board Dialogue

Board President: The strategic planning process shows us that the agency is facing a number of challenges that it must successfully address in the next two years in order for it to be successful.

Board Member: Well, we all understand this, so what changes will the executive director make in order to meet these challenges?

Board President: The executive director has a very clear agenda. But what isn't clear is our own agenda. A critical question for us—the board—is how do we need to develop in order to meet these challenges so the agency will be successful?

Board Member: What do you mean, the board needs to change? Isn't it our responsibility to make sure that the agency changes? I think you are off track here.

Factors Creating a Need for Board Development

This segment of dialogue reveals a board that may be unattached or disconnected from the agency. Ignoring the challenge of board development can place any community service board in jeopardy. Indeed, board development may be one of the principal responsibilities a board must execute to ensure the viability of the nonprofit or public service agency it oversees. Its importance cannot be denied. And its execution cannot be ignored lest the agency find itself in peril. The dialogue illustrates a board that is unprepared for undertaking board development and it suggests that this particular board may fail to see itself as a fundamental system of the whole organization.

But the idea of board development is most likely familiar to numerous boards and their members who recognize the importance or perhaps the necessity of intentionally changing in service to higher levels of agency performance. This higher level of performance may be induced by internal sentiment among board members that more needs to be undertaken by the board to improve the performance of the nonprofit or public service organization it sponsors and governs (B. Collins & Huge, 1993). Some board members may be dissatisfied with the performance of the board and anxious to resolve those issues standing in the way of better performance or to enhanced functioning on part of the board. However, it is more likely that changes to the board—in terms of how it functions and undertakes its work—are not exclusively motivated by member dissatisfaction although this should not be discounted as a powerful factor.

There are likely a number of factors—especially those involving changes in the agency's external environment and those involving changes in the organization—that push for development of the board and the enhancement of its performance (Holland, Leslie, & Holzhalb, 1993). Those factors in the organization's environment, like new ways of funding or financing services, new technologies, emergent social problems, or community and political changes may suggest with some urgency that changes must occur to the board or the agency will not survive or will not prosper. These changes or developments in the agency's environment may be reflected in events that occur internally within the organization. There are numerous events: the recruitment of a new chief executive officer; the emergence of new service populations that want the services the agency offers, or technological changes requiring new capital equipment like computers and telecommunications; growth of the agency that requires new facilities or changes to physical plant; the need for new resources to address service populations in flexible and innovative ways. These are just a handful of examples.

Changes or developments in the agency's environment may change the composition of the board, such as when new members join bringing with them new perspectives about agency purpose, mission, or aims. These new perspectives may be products of the roles new board members hold within the community (for example, as a consumer representative or as a representative of the business community). Or they may be products of the previous experience these board members have had with other community service boards or with the problem or need addressed by the agency.

A survey of board development practices undertaken by Brudney and Murray (1997) validate my own observations from board development projects: There is never one motivating factor for board development. Motivation for board development comes from a combination of factors that trigger a perceived need for improvement among board leaders. This perception can alter the attitudes of board members and legitimize board development as a responsibility of the board. One thing is certain—board development does not emerge in a vacuum but is stimulated by critical changes to the agency in the context of its environment (Harris, 1993). It is in this sense, therefore, that board development is one of the most important undertakings of an agency because it has the potential of assisting it to achieve a stronger or a higher level of performance within a given environment. In other words, board development is linked to agency performance and from a strategic perspective it is a principal means to position the community service agency on the path to relevance (Levitt, 2008).

Board as a System of Governance

The board is the principal system of governance of the community and public service agency. Often textbooks on social administration refer to the board as the strategic apex of the agency responsible for major decisions that influence what the agency is, how it conducts its business, and what outcomes it achieves.

As the system of governance within the agency, the board performs like any other system of governance. It oversees the performance of the agency that often involves monitoring the work and performance of the chief executive officer and sets and controls the budget of the agency. But, as noted above, these are ordinary tasks and responsibilities. They are consistent with governance as trusteeship. We can also broaden the scope of the board by considering its responsibilities as a policy-making body committed to steering and influencing the agency through the formulation and evaluation of policy that guides the substantive work and direction of the community and public service organization (Middleton, 1987). As a policy-making body, the board offers to the agency broad guidelines, priorities, and prescriptive statements that establish how the agency will achieve both its purpose and mission (Levitt, 2008). The board also can be instrumental in helping the agency shape its value proposition: the value it brings to the community to advance its quality of life (Joyce, Nohria, & Roberson, 2003).

We can continue to broaden the scope of the board by identifying its key responsibilities involving the shaping of organizational image, identity, and character. Boards often execute these institutional features through the identification of critical values and beliefs and their use in practice to shape agency identity and character. To build the institutional dimension of the board, it must function as a system of governance. The board must have the capacity to perform as a system of governance (Houle, 1989, 1997). It must also change as the community and public service agency changes in response to new needs, new problems and issues, new environments and policies, and new technologies (Holland et al., 1993). Thus, we cannot separate what the board is from where it stands in the lifespan of the agency.

A basic premise of this volume is that we cannot give a simple definition to what a board is other than to identify it as a principal if not the principal governance structure of the community and public service agency. But to truly understand the board as a governance system we must understand each of its four dimensions and how these dimensions are executed in practice:

1. The *institutional dimension* focuses on the role of the board in developing and establishing an overall framework of agency identity that informs and guides organizational purpose, mission, and performance.
2. The *functional dimension* focuses on the board's development of those core functions that are needed to actually govern the community and public service agency.
3. The *performance dimension* focuses on how the board organizes to undertake its work so it can produce what the organization requires.
4. The *lifespan dimension* requires the board to be sensitive to how the phase of agency lifespan influences the work and organization of the board.

Taken collectively, these four dimensions define what a board is as a system and how it governs the community and public service organization. Their formation creates a number of challenges to board development. These challenges are addressed in subsequent chapters of the book, especially in section 2.

Definition of Board Development

Boards of nonprofit and public service agencies grapple with numerous changes and the forces motivating their adoption. Table 1-1 identifies five examples of these changes and the factors motivating them. They reveal that board development can focus on a number of different dimensions. Yet an inspection of the factors motivating change suggest that a board engages in its own development because this work advances the performance of the agency by meeting new needs, successfully meeting challenges, and addressing those critical issues that, if left unresolved, will compromise the effectiveness of the agency.

The scope of these changes identified in Table 1-1 is somewhat different, but the changes themselves are profound. They are profound because they can—and often do—demand new performance on part of the board, and this new performance raises the question of whether the board is actually prepared to meet the challenges of agency change by focusing on its own change. This is the essence of board development. This means that the board has the abilities, competencies, and motivation to change or alter itself intentionally. It does so to meet the challenges faced by the agency the board sponsors and governs and the challenges the board faces in executing effectively its sponsorship and governance of the agency.

Board as an Organizational System

The board can be an ordinary or extraordinary system depending on the perspective and motivation of the board as a whole and of its individual members. The meaning of the word *ordinary* is found in the concepts of "giving order" and

TABLE 1-1: Five Examples of Changes to an Agency Board and Factors Motivating These Changes

I. **The Size of the Board Increases**

A self-audit of the board revealed that the agency's environment has changed, revealing board development needs:

- The board needs technical expertise essential to mission performance.
- The board needs linkages to its essential social markets, recipient groups, and community groups.
- The board needs to harness the energy of advocates for the people it serves.

II. **The Board Endorses an Agency Outcome Evaluation System**

Purchasers are demanding outcome accountability, and recipients want greater choice over service selection and outcomes.

III. **The Board Expands Its Role to Incorporate Resource Development**

Funding streams limit agency discretion over the use of funds at a time when the agency has a number of needs that, if left unfulfilled, can compromise its mission.

IV. **The Board Adopts a Strategy and Task Force on Information Technology**

The agency is lagging behind in the acquisition and use of information technology, and this jeopardizes the quality of all agency services and the ability of the agency to achieve its mission.

V. **The Board Adopts a Code of Ethical Conduct on the Part of All Who Are Affiliated with the Agency**

Several incidents have compromised the reputation of the agency and have placed it in political and legal jeopardy.

"offering or achieving routine." In this sense, the board as an ordinary organizational system means that it links with other internal organizational systems such as the executive system, the supervisory system, and the planning system to assist the agency to achieve order and routine.

The board as an ordinary organizational system is consistent with the idea of trusteeship. Board members as trustees oversee the agency as a whole offering guidance and direction and achieving regularity, accountability, and propriety (Neugeboren, 1985). Development of the board as an "ordinary system" requires the board to acquire those skills, competencies, and resources the agency needs to perform and remain legal. *Performance,* here, means to achieve those standards external bodies establish that legitimate the agency through funding, contractual relations, accreditation, certification, and licensure (Rosenthal & Young, 1980).

Those boards that are "extraordinary systems" go beyond the offer of order and routine to the community service agency to initiate conditions of high performance (Hanna, 1988). The idea of high performance means the nonprofit or public service agency has the skills, competencies, resources, and motivation to make a profound impact on the problem or need that it seeks to address or fulfill. In other words, the board ensures that the agency adds considerable value to the life of the community (Egan, 1993) and can sustain this value over time.

The pursuit of high performance by a board is justified by a number of different social forces. The seriousness of social problems many nonprofit and public service organizations address demands exceptional or extraordinary performance on the part of these agencies (Garr, 1995). Creativity, innovation, and dedicated service are required to make an impact on these problems (Kramer, 1981; Perlmutter, 1988). These social problems—like school dropout, community violence, and homelessness, to identify just a few—must be addressed by highly motivated organizations that go beyond a level of ordinary performance to achieve a level of extraordinary performance (Behn, 1991).

We can also recognize a rationale for high performance based on consumerism. Many people who receive service and support from nonprofit and public service organizations are the most stigmatized and neglected citizens in our communities. Often, it is the nonprofit or public service organization that voluntarily accepts the responsibility for serving people of diminished status (Lee, 1989). The board recognizes that it is essential to assist these individuals to address the needs and problems they experience in the community in the most effective manner possible because without such a commitment people can actually suffer.

The transfer of the responsibility for meeting social needs from government to nonprofit and public service organizations through privatization is another motivating factor necessitating the achievement of high performance (S. Smith & Lipsky, 1993). Privatization means that nonprofit and public service organizations are executing those responsibilities once undertaken solely by governments such as cultural enrichment and the arts, public information, housing, education, health care, and recreation (Salamon & Anheier, 1996). This transfer of responsibility has been advocated on the basis that these organizations can get closer to consumers, perform less bureaucratically, and deliver a service with more quality, innovation, and creativity compared with the public sector (Osborne & Gaebler, 1992). Thus, the expectation for higher performance is embedded in the actual policy of privatization.

And last, the expectation of high performance is framed by the idealism many community service agencies express (Gawthrop, 1984). This self-defined idealism can establish high expectations, in the form of standards, and high aspirations as well. This idealism extends from the board's establishment of high expectations of performance based on a commitment to civil society, the stewardship of individuals and groups of people who may face rejection and discrimination in their daily lives, and the fostering of a richer or more varied community life (Selznick, 1992). The quality of idealism can invigorate the work of a board and can infuse meaning into its work. In a sense, it may be the most critical attribute to develop within a board because it forms the essence of community and public service (Raskin, 1986).

Conclusion

From my own work as a board consultant, I have found that a board committed to extraordinary performance will likely adopt a board development agenda that is more ambitious, focused, strategic, and dynamic than a board that conceives of its performance in ordinary ways (Kiefer & Senge, 1984). The rationale for board development adopted by the extraordinary board is based on a sense of purpose and a sense of commitment to high performance for without such purpose and commitment the board recognizes that the ultimate measure of agency effectiveness will go unrealized (Pascarella & Frohman, 1989). That is, the board in conjunction with the agency as a whole fails to achieve those outcomes that are needed to improve the life situations of the people, groups, and communities it serves.

The board can and should be a high-performance system with expectations of itself that meet or exceed those it holds for the chief executive officer as well as for other parts of the agency. In addition, as a high-performance system the board should look to itself to see that it is setting the tone and momentum for agency performance as a whole. In this sense, the board as an organizational system is a "leading part" (Ackoff, 1991). Its purpose is to lead the agency to higher levels of performance, to lead the agency to execute its purpose, and to lead the agency toward mission effectiveness (Bennis & Nanus, 1985). The "developing" board finds its own purpose in this leadership—to anticipate agency change through its own functioning and to strengthen the performance of the agency by infusing into the organization new leadership skills, competencies, and resources at the highest level of agency purpose.

Questions for Board Discussion

1. What are the principal responsibilities of your board? How does board development fit into these responsibilities?
2. How strong is the motivation for board development within the board? Within the executive committee of the board? Among the leadership of the board?
3. What is your board's definition of board development? How does it compare or differ from the one this chapter offers?

4. What are the core expectations the board holds for itself? What are the core expectations the board holds for the members of the board? What are the core expectations the board holds for the committees of the board?
5. If your board decides that board development is a need, what do you hope to achieve through such a program? What is the vision among board members about how the board will look and function at the end of this program?
6. What developmental needs does this chapter illuminate for the board? How will the board act on these needs?

■2■

Five Properties of the Developing Board

Executive Director: The board is an outstanding role model for the staff. Whenever a staff member asks why we are working so hard I just say, "Look at the board. They show us the kind of commitment that is needed to really serve people who are challenged by AIDS."

Board Member: I am happy to hear this. As you know, most board members come to the board because they have been personally touched by this pandemic. But many of them felt that they didn't have the technical business skills to oversee the agency. You know, I tell them that the energy they have, the vision they have about improving people's lives, and their deep ethical commitment to accessible and responsive health care, will make them successful as a board.

Executive Director: More and more of my time is devoted to working with the board. It has been very concerned with improving its own performance and with learning as much as it can about how this agency can better serve people and their families. I've never seen a board more dedicated to achieving higher and higher performance.

Board Member: We know the stakes are high. If the board and the agency are not successful, what will people do?

As emphasized in the previous chapter, effective boards are vital to the work of community service agencies. The board represents a key organizational system and without this system working effectively the realization of an agency's mission may be severely compromised. We can think of the developing board as a high-performance system—one committed to the development of the agency through its own development.

High-performance systems are highly productive and their work results in the achievement of highly valued outcomes (Katzenbach & Smith, 1993). High-performance systems have the energy to undertake their work and are able to use their aspirations, vision, and ethical commitments to frame and direct this energy. Understanding that it cannot get to its preferred destination without considerable ongoing improvement, the high-performance system understands that success will require it to improve as it pursues its vision (Bergquist, 1993). Progressive learning becomes an essential feature of high performance (Kline & Saunders, 1993).

Those properties useful in thinking about a high-performance organizational system are also useful in thinking about board development. A framework organizing these five dimensions is presented in Figure 2-1, a pictorial representation of board development. The five dimensions are (1) energy or aspirations, (2) vision, (3) moral–ethical commitment, (4) continuous improvement, and (5) progressive learning. Bringing these properties together into a single board is a challenge but it is possible.

Property 1: The Board Has Energy to Invest in Its Development

The motivation of the board to engage in board development is based on the energy brought to the situation by individual members and the board as a group. Certainly, to engage in any kind of developmental activity, the system must have available to it the energy to undertake the necessary changes (Gawthrop, 1984). Boards with high energy will be looking for work and responsibilities to undertake and although a board may err on the side of being overzealous, it is probably easier to address this excess than it is to try to motivate a board that does not have much energy.

The direction of this energy is as important as the amount of it. Raw energy undirected can be destructive and can lead a board into disarray, into unproductive

FIGURE 2-1: A Pictorial Representation of the Properties of Board Development

I. Energy/Aspirations	II. Vision
The Board has Energy to Invest in Its Development	The Board has a Clear Conception of a Highly Valued End State

V. Progressive Learning

The Board Commits to Its Own Learning

III. Moral-Ethical Commitments	IV. Continuous Improvement
The Board has a Strong Belief System to Steer Its Work	The Board Acts to Improve Continuously

conflict, into micromanagement, and into disjointed or fragmented action (Eadie, 1991). Energy, however, is harnessed and directed through the aspirations of board members. These aspirations are found, in part, in what motivates people to join a board. However, these motivations usually are not enough to give direction to the energy of board members. Some board members aspire to be members of elite boards in which they can make connections and network for personal or business interests whereas other members aspire to the board to earn recognition. Although the board recognizes and accepts these motivations, board development requires that the board uses its energy to create and foster aspirations among its members that are in line with the purpose and distinctiveness of the agency (Wilkins, 1989).

There are three crucial aspirations that establish among the board expectations about agency performance: (1) aspirations for the people the agency serves, (2) aspirations for agency performance, and (3) aspirations for the impact of the agency on the problems and needs it has been founded to address. These collective aspirations are crucial. They relegate to a secondary level those motivations or aspirations of board members based on self-interest (for example, service on the board leads to status enhancement). They help the board to channel the energy of board members as individuals and as a group into achieving outcomes for the agency as a whole (Senge, 1990). And the emergence of collective aspiration—those held by the board as a whole—supports the formation of a focused vision of what the nonprofit or public service agency can do in its community (SANNO, 1992).

Aspirations for the People Served by the Agency

These aspirations awaken board members to the essential bottom line of the agency. Organizational effectiveness involves the ability of the agency to make a positive and enduring difference in the lives of the people it is chartered to serve (Dykstra, 1995). It is up to board members to decide whether this difference is profound or minimal, a decision that is critical because it will serve to define the energy, momentum, achievements, and reputation of the agency. These are all elements of the agency's institutional character (Selznick, 1957). The board of an agency whose purpose is to increase employment among people with disabilities may be satisfied with entry-level and minimum-pay positions for the people it serves. Another board may aspire to more significant employment outcomes involving career development, training, and entry into higher level positions. The board of a nonprofit arts organization may aspire only to expose secondary students to the arts whereas another board aspires to help students, teachers, school personnel, and parents to value the arts as much as they value, for example, science education or athletics. These contrasting scenarios demonstrate that boards can have different aspiration levels, but whatever level the board chooses will have important performance-defining implications for the agency (Knauft, Berger, & Gray, 1991). An important caveat here: The level of aspiration can dramatically influence performance. High aspirations can induce high performance (J. Hall, 1980). Low aspirations will most likely fail to inspire high performance on part of either the board or the agency (King, 1980; Livingston, 1980).

A board without high aspirations may simply lack the energy to move the agency to higher levels of performance. The agency as a whole may sense this lack of energy and adopt correspondingly low aspirations.

Aspirations for Agency Performance

These aspirations involve board members in examining their hopes for what the agency will do and how it will do it. Positive aspirations held by board members can involve the use of progressive state of the art service concepts and philosophical frameworks, and the incorporation of best practices into service and into agency administration. The board may identify and adopt aspirations involving the quality of service delivery, benchmarks of exemplary service, the achievement of an outstanding reputation among the agency's peer group, or the attainment of state and national recognition (Cohen & Brand, 1993). The agency as a whole is a means to achieve positive outcomes for the people the organization serves, and the aspirations board members hold for the entire agency are no less important than those aspirations they hold for the people it serves. The board must recognize that outcomes achieved for the people the agency serves are not achieved in a vacuum but require a set of aspirations that establish among board members a sense of how well the agency will actually perform to achieve desired client or consumer outcomes. Aspirations for the performance of the agency go hand in hand with aspirations for the benefits that consumers, clients, and communities will experience (Hardy & Schwartz, 1996).

Aspirations for the Impact of the Agency on the Problems and Needs It Has Been Founded to Address

These aspirations motivate board members to establish their hopes for how much or to what extent the agency will make an impact on the actual social problem or social need it is chartered to address (Markowitz & Rosner, 1996). The board of an agency responding to the employment needs of people with disabilities may not only aspire to help people get the very best jobs, but also to decrease significantly the unemployment or underemployment rate among people with disabilities in the geographic locale served by the agency. Is this unrealistic? Maybe so, but maybe not. Certainly, these kinds of aspirations compare favorably with the desire of a large financial service agency in the private sector to attract 90 percent of the consumer credit business within the next five years. The board of a nonprofit arts council may look at what it aspires to within a community in the area of cultural enrichment. "What does the board aspire to achieve in helping a community to become culturally enriched?" The board may set its aspirations very high. Its aspiration is to help every major demographic group within a community to enjoy the arts. The board aspires to have an increasing number of people within the community identify the arts as part of their lifestyles and quality of life. Another board may not be so ambitious and define its own aspirations as having a presence in the community so that people can take advantage of these opportunities. Here again, we have contrasting aspirations—two boards with very different conceptions of what they aspire to do.

These aspirations indicate how very important it is for the board to think about what its impact is intended to be in the community as a whole. It means going beyond benefits created for individuals to an aspiration for the community as a whole or the population as a whole (Lappe & Du Bois, 1994).

Aspirations are a good place to begin board development. Their clarification is fundamental both to board and agency performance. The identification and the clarification of board aspirations provide a reference point for how well the agency should do in relationship to the people it serves, organizational performance, and the problem or need the agency addresses. They also offer an understanding about how much energy is needed by the board as a whole while they make visible the kind of energy and beliefs individual board members need to bring to the board. Energy and aspirations form an essential quality of a high-performance system and are needed for the board to actually make an impact on the community service agency.

Property 2: The Board Has a Clear Conception of a Highly Valued End State

A high-performance system possesses a clear sense of where it wants to go and how it wants to get there—that is, it has a vision both of its journey and its destination (P. Schwartz, 1991). Boards must understand that a vision is both end state and journey, and without making both clear development will be difficult if not impossible for the board (Schon, 1971). At least, it will not be intentional and any development that actually does occur perhaps will be a result of accident or, at best, of good fortune. A clear and unambiguous conclusion concerning planned organizational change is that many systems focus on defining their end state without paying much attention to how they are going to achieve this end. They do not clarify the actual core and general strategies that they will use to negotiate the sometimes long-term process of achieving their destination (Cunningham, 1994). A high-performance system understands both its end and the process for achieving this end (Hanna, 1988).

Vision of the Destination

Board development is problematic without a conception of the end state or the destination. Indeed, we can assert that the purpose of board development is in service to the achievement of organizational destination. In many ways, the vision is an extension of the board's aspirations for the people the agency serves, for the agency itself, and for the impact of the agency. However, I should draw another caveat here so as not to make vision self-serving to agency self-interest. The board's crafting of vision forces it to not only look at its mission (that is, what it wants to achieve as an organization), but also at its purpose (that is, how it conceives of the problem or need it seeks to address from which mission will flow).

Participants in high-performance systems understand that a vision is not framed as merely the system's own success. Rather, participants find their meaning in the difference the system can or should make in its environment. The formation of vision is based on the organization's conception of how well the people the agency serves will prosper and the impact the agency will make on its community—that is, by reducing a problem or fulfilling a need. Indeed, we can sort out the aspirations discussed previously by linking those aspirations for the well-being of people served by the agency and aspirations for the impact of the agency on the community to the actual long-term vision of the agency's destination. Those aspirations linked to the performance of the agency can actually serve as a conception of the means for getting to the destination.

A vision of the agency's destination does not have to be a long document or statement. The vision can and should be a succinct statement written in a manner to delight people and to form a challenge to agency performance (Nanus, 1992). It should offer board members a sense of challenge and initiate the best thinking on the part of the board about how it is going to develop itself to meet the challenge. I will not offer specific examples here of vision statements because this is a topic of discussion in chapter 8. However, I do want to emphasize that a vision is not a story of the success of the agency. It is a story of the success of the people and community the agency serves.

In addition to the emotional or affective qualities of the vision (for example, it is found to be exciting) the vision is framed from the perspective of those people who are to be beneficiaries of the agency's performance. An agency devoted to offering schools exposure to the performing arts will frame its vision not in terms of how well the agency does fiscally or programmatically. Rather, the board of the agency will frame the vision in terms of how students will benefit from the exposure—how they will change emotionally, intellectually, socially, and culturally from the experiences that the agency offers. An agency that offers housing opportunities for people with AIDS offers a vision of how people benefit from this resource and perhaps how their health is stabilized or improved because their housing status improves. The "vision of destination" not only has an emotional quality, but also a compelling one. It can drive action, and, thus, the formulation of this aspect of vision is linked to the energy and aspirations of the board. "Why do we need to commit this energy?" asks a new board member. "Why?" replies a more seasoned member. "Because look what we can achieve or do for people. Isn't this exciting? Isn't this what brought you to the board?" The vision gives meaning to action and builds on aspirations.

Vision of the Journey

The vision of destination focuses the attention of the high-performance system on what it must undertake—that is, the process it must execute—to get to the destination. There are numerous pathways to a destination—many different routes and many different means. Starting off in Boston with the destination of San Francisco in mind can take a traveler along various routes using various modes of transportation. The goal of San Francisco linked to the route for getting there and to a mode of transportation chosen by the traveler forms a strategy (Judson, 1990). It is interesting to note that the journey itself, or the execution of the strategy itself, can help the traveler develop as new situations are experienced, new challenges mastered, and new competencies developed (Bateson, 1994). For the board, clarity about destination raises questions about how the board will undertake the journey, that is, what its basic strategies are for achieving its destination.

Of course, clarification of the destination helps the board to understand why it is undertaking the journey ("People coping with HIV/AIDS need stable, safe, and good housing and without it will likely experience harm. We can prevent this harm and help people to maintain their health."). A key to understanding what journey is needed is found in the board's own aspirations about agency performance. Thus, the board develops further by gaining an understanding about how the process of change will occur and the principal strategies that it needs to undertake to reach its desired destination. Strategies dealing with such things as best practices, benchmarking, quality improvement, human resources, service technologies, information technologies, marketing and image development, financial and resource development, corporate planning, and risk management are identified in service to the destination. The formation and execution of these strategies are the content of the journey and they require the board to become increasingly well versed in what the agency does and how the agency does it.

"Ordinary" conceptions of board functioning may say the conception of this journey is not within the scope of the board and infringes on the performance of the chief executive officer and the staff (Weissman, 1973). But a vision of the journey does not get the board into micromanagement. It offers the board a framework for how it needs to develop to, in turn, support high performance within the agency. "What do we need to get good at" board members ask, "so that we can actually achieve our destination?"

In terms of board development, the vision of destination and journey helps position the board and to use its energy and aspirations in service to supporting agency performance (Rummler & Brache, 1991). Thus, the formation of agency vision is not an executive task. It can be framed as a board development task for without this understanding the board cannot be reasonably expected to know how to move the agency toward its future (Eadie, 1991). Initiating and preparing the vision is essential to high performance and it is within the domain of board responsibility and development. The product of this work is a more informed and understanding board. As a consequence of this work, board members are better prepared to meet the challenge established by the vision. The board is developing a clearer understanding of who to recruit as members, what kind of contribution to expect from individual board members, and how board members can be organized to undertake the leadership work needed to bring a vision to fruition.

Property 3: The Board Has a Strong Belief System to Steer Its Work and the Work of the Agency

There is no legal reason that nonprofit or public service organizations must exist. Their existence is founded in law—for instance, in recognition by the Internal Revenue Service—but their existence is not required by law. Their existence is useful to government and the public sector. Yet they are not established by policy edict even though government likely regulates them.

A captivating quality of nonprofit and public service organizations is that their existence is a product of voluntary initiative and voluntary sustenance. A complex mixture of public and private resources maintains these agencies. The leadership of these agencies perpetuates them because of a fundamental purpose or commitment to the advancement of a cause, a group, a population, a locale, or a need. This makes nonprofit or public service organizations both remarkable and precarious. They are remarkable because their existence is not coerced. They are precarious because the leadership of an agency may decide not to perpetuate the organization and its work (Selznick, 1957).

A high-performance system does not base its work solely on energy or on vision. The power of the system is founded in the linkage of energy and vision to the animating quality of the moral and ethical commitment of the entity. I use the term *animating* to suggest that there is a value of empowerment that supports the energy and vision of the nonprofit or public service agency and it is this value of empowerment that moves the agency to act (Moxley & Jacobs, 1992). Certainly, organizational theorists point to animation based on organizational self-interest and self-perpetuation. But self-interest and self-perpetuation alone do not explain the motivation of nonprofit and public service agencies.

Animation suggests that there is a "call to action" that is visible in the behavior of the actual system (Lauffer, 1993). For those boards seeking to craft themselves as high-performance systems, a moral–ethical commitment informs and directs agency action. An alternative service organization that prides itself on its history and competencies in helping youths who are considered to be troubled to resolve problems with their families, prevent drug use and homelessness, and foster positive transitions to adulthood bases its work on an ethic of intergenerational responsibility. The "ethic" of the board is to foster the ability of the agency to meet this responsibility based on a moral understanding of stewardship. Adults have the responsibility for assuring that young people develop and become successful. It is immoral to allow young people to fail and to harm themselves.

Another nonprofit agency bases its work on an ethic of civic responsibility to a local community (Chandler, 1987). This neighborhood-based organization is devoted to the improvement of the quality of life within a specific geographic area. It prides itself in its ethical commitment to beautifying the area, augmenting safety in collaboration with the city police force, and helping people to hold on to their homes during rough economic periods. The agency does not see itself as replacing city government or displacing city resources. It sees itself as holding the responsibility for its own fate in partnership with residents and the local government. Its ethic is based on values of mutual support, collaborative enterprise, and civic commitment (Glassman, 1998).

More than any other dimension of high-performance systems, moral–ethical commitment offers a rationale for why the board is undertaking its work (Gillies, 1992). From the perspective of board development, this commitment offers an explanation that informs the vision adopted by the board and gives relevance and meaning to the investment of energy by board members. Whether animated by religious commitment and values, a secular commitment to humanism, concern for a specific group, or a value like intergenerational equity or stewardship, moral–ethical commitment gives a special meaning to the work of the board and to the work of the agency. System development requires this commitment for without it, the system is likely to run out of energy because it has run out of meaning (Gawthrop, 1984).

For board development, moral–ethical commitments require board members to gain an understanding of what the agency stands for and why it is undertaking its work. These commitments mean that strong and meaningful beliefs are essential to board functioning and board development. As a result an understanding of these commitments can strengthen the normative basis of the board as a group and help the board to integrate its members into a stronger performance system. It is not necessary for everyone to consent to the beliefs of the group. But some level of agreement on the essential beliefs of the agency can be a resource to board development when development is now seen as the ability of the board to form as an effective group or team (Gastil, 1993).

Civic and social responsibility, as part of an ethical commitment, helps the board as a system to understand that it must perform for a greater purpose and in service to a higher ideal. It also reminds the board that it has chosen to perpetuate the agency and to do so effectively requires a calling to a greater purpose (Pascarella & Frohman, 1989). Nonprofit agencies—whether in the arts, human services, education, or health care—are truly public in spirit and character. Their "public" character is based on the idea that their purpose is founded in the involvement of citizens to advance the quality of life and well-being of other citizens through involvement and participation, civic education, cultural enrichment, and human and social services (Riesenberg, 1992). This democratic ideal defines the very purpose of nonprofit and public service agencies. It suggests that their moral–ethical commitment is tied very much to the advancement of the common or public good (Ackoff, 1994). Board development in this dimension requires the board as a system to further think through and clarify its social or public purpose.

Property 4: The Board Embraces and Acts on Continuous Improvement

A high-performance system recognizes the importance of improvement, for without this recognition the system can lose energy as well as fail to achieve its purpose or simply stagnate. High-performance systems are not perfect entities. Indeed, such systems recognize their own flaws because they are vigilant about their own development (Bennis, 1993b). The idea of development means that the system continuously identifies how it can improve its own functioning and purpose using the reference point of an ideal against which it can measure itself.

Continuous improvement requires a certain demeanor on the part of the board of the nonprofit and public service organization. The idea of improvement and its necessity suggests that the board understands its own imperfections and, most important, understands the challenges it faces and the issues it must resolve to improve. The idea of improvement reinforces in the board the "pursuit of the ideal" and therefore has a strong connection with the dimensions of vision and moral–ethical commitment discussed previously. The idea of improvement also involves the board's appraisal of its energy and a developing sensitivity to the need for momentum because improvement will not and cannot occur without the investment of energy. And the idea of improvement requires the board to develop an understanding of the issues it faces and must resolve to be successful as a board.

Continuous improvement therefore brings into focus the imperative of board development as well as the substance of board development. As a high-performance or extraordinary system, the board finds that an intentional commitment to its own development requires an improvement agenda. It is this agenda of improvement that gives considerable substance to board development because it requires the board and its members to identify and think through those issues it must address to improve and to develop (Schmidt & Finnigan, 1992). The concept of "issue" is important here because each board will develop differently and individually on the basis of its own membership, its configuration, its stage of development, and the history, traditions, and character of the organization it sponsors and governs.

"Issues" are those concerns identified by the board the resolution of which will improve the performance of the board and the mastery of which will help the board develop as an essential leadership system of the nonprofit or public service organization (B. Collins & Huge, 1993). The identification of this agenda and the resolution of these issues propel the board forward in its own development. Issues can involve such concerns as the stability of revenue sources, overdependence on one form or source of revenue, the absence of adequate or useful information about agency outcome and performance, the instability of human resources, or a legal threat to the agency. These are substantive agency or organizational issues. They hold very significant, if not substantial, implications for board development and improvement, particularly if the board does not have systems or processes in place to address them successfully.

We must address another key concept here if an improvement agenda composed of vital issues is to have a desirable effect on board development. The improvement agenda cannot be static for true development to be realized (Schmidt & Finnigan, 1992). The agenda must be dynamic and continuous because the situation of the board and the organization it governs is always changing. A dynamic situation created by a changing and perhaps turbulent board creates the need for a dynamic agenda of improvement issues (Vaill, 1989). The board as a high-performance system recognizes and understands the dynamism of its situation and oversees the continuous identification of issues that must be resolved (Waterman, 1990). The management of these issues influences many aspects of the board and its development. It can influence the substance of the board's agenda, the charters of its committees, the creation of task forces, membership recruitment, the formation of board information systems, and the evaluation of board performance. Without a sense of these issues and a structure for managing or addressing them, a board is not continuously involved in tracking its environment and situation. Therefore, it is not really addressing those challenges to board development that emerge over time in what appears to be a chaotic environment (Wheatley, 1992). It benefits a board to pay attention to the agency's environment (Lawrence & Lorsch, 1986).

The pursuit of continuous improvement by the board as a high-performance or extraordinary system raises at least three questions within the board: (1) What is the board seeking to improve? (2) Why is the board seeking to improve this? (3) How is the board improving this? Improvement continuously undertaken by the board will result in development precisely because the board will have to undertake intentional change to meet the challenges created by improvement. Continuous improvement is board development in action.

Property 5: The Board Possesses a Commitment to Its Own Learning

The fifth and final dimension of a high-performance system resides in the posture the system takes vis-à-vis its own learning. The other four dimensions rest on the ability of the board to develop as a learning system. The board as a system or group, as well as individual board members, must learn on a continuous basis. Hopefully, this learning is well designed and implemented so that it results in more than just the acquisition of information about the board, the agency it sponsors and governs, the people the agency serves, and the problem or need the agency addresses. The acquisition of information is necessary but not sufficient for board development. Board development requires knowledge and understanding.

"Knowing" the agency requires the board and its members to become grounded in what the agency does, how it does it, and the challenges it faces in executing its purpose and in achieving its mission. Such knowing is very much about understanding the influence of those forces shaping the agency (Senge, Laur, Schley, & Smith, 2006). Knowing emerges from the vigorous exposure of board members to what the agency is in terms of its history, traditions, technologies, culture, and the need it is filling within the community (Nonaka, 1998). The danger here is that board members are quite removed from the day-to-day action and this social and organizational distance may make them remote not only emotionally, but also intellectually. But in depth knowledge here among board members can help them anticipate what is needed, and even come to see those needs emerge on the horizon (Senge, Smith, Kruschwitz, Laur, & Schley, 2008). The board itself can emerge as a community of practice the members of which are engaged together in the pursuit of expertise concerning the work of the agency (Wenger, McDermott, & Snyder, 2002).

After an in-depth review of an agency completed during a retreat, a board member confessed that she was not "in tune" with what the agency was doing and why a feminist orientation to service was so important in helping women with recovery or healing from sexual abuse and exploitation. As an attorney, she often heard from prosecutors and police about the conflict that existed between their organizations and the agency. Before the retreat, she often heard in the community that agency personnel were basically hostile. After the retreat, she was more understanding of why this conflict existed and the changes that were needed by personnel in the prosecutor's office and police department to make recovery and healing possible for the people the agency serves.

Unfortunately, this education came well into the attorney's third year of service on the board. Without this knowledge she could not really execute her role as a chief policy maker and strategist for the agency as a whole. Multiplied by 15 other members, the absence of progressive learning on the part of the board meant that there was a substantial knowledge deficit operating in this board system. There is no reason why this deficit should exist within a board. Through a commitment to board development, members can take action to ensure that it does not exist.

There are several practical outcomes the board can realize through progressive learning. Developing empathy for what the agency does and the many challenges it faces is one of these outcomes. Board members can develop an emotional appreciation for the people served by the agency and move beyond stereotypes about recipients as individuals and as members of the community (Weick, 1995). Board members can also develop an emotional appreciation for how staff members feel about their work, their sense of professionalism, their commitment, and the issues staff members face in sustaining themselves and in feeling effective. Without this empathy and the knowledge that undergirds it, board members may find it difficult to relate to the actual people the agency serves and to the actual people who offer services.

Another practical outcome of progressive learning involves gaining knowledge of the actual social problem or need the agency addresses. Most agencies cannot simply isolate the problem or need they address from other problems and issues because most social problems or needs involve many interacting factors. The community service agency that develops housing options for people with HIV/AIDS is not merely focusing on housing and HIV/AIDS but, rather, is likely involved in addressing factors associated with successful community or independent living. As a result, the agency must address aspects of the problem involving transportation, medical care, health promotion, advocacy, self-help, nutrition, and social support and involvement. Thus, like it or not, the agency is involved in an array of social support and social services that are linked to successful housing development. The provision of housing masks the complexity of the agency's purpose (Stacey, 1996). Board members need an understanding of this complex matrix of the problem addressed by the agency so they have a better grasp of the agency's purpose and can understand the mission of the agency within the context of this purpose.

By *purpose* I refer to the board's understanding of the actual social problem addressed by the agency and the reason there is a need for the community service. A thorough understanding of purpose is essential to board development. Such knowledge can illuminate or enlighten board members. This knowledge can open the eyes and minds of board members to issues or concerns they had previously not considered. As a consequence of a thorough orientation to the housing challenges created by living with HIV/AIDS, board members may begin to say, "Now I understand why we need to link people to support groups and to transportation. They can get very isolated in their housing situations." Thus, the third practice outcome of progressive learning is the enlightenment of board members.

Gaining empathy, an understanding of the complexity of the social problem or need, and becoming enlightened are not trivial board development outcomes. They are all essential to the formation of agency purpose and mission, strategy, and policy making. Without these outcomes the board may simply be conducting its business in a vacuum and may earn a reputation among agency staff and clients as a marginal group that lacks relevance to the actual work of the agency (Eadie, 1991).

These aspects of board knowledge suggest that members invest a considerable amount of effort in planning and implementing events that support progressive learning. Thus, through special briefings, retreats, continuing board education, conferences, and ongoing orientation, the board develops its knowledge base and understanding of what the agency is, what it seeks to achieve, and how it goes about effecting change through community service.

Progressive learning is the centerpiece of the board development framework presented in Figure 2-1. Without it, the board will be unsuccessful in shaping its aspirations, vision, ethical commitments, and improvement agenda. With it, however, the board develops as a stronger system because it increasingly gains more insight into what the agency is all about and how the board needs to develop to better serve the agency. The adjective *progressive* like the adjective *continuous* that is linked to improvement suggests an ongoing intentional process. Learning is not a one shot event for the board and cannot be limited to a short preservice orientation event. The complexity and challenges of board work with community service agencies really do demand an ongoing process of education and knowledge development. This kind of development will be worth the investment in effort when it results in board members who are empathic, who understand agency purpose, and who are enlightened about the work of the agency. The board as a whole will be better prepared to execute its responsibilities as a principal leadership structure of the organization.

Conclusion

This chapter has given a complexity to board development that may put off some readers. Why does it have to be so complex—that is, why does it have so many dimensions? One response to this very important question is quite simple. The work of the community service agency is so complex! The problems, issues, or needs the agency seeks to address or resolve or fulfill are not easily tackled! Government, the private sector, and public opinion have decided that some issues or concerns having to do with our collective life are better left to these entities—organizations that many of you who are reading this volume lead as board members.

Reflect on the complexity of the agencies you serve. Reflect on the complexity of the work of your board. Reflect on the complexity of your work as a board member. This reflection may underscore just how important or vital board development is to the continuation of the agency you serve.

The idea of board development is complex but it is also rich and fascinating. People come together as a voluntary entity to lead an agency committed to some form of community service—whether in health care, social service, neighborhood development, or the arts. In large part, the fate of this organization is in the hands of these leaders. That is, the continuation of the agency and its performance and effectiveness does or can lie in the hands of an entity referred to as a board. And, as a consequence, if the board does not intentionally develop over the short and long run, the current performance and future effectiveness of the agency can be threatened. Even worse is the scenario of the agency surviving but failing to do anything meaningful in addressing its purpose, that is, in addressing the problem or need that legitimizes the existence of the community service organization.

Board development is complex and should be complex. Board service is challenging because community service is challenging. This does not mean, however, that it cannot be efficient and effective. The idea of board development requires board members to think of their boards as systems—and particularly as extraordinary systems that incorporate high performance expectations for themselves and for the agencies they sponsor and govern.

A framework of high performance is useful to thinking about board development and the properties needed by the board to develop:

- The board develops through its aspirations for the people the agency serves, the agency and its staff, and the impact of the agency.
- The board develops through the formation of a vision of how people benefit from the work of the agency and through the strategies the board adopts to progress toward this vision.
- The board develops through a moral–ethical commitment to its work and the action it takes to bring about this commitment.
- The board develops through continuous improvement by successfully addressing those issues that challenge board and agency performance.
- The board develops through progressive learning by helping board members to develop empathy, sense of purpose, and enlightenment.

We will stay with the theme of complexity as we move into a consideration of the complexity of the board as an organizational system. Through the explication of five essential subsystems, we can obtain a better understanding of why boards are complex and why board development is a complex and continuous undertaking.

Questions for Board Discussion

1. Assess the energy level of the current board. How much energy does the board possess to invest in board development? Is it willing to invest this energy in its own development?

2. What aspirations does the board hold for the people who are served by the community service agency? Are these aspirations weak or strong? Do they energize action?

3. What aspirations does the board hold for the social need or problem that it seeks to improve? Are these aspirations weak or strong? Do they energize action?

4. What aspirations does the board hold for the performance of the agency? Are these aspirations weak or strong? Do they inspire action on part of the board? Do they inspire action on part of agency personnel?

5. Does the board possess a vision of how the agency is to perform and to make an impact on its community and on the people it serves? What is this vision? Does it inspire action?

6. What are the core beliefs held by the board that make the community service agency distinctive? Do these beliefs inspire and sustain action on part of board members and agency personnel?

7. Does the board have an agenda of quality improvement for itself and the agency?

8. How do board members learn about the work of the agency? About the role of the board in the community and within the agency? How is knowledge developed and maintained by board members on a continuous basis?

9. What developmental needs does this chapter illuminate for the board? How will the board act on these needs?

■ SECTION TWO ■

DEVELOPING THE BOARD AS A MULTIDIMENSIONAL SYSTEM

The four chapters composing this section examine the idea of the development of the community service board as a multidimensional system. Each chapter explores one dimension of this system. The institutional dimension is explored in chapter 3. The board's institutional dimension addresses the incorporation of the overarching framework of the community service agency, which involves (1) the agency's conception and interpretation of the community problem or need it seeks to address, (2) the agency's conception and interpretation of its purpose and aims, and (3) the agency's conception of its basic enterprise. The institutional dimension offers the community service board and the agency it governs its organizational identity.

Chapter 4 recognizes that a board must incorporate a plurality of functions to govern well, and it is these functions that offer various governance roles to the members of the community service board. Development, here, involves the integration of the agency's sense of history (the ancestral function), future (the generative function), environmental demand and challenge (the strategic function), policy requirements (the adaptive function), and civic involvement (the civil function). Chapter 5 focuses on the performance dimension, involving how the board organizes and executes its work. This chapter incorporates what is most likely considered the most concrete aspects of board development, involving such elements as board membership, group life, committee structure, networking, task performance, and board products. These elements represent the basic inputs, processes, and outcomes the board undertakes to govern the community service agency.

Chapter 6 places board development in the context of the lifespan of the community service agency. Developmental tasks are organized by major stages of organizational lifespan involving the founding of the agency, growth and maturation, stabilization, and decline and renewal. The content presented in this chapter reminds us that board development is never ending—it is differential, geared to the stage of development the agency and the board are negotiating.

Taken collectively, these chapters underscore the systemic focus of board development and the linkage of these various dimensions to the advancement of the purpose of community service held by the agency—its staff, leaders, and stewards. The chapters remind us that board development cannot be separated from the quest to fulfill a vision of community service. This quest really forms the essence of board development.

■ 3 ■

Institutional Dimension

Thank you for the opportunity to serve the Heritage Center. It is now time for me to resign from the board. I do so with great personal disappointment. Board members insist on getting into the detail and day-to-day work of the agency, and this strikes me as improper. On many occasions I have pointed out that the board needs to prepare the agency for the future, not to get into the job of the executive director. It is the job of board members to ensure the community of families with children who are disabled that this agency not only stands for something but that it acts on what it stands for. The source of my frustration is the unwillingness (or inability, I can't decide which) of the board to take a long-term perspective. I am also frustrated by the unwillingness of the board to put in place those resources (including a strong board that knows how to perform) that will make the agency a purposeful agent in strengthening families of children with disabilities. The board does not recognize its institutional purpose and responsibilities. This is a serious shortcoming, the responsibility for which I share.

As the chair of the planning committee, I have tried on repeated occasions to help the board to get on this pathway. I just do not have the skills to motivate a board that does not want to go in this direction. We waste energy on telling very qualified staff members how to do their jobs. And we blame the staff for being somewhat undirected and unproductive. The board really does need "to get with it." We need to steward this agency rather than keep it hostage to our mediocrity. We need to prepare it for a productive future if not an exemplary one.

One of the most important responsibilities of the community service board is to foster and strengthen the agency as an institution. This basically means that the community service agency, under the leadership of its board, emerges as an enduring, viable, and respected force in the life of the community to which the agency offers service. As noted in previous chapters, nonprofit and public service organizations are becoming increasingly important in the provision of a range of services, amenities, and social products designed ultimately to advance the quality of life of specific groups of people as well as the community at large.

However, a community service board must understand that it is not merely overseeing the agency in this most important responsibility. The board must recognize that the agency, as a nonprofit or public organization, serves a greater purpose as recognized by prevailing federal and state laws. These agencies serve a special purpose in local communities, obtain special tax exemptions to perform and execute this purpose, and receive resources in the form of contracts, grants, donations, and gifts to implement their work (O'Neill, 1989).

There are many expectations that come with this recognition and the resources that are provided to community service agencies. Certainly some agencies may interpret their responsibilities in very narrow ways—as performing some kind of discrete service, or in executing some kind of task. Community service agencies that operate in this manner probably will not receive much positive recognition for what they do. And they most likely will fail to become truly viable entities within their communities.

Becoming an established, viable organization within the community requires community service agencies to become institutionalized. And institutionalization requires an agency to become known as an enduring entity within the community and to become recognized within its community for offering help, assistance, and valued products that advance the quality of life of the community. The substance of institutionalization is hard to capture. But allow me to offer three qualities that the board can incorporate into its role as the steward of the community service agency. These qualities are

- ■ the purposeful shaping of the identity of the community service agency as a whole in order to build meaning both within the agency and within the community that the agency serves (Pascarella & Frohman, 1989),
- ■ the adoption of a long-term perspective within the board that offers continuity to the organization and ensures its perpetuation (P. Schwartz, 1991),
- ■ the capacity to develop the resources needed by the agency to support its work within the community (Herman & Heimovics, 1991).

Building the community service agency as an institution is not an easy task for the board. It is a principal responsibility as well as an ongoing responsibility of board development. The community service board must become conscious of this responsibility. The board cannot neglect it for this will only mean that the agency itself will fail in its vision, mission, and ultimate purpose. From my perspective, the institutional dimension holds one of the greatest hopes for responding effectively to the complex social problems or social needs that most community service agencies must address. It is this dimension that actually frames the entire work of the board and agency. And it is this dimension that frames how the board will subsequently choose to function and to perform.

Purposeful Shaping of Identity

Importance of Identity

Creating a viable social institution within a community begins with the shaping of the identity of the community service agency by its board. This is one of the principal responsibilities of the board because without a strong identity the agency risks the misuse and misallocation of the precious resources it receives to perform its work. Identity is just as important to an organization as it is to a person. Identity offers the organization a compass useful to the establishment of direction. Identity offers the community service agency a sense of what is "right" in the performance of its duties. As amplified in the chapters composing section 3 of the book, the shaping of identity results in a framework that gives an overall sense of direction to community service and to what the agency is trying to achieve in responding to a particular social problem or in fulfilling a social need.

Community service boards will likely find themselves in situations where there are numerous opportunities and numerous demands placed on the agencies they sponsor. Some of these opportunities and demands will not be consistent with what the agency seeks to do and what it seeks to achieve. It may not be clear which opportunities to select or which demands to respond to for those community service agencies with weak identities. But for the community service agency with a clear sense of identity, opportunities and demands can be evaluated with some confidence. The framework the board establishes allows the agency leadership to select those opportunities that are most relevant to what the agency is seeking to do within its community (Eadie, 1991).

Board development in this area requires the community service board to contemplate and establish the core identity of the agency. This board development work may require some basic definitions to offer meaning to the agency as a whole and to define the agency to its various stakeholders who most likely have great expectations for what the agency will achieve and how it will perform. One of these basic definitions involves what community service means to the board. After all, it is in the realm of community service in which the agency has been founded. And it is in the realm of community service that the agency has grown and developed.

Some boards may not want to invest much energy in this task, but they risk undermining the process of institutionalization (Selznick, 1957). This process does require a basic meaning that infuses energy into the process of community service. Other boards will undertake this task with some enthusiasm and much energy. They understand that agency leadership, personnel, consumers, and other stakeholders want to hear what community service is all about (Chappell, 1993). They also want to have input into what it means and what form or shape it takes within the board.

Definition of Community Service

Creating an overarching definition of community service is a linchpin in the structure of governance created by the community service board. Creating this definition offers the board opportunities to involve representatives from many different groups in crafting a sense of community service that unifies, integrates, and joins these various groups into a common social enterprise (Herman & Heimovics, 1991). I actually elaborate this process in chapter 7 ("Understanding 'Who We Are'"), but for now let me emphasize that a definition of community service that unites different stakeholder groups can institutionalize the relationships between the community service agency and the groups that compose what we often refer to as "community."

This cornerstone definition can be brief or long. It can be romantic and idealistic or quite pragmatic and utilitarian. The nature of the definition is up to the board and its understanding of the character of the agency (Kiefer & Senge, 1984). However, the definition itself possesses several attributes. First, it communicates what the agency sees as the value it produces for the community. Second, it articulates what the agency stands for in relationship to the social problem it seeks to address or the social need it seeks to fulfill. And, third, it interprets for the agency and for the community how the organization will go about its work.

Articulation of fundamental values becomes important to the definition of community service by the board (Selznick, 1957; Stacey, 1996). These values can be identified as critical ones because they give substantive character to the board and to the agency. They give meaning to what community service is all about. And they communicate what the agency stands for.

For the Braddock Community Arts Outreach Center (hereafter, "Braddock Center"), the basic definition of community service went a long way in enabling the board to set itself apart from other arts organizations. The board and chief executive officer always saw the agency as distinctive but it faced great challenges in defining this distinctiveness for principal stakeholder groups within the community. Several donors to the agency began to reconsider their annual gifts because they did not clearly understand the differences between the agency and other nonprofit arts organizations, including several museums that required an infusion of resources at the time. Braddock Center did not want to compete with these other organizations, but it also did not want its distinctiveness to go unrecognized. In previous times, when resources for the arts were more plentiful, the idea of agency distinctiveness was not really challenged. Now it was. And Braddock Center found that it was ill prepared to interpret its identity to the community.

The center defined and described what it meant by outreach. Indeed, outreach in the arts takes on special meaning at Braddock Center. Taking the arts into homes, neighborhoods, schools, hospitals, nursing homes, residential care centers, and even jails and homeless centers defines how Braddock Center goes about its work. The center stands for the arts as a fundamental human experience that can humanize both people and environments, and enrich the quality of life of people who are at risk of social neglect. Whereas other arts organizations offer standing, fixed resources to which people come to take advantage of various offerings, Braddock Center brings these resources to people and seeks to make the arts a part of their living, work, or educational environments. The center itself is very much on the cutting edge formed through the integration of the arts and healing (McNiff, 1992), realizing community through the arts (Freedman, 2003), and fostering self-development and personal transformation among those the agency serves (Belfiore & Bennett, 2008; Eisner, 2002).

For Braddock Center, the metaphor of outreach serves as a fundamental concept of the agency's identity. This metaphor, framed as "taking the arts to our customers," communicates what the agency produces. It communicates social involvement, social participation, and social enrichment.

In the purposeful shaping of identity it is not unusual for community service boards to work with metaphor (Whitmont, 1978). These metaphors add meaning to institutional identity, such as when the board of Braddock Center becomes conscious of just how important outreach is to the work of the agency. Outreach becomes an idea that encompasses what the agency is all about.

Clarification of Identity through Stories

The institutional dimension of board development also involves the growing consciousness among board members of grand narrative or story (Czarniawska, 1997). This grand narrative helps the board to define the purpose of the agency and to further define and deploy identity through the stories that enrich the understanding of groups and people about what the agency stands for in the community. Stories can give meaning and coherence to community service and to the agency that performs it (Chappell, 1993). Board members who have opportunities to hear these stories are themselves enriched in terms of their understanding of the agency and the community service it performs.

Board members, who founded the agency, administrators of long standing and key service personnel may serve as storytellers. But it is the substance and content

of the stories they tell that can enrich the perspective and understanding of decision makers (Coles, 1989). Take, for example, the "breakaway" story told by the
founding member of a vocational service agency. He proudly recounts how the
agency was created after the existing chief executive officer and two other board
members removed the organization out from under the umbrella of another corporation. The story has a David and Goliath motif complete with a hero and villain
(Campbell, 1972). The board member tells the story to remind the board and the
agency why the organization withdrew from this parent corporation. He tells the
story to emphasize the frustrations the agency experienced in its efforts to become
an exemplary service provider and to pioneer an area of psychiatric services—that
is, vocational development of people coping with serious mental illness—that was
ill-defined and poorly performed at the time. The story is told by this board member to increase the expectations about agency performance and agency value. The
story not only enriches the board members' understanding of the agency's history,
but also, more important, enriches board members' understanding of institutional
performance. That is, this agency is in the business of becoming exemplary in its
chosen service area.

Commitment to Quality

Another consideration involved in shaping the identity of the community service
agency is the level of quality that the board and agency seek to achieve in addressing social problems or social needs. Quality becomes a critical aspect of identity
given the challenging nature of most social problems or social needs community
service agencies seek to address. Modern conceptions of quality management
require institutional commitment (Creech, 1994). Modern conceptions of quality require organizations to define the expectations for their work and what their
work will produce in the fulfillment of needs (Gunther & Hawkins, 1996). Modern
conceptions of quality also require organizations to become knowledgeable of the
prevailing perception people or groups hold about the work performed by an organization. Quality, therefore, is the discrepancy that exists between expectations of
performance and the perceptions of whether these expectations are achieved in
practice. Quality management involves institutional action to reduce this discrepancy (Sashkin & Kiser, 1993).

The level of quality sought by the board becomes an instrumental aspect of
agency identity. It helps define how "good" the agency seeks to become in making
an impact on the social problem or social need selected by the organization (McInerney & White, 1995). It sets the standard of expectation within the agency. The
selection of a high expectation of quality requires the agency to use those service
processes that can be considered best practice or exemplary. And the selection of a
high expectation of quality requires the agency to achieve meaningful outcomes at

a level that earns the agency a reputation for doing good or excellent work. Building an identity of high quality also requires the board to become conscious of the perceptions of agency service and product held by the people who use or fund these services or outcomes. Thus, shaping identity through quality management requires the community service board to become conscious of what it wants to achieve and whether the agency actually achieves these ideals in practice.

In executing its responsibilities for building the community service agency as a community institution, the board sets in place a basic definition of community service that offers meaning to the various stakeholder groups involved in the work of the agency (S. J. Taylor, Bogdan, & Racino, 1991). The board clarifies the fundamental values that define for these stakeholder groups what the agency considers to be critical in giving substance to this identity. The definition of community service and the values that compose it are further communicated through the use of a grand narrative or a set of meaningful stories. And, finally, the board's commitment to quality further defines the identity of the community service agency.

This work is not trivial. When undertaken collaboratively within the executive leadership of the agency it truly becomes the work of institution building. There is a unified set of expectations about quality, what it is, and how to achieve it (Herman & Heimovics, 1991).

Adopting a Long-Term Perspective

Focusing on the Future of the Community Service Agency

One of the most important responsibilities of the community service board is to link the current situation of the agency to the future of the agency. This means that the community service board in the execution of its institutional responsibilities is more concerned about where the agency is going, how it will get there, and what it needs to fulfill its purpose in the future (Burton & Moran, 1995). This institutional requirement does not mean that the board either neglects or overlooks its trustee responsibilities typically found in monitoring the current performance of the agency. It means that the board does not exclusively confine its vision or attention to the present circumstances of the agency.

The adoption of a long-term perspective, even one that is balanced by a more pragmatic or utilitarian focus on the present, is a challenge to the institutional development of the community service board. The contemporary dialogue regarding character formation in individuals or organizations points to the importance of the adoption of a long-term perspective as opposed to short-term considerations or a preoccupation with the present (Wilson, 1995). Community service boards can get overly involved in the present, here-and-now management of the agencies for which they are responsible. In those agencies in which resources are scarce or limited, board members may find themselves filling consulting or technical assistance roles. Or they may find themselves in ad hoc managerial or supervisory roles. There can be a blurring of roles and responsibilities between board members and agency personnel—a blurring that can be quite destructive to the administration and governance of the agency. Boards can become preoccupied with immediate crises and, as a consequence, confine their vision and attention span to the short run.

The institutional dimension of board development reminds board members that one of their principal responsibilities is to foster the longevity of the agency based on an evolving sense of organizational relevance. Long-term and visionary thinking become critical competencies to the institutional development of the board.

The institutional dimension requires the board to identify those structures and capacities it requires to make community service viable. The board does this through the framing and execution of sound decisions, relevant policies, and informed actions that together perpetuate the agency and that strengthen its viability. Thus, a future focus within the board is critical to the advancement of the community service agency.

This orientation to the perpetuation of the community service agency requires the board to think and act in a future-oriented manner. It is not enough for the community service board to establish a board-level committee or task force on long-range planning. It requires that all active board members become sensitive to the future evolution of the agency. Board members must also understand the community in which the agency is working, and the problem or need addressed by the agency so that they can frame and execute the decisions that are needed to perpetuate the agency (Eadie, 1991; Herman & Heimovics, 1991).

Several agencies I work with are celebrating 30-, 40-, and 50-year anniversaries. Invariably, when I explore with these boards the reasons for their success, board members note that the members who came before them executed their generative functions well. Every generation of board consciously, and with foresight, prepared the agency for the next five to 10 years. They did so through the formation of endowments, acquisition of assets, and strengthening of infrastructure. But these actions were all influenced by a basic temperament and belief system within the board: that the agency fulfilled a critical purpose within the community and, as a consequence, the community needed the agency. Thus, the board established an institutional commitment to the perpetuation of the agency by defining the role of the agency in the community.

The long-range perspective is established within the community service board first through the commitment of the board members to the responsibility of fostering the viability of the agency and, second, by acting on this commitment. Making explicit this commitment in the board mission, in the by-laws of the board, and in principal board policies underscores this responsibility in an unambiguous manner. Acting on this commitment, however, is much more demanding. It requires the community service board to increase its knowledge of the future circumstances of the agency, the challenges the agency faces, and the resources needed by the agency to remain viable in the future.

Tracking and Responding to Change

A principal competency of the board lies in tracking the future change the community service agency anticipates. The future-focused board becomes comfortable tracking how the social problem or social need it addresses is changing and will change in the near future. This requires the board to obtain information and knowledge of changing demographics, changing manifestations of the problem or need, and emerging policy issues and policy changes. Knowledge is as essential to sound board performance as it is to the execution of any worthy activity (Nonaka & Takeuchi, 1995). It is not enough to say, for example, that the arts are changing. It is critical for the board to have a substantive understanding of how the arts are changing and the social dynamics that are influencing this change.

Those agencies responding to the problem of homelessness have seen this very serious problem change its demographic and social dimensions radically over the past 10 years. These agencies find themselves now addressing the needs of several different populations formed by the same social and economic circumstances but who require very different substantive responses. Adolescents and young adults, young families with children, and people coping with substance issues require different kinds of responses. Failing to differentiate among these groups can create a crisis of relevance for an agency.

A community service board must become aware of the changing nature of the response to the problem. The manifestation of such change may be found on a policy level as well as within the practice technology that is applied to the problem or need that is of interest to the agency. Board members do not have to become substantive experts in such policy or practice changes, although some may find themselves becoming quite knowledgeable. They do have to become aware of these changes and the implications they hold for the future relevance or even identity of the agency. The mental health agency that does not prepare for the emergence of a recovery paradigm in psychiatric rehabilitation may find that its day treatment programs and residential services have become obsolete. The vocational development agency that ignores inclusive employment options may fail to attract the interest of new and different donors. The arts center that does not identify how it will perform in an outcome-based policy environment may fall by the wayside.

These changes taken collectively are challenges to the identity and the viability of a community service agency. An institutional aim of the board is to steer the agency through the thicket that the future creates. Of course, this is not done alone. It is done in partnership with the executive director and with senior administrators

(Herman & Heimovics, 1991). But the board needs to be sensitive to the changing nature of social problem or social need as well as to the changing nature of good practice in the agency's chosen area of service.

Anticipating and becoming knowledgeable of this changing context of community service links naturally to the future-focused board's growing understanding of the emerging needs of the community service agency. These needs can involve new personnel with new kinds of expertise, new equipment and tools, new facilities, new locations, or a new set of goals or aims. Typically, the list of agency needs is unlimited, but the community service board must identify what is essential and what will add value to the achievement of agency purpose, vision, and mission. The growing list of needs reminds the community service board that the social problem or social issue addressed by the agency is dynamic. And so is the agency. The dynamic nature of organizational needs must become a focus of the board's work as it seeks to perpetuate the agency and make it a truly viable institution in the community.

Importance of Resource Development

The adoption of a long-term perspective by the board also requires it to become involved in resource development (Chait et al., 1996). Sensitivity to the changes the community service agency must respond to in the distant and near future will require new and diverse resources. Public and other revenue sources are unlikely to support fully the aspirations of the agency and the fulfillment of its vision, particularly if the agency is committed to an agenda of high quality and innovation. Such an agency will simply require additional and more flexible resources.

A long-term perspective links naturally with resource development. The board committed to creating a community institution will learn the importance of anticipatory resource development and the competencies needed to expand the agency resources.

As the board becomes increasingly involved in the long-term planning of the community service agency, it naturally focuses on resource development. The board will examine its own structure, membership, and competencies in relationship to the ability to execute complex resource development activities. The basic question here is whether the board is able to raise the resources the agency will need in the long run. Not all boards are prepared to conduct long-term resource campaigns.

Alternatives such as the creation of endowments, capital campaigns, annual drives and giving programs, and event planning all require the agency to have a clear sense of purpose and a good reputation within the community as an established institution (Grace, 1997a). Some boards will become frustrated when they move quickly into fund development without much institutional preparation. Members can become easily disillusioned when their work fails to show immediate results.

Here, again, the long-term perspective within the board becomes important. The board creating an enduring community institution is not in a hurry and understands the importance of preparing itself for effective resource development. An agency committed to housing development for people with HIV and AIDS prepared diligently for four years before it realized success in the area of resource development. I recorded 10 crucial steps the agency negotiated successfully to engage in an effective, ongoing, and long-term resource development campaign. The board

1. invested at least one full year in the formation of the institutional identity of the agency that resulted in clear identification of agency purpose, values, and commitments;
2. created an ongoing board education program that defined the changing character of HIV and AIDS and the changing housing needs among people coping with this medical concern at different stages of their illness;
3. formulated a clear sense of organizational service quality that was linked to the achievement of housing outcomes for the people served by the agency;
4. identified the pressing needs that would be fulfilled through resource development and translated these into a long-term resource development budget;
5. identified the expertise the board required to engage in resource development and recruited people to the board who possessed the competencies needed by the agency;
6. created a standing board committee on the long-term viability of the agency that was charged with the responsibility for planning and executing the agency's resource development campaigns;
7. trained all board members in core resource development skills, including the planning, monitoring, and execution of resource development;
8. executed one pilot project that initiated board members into resource development activities and evaluated the success of this project at the board level;
9. formulated a comprehensive, long-term resource development plan that was formally adopted by the board as a whole; and
10. integrated resource development activities and projects into the two year calendar of the board.

These steps were laborious but productive. The board adopted a "whole system" approach to resource development. First, the board identified this activity as part of its institutional activities. Second, it refined a framework of identity within which resource development was executed. Third, a fixed point of responsibility within the board was established for resource development, but all board members were trained to become aware of and comfortable and active in resource development.

The motivation for this activity among board members came from their deep commitment to fulfilling the housing needs of people impoverished because of HIV and AIDS. Board members came from all walks of life, including human services, education, business, and the arts. However, consumers and consumers advocates were well represented on the board, which added energy and urgency to the work of this agency (D. B. Schwartz, 1997). The long-term perspective adopted by this board was a product of the board members' recognition that the problem of HIV and AIDS was not going to disappear in the foreseeable future. Indeed, the field was about to enter a new phase of long-term community care. The board wants to expand its resource base so that the agency can offer these supports to people in a relevant and meaningful manner.

Conclusion

The institutional dimension of the board is an important one. However, it is one that probably emerges over the long term itself. As emphasized in the chapter discussing the lifespan dimension of the board, institutional work is performed in the long haul. It requires the board to make explicit efforts to frame the identity of the agency, and then to use this identity in service to creating continuity and viability within the community. The institutional dimension emerges as a positive organizational character that earns the community service agency a high standing in terms of its reputation within the community. Character is shaped by this long-haul work, by the decisions that are made, and by the values the agency puts into action that supports its conception or vision of community service. A strong, positive character means that the agency stands for something of substance in relationship to what it is trying to achieve. The public recognizes that the agency adds something important to community life. Character, in turn, is linked to reputation. People, groups, and organizations within the community begin to recognize the agency as an institution: as something enduring that can be relied on in the improvement of the quality of life for specific groups and for the community as a whole. Quality then becomes the ability on the part of the community service agency and its board to offer sustained value to the community.

The institutional dimension, however, cannot be viewed in isolation from the other dimensions of the board system. Certainly, the institutional dimension benefits from a well-thought-out system of functions within the community service board as well as an explicit framework of performance that guides the work of the board. The institutional dimension cannot be viewed independently from the lifespan dimension. After all, it takes time for the community service agency to emerge as an institution and this occurs through deliberate work over the lifespan of the agency and of the board that sponsors it.

Questions for Board Discussion

1. What is the greater community or societal purpose undertaken by your board? How do board members interpret this purpose? How does the board act on this purpose?

2. How does the board define community service? What fundamental values are incorporated into this definition?

3. What stories do board members share that communicate the substance and importance of its community or societal purpose? How do these stories offer meaning to the work of the board?

4. How does the board conceive of quality? To what extent is there a connection within the board between its conception of purpose and its conception of quality?

5. How does the current board foster the longevity of the community service agency? What specific activities does it undertake to make the agency a permanent community resource?

6. How does the current board track and monitor changes in the agency's environment? Are there structures or procedures within the board that enable it to stay on top of environmental change?

7. How does the board link its purpose to resource development on behalf of the agency? What is the resource development agenda of the board? How is resource development used to perpetuate the agency as a community institution?

8. What developmental needs does this chapter illuminate for the board? How will the board act on these needs?

4

Functional Dimension

Five Board Members Debate the Job of the Board

The Adaptive Board Member: We have one and only one job—we need to assure that the books balance, that we stay legal, and we do what our funders want. The rest is up to the staff.

The Strategic Board Member: We really need to stay attuned to the environment and figure out our strategies since everything is changing so much. There is a lot of opportunity out there and we should try to take advantage of it. Yes, we need to pay attention to the bottom line but if we don't strategize, strategize, and strategize there will be no bottom line.

The Generative Board Member: Who is to say that our current environment is all that stable and that doing only what our funders want us to do will make us viable? This agency has been around for 20 years. This board needs to concentrate on the future, making sure we have the resources and skills to meet this future. We have to have foresight and wisdom to guide the agency in the long run.

The Civil Board Member: We are here because of a community and our principal function is to involve community members in this agency. We can't stray far from our community and much of our purpose lies in getting people involved.

The Ancestral Board Member: I've served on this board now for what seems an eternity and we have some really good traditions here. The board needs to preserve these and to make sure that our philosophy endures now and into the future and that the essential values on which we were founded guide us. If we do not use these values, how true will we be to our founding purpose?

These five board members are in a heated debate. I have heard this kind of debate many times in board forums. Time is spent examining and debating the larger issues of what the board is all about, what board purpose is, and what essential functions a board needs to serve in relationship to the community and public service agency it serves and governs. On first blush, this dialogue may seem disjointed and fragmented. The reader may think that this is not a board that really knows itself and may lack a center. Actually, this dialogue is summarized from a discussion I facilitated with a very competent board, a board that has given careful thought to its governance and leadership functions. It is a board of a nonprofit human service organization that formed 20 years ago to respond to the community and independent living needs of people with developmental disabilities through advocacy, protective services, and guardianship. Over the past twenty years, the small struggling agency has emerged to become a national leader in rights protection and advocacy.

Not only did the size of agency and administrative staff grow tremendously with a corresponding growth in contracts and budget, but the board grew as well. At this writing the board is well over 25 members who represent a variety of advocates from consumer organizations, progressive social service agencies, public interest law, and the academic community. Growth in board size and the diversification of board membership (20 years ago the board was only about seven people) were not accompanied by a corresponding dialogue about what the board was all about. Only recently—within the past three years—did the board begin to recognize that it served many different functions for the agency, and that somehow all of these functions had to be integrated into the "whole of the board."

Functional Basis of the Board System

The complexity of the boards of community service agencies is reflected by these multiple functions. There is really no one right or wrong answer to the debate that introduces this chapter. All of these board members may be right. But in their eagerness to clarify their position and their focus, they reduce the salience and importance of the positions taken by their colleagues. Are we in the proverbial position of the wise men who blindfolded are trying to describe the elephant by extrapolating from the part they are touching to the animal as a whole?

The board is not limited to one function. Indeed, boards are complex because they serve many functions and a board can be defined as an integration or collection of these functions (Hackman, 1990). Some of these functions are nascent, others juvenile, while others are mature, and still others are overdeveloped. Some boards identify with one or two functions while leaving the others ambiguous or ill defined. Witness the board that is dominated by housing developers who have been so successful in financially managing the development of housing for people with serious and life-threatening health conditions that they did not see the need for social services and social supports. People's housing needs were met but people were basically isolated from the larger community and many of their other needs went unaddressed. Or witness the board that adapted to a fiscal and resource environment that seemed to change over night and resulted in the agency's loss of relevance.

The board as a high-performance system is committed to establishing, nurturing, and developing the five critical functions identified in the previous dialogue (Buchholz & Roth, 1987). The functions are not all necessarily compatible. They can indeed create a tension within the board, and this tension may result in conflict at times when a board is struggling with important questions concerning viability, relevance, and performance (Hackman, 1990). But this conflict is essential to any developing system. The multiple functions identified in the board dialogue introduce different perspectives often based on different values and different priorities about how the board should take action. The multiple functions also highlight the real work of the board of any community or public service organization. These boards govern by steering and stewarding the agency as a whole within often-conflicting or challenging or contradictory policy, political, economic, and legal environments. A vital board recognizes the importance of developing these functions so that the board gains greater competence in navigating the various environments within which the agency must perform. The proof that these functions serve the board well is found in the board's ability to produce better decisions that shape the competence of the agency to realize mission effectiveness and to attain its ultimate purpose (Buchholz & Roth, 1987).

In this chapter, I further expand the idea of board development by getting into the five functions that compose the performance of the board as a principal agency system. I look at what is distinctive about these functions and how the board develops each of them. I then look at the tensions these functions can create within the board and how the board can develop to handle these tensions successfully.

Orientation to the Five Principal Functions of the Board System

Adaptive Function

The adaptive function of the board addresses the ability of the community and public service organization to adapt to its current circumstances. The board exercising this function is concerned about the accountability of the agency typically to external sources—those entities that fund, license, or certify the agency. The adaptive function is a conservative one but is needed because the survival of the agency is at stake. This function comes into play within the board as it oversees and controls the budget of the agency, enters into contractual relations with external sources, monitors the chief executive officer, and generally monitors the performance of the agency.

The principal values of the adaptive function involve security, safety, and stability of the organization. This function comes to the foreground when board members serve as trustees. What are board members trustees of? The adaptive function suggests that board members serve as trustees of those donors who contribute resources to help the agency execute its mission or of those funders who contract with the agency to offer a set of services.

Board members must "conserve" the agency and ensure that the agency performs adequately and correctly and in a manner that is found acceptable by its current donors and funders. The adaptive function also recognizes that community and public service agencies have specific dependencies on other organizations within the community, especially those that fund their services (Mintzberg, 1983). These dependencies require the agency to adapt to these entities and to their conceptions of what the agency should be doing vis-à-vis the social problem or social need it is chartered to address (R. Scott, 1994). The adaptive function is consistent with a regulatory approach to human services.

The adaptive function can focus the attention of the board on the needs and perspectives of these external entities and develop a worldview that is structured by these entities (Tolbert & Zucker, 1996). Thus, a mental health agency board recognizes that 80 percent of its funding comes from the county mental health authority and is almost totally absorbed by the politics of this entity and by responding to the policies of this authority. The values of safety, security, and stability come to the fore as the board adopts information systems, budgeting approaches, performance monitoring approaches, networking, and risk management approaches that enable it to be successful in adapting to the policy environment created by the mental health authority. The resource dependency of the agency clearly indicates to the board that it cannot do much more than adapt, although it may seek to shape or otherwise influence these regulatory entities and forces (R. Scott, 1994).

Certainly the adaptive function is essential to any community and public service agency. But in the example offered above, the board has overdeveloped this function and has not really examined its other functions resulting in the need for new resources and new relationships. The adaptive function is critical to board performance because of its conservative nature. This function alerts the board to the reality of its business the purpose of which is to ensure that the agency is stable in its current environment.

The adaptive function, however, can conflict with other functions. It may suggest to the board that the security or stability of the agency can be compromised if the agency acts on its traditional or founding values (the ancestral function). Or the security or stability of the agency can be compromised if the agency takes advantage of opportunities that lead to new funding relationships and new populations to serve (the strategic function). The board may not want to compromise its security or stability by becoming more innovative (the generative function) in ways that are not recognized as needed or legitimate by the agency's sponsoring organizations or entities. And the board may not undertake effort to involve representatives of community or consumer groups or other stakeholders (the civil function) because the involvement in the board of these groups may be too controversial to those external entities that contribute resources to the agency. As asserted earlier, the function of adaptation makes the board somewhat wary of these other functions, which imbues the board with a conservative posture.

The adaptive function can also create a significant contradiction in how the board performs. The adaptive function may be so strong within the board that it actually earns the agency a positive or strong reputation among funding sources for its management ability. Yet the board may be unprepared to anticipate changes in its environment and may limit its attention to those "here-and-now" issues that are generated by the entities and the environment to which it is adapting. The board may spend very little time anticipating the agency's future and how this will be influenced by political and policy change, demographic and economic change, the emergence of new needs and service populations, and technological change. Fortunately through the development of other board functions these potential blind spots in board performance can be avoided.

Strategic Function

The strategic function of the board addresses the "here-and-now" situation of the agency differently than the adaptive function. The board's principal concern in exercising this function is with the positioning of the agency in its environment not merely or necessarily to adapt to existing funders, donors, or regulatory entities, but to identify and take advantage of emergent opportunities using the core competencies of the agency (Hosmer, 1987). The board seeks to position the agency to make a more significant impact on the problem or need that it was founded to address (Grace, 1997b), that is, to execute its mission.

A more opportunistic approach to strategy may be undertaken by the board when it searches for new opportunities in which it can use its core competencies for the purpose of advancing the well-being of the agency. This opportunistic approach to strategy can actually take the agency away from its founding idea and its founding vision. For example, an agency committed to bringing the performing arts to children and young people living in poverty takes advantage of cutbacks in school systems by contracting with these systems to provide a minimal exposure to the arts. Before long the board finds that its new business is to offer exposure to the arts to middle-class and upper-middle-class communities resulting in less responsiveness to impoverished communities.

Whichever approach the board takes to strategy, however, will not obscure the fundamental values of this function. The strategic function values opportunity, risk taking, and change. The strategic function exercises these values through board competencies involving environmental sensitivity, environmental surveillance, policy management, and policy change (Howe, 1997). This function, unlike the adaptive one, requires the agency to purposefully embrace change and to assess the implications of the environmental change facing the agency for the organization's principal policies, especially those that define agency purpose, mission, aims, service populations, and service structure (Carroll & Hall, 1987). The opportunistic nature of strategy requires the board to be sensitive to its environmental situation and to be willing to make appropriate changes that reflect the opportunities that the board identifies (Howe, 1997). Thus, unlike the adaptive function, the strategic function is wary of stability, security, and safety. This does not mean that the board acts in a cavalier or impulsive manner. It just means that the board is willing to change the agency intentionally so that the agency can take advantage of its environment (Carroll & Hall, 1987).

The strategic function is often expressed within the board through the adoption of a strategic management approach that involves three principal components: (1) strategy formulation and planning, (2) strategy implementation, and (3) strategy evaluation (Eadie, 1991). The formulation and planning component may or may not be undertaken in a formulaic way. Indeed, there is considerable variation in how community and public service organizations undertake strategy formulation and planning (B. Taylor, 1987). But strategy typically includes the formulation of an actual written and explicit plan based on the appraisal of the agency's environment, including the rate and kinds of changes that are currently experienced by the organization. It also can include an appraisal of threats and opportunities; the creation of scenarios; the evaluation of mission; the identification of core organizational competencies and assets; the identification of organizational needs; the formulation, evaluation, and selection of strategies; and the linkage of strategy to agency budget. The strategic function involves the oversight of strategy implementation by the chief executive officer and other agency executives and involves periodic evaluation of the strategy leading to its revision within a context of a board or organizational planning cycle.

But this framework is even a formalism that some boards may eschew while they maintain a strategic posture and approach (Lewis, 1991). The strategic function is as much a mindset within the board as it is a formal document to be formulated, monitored, evaluated, and revised. As a mindset, the board develops a keen sensitivity to the various environments within which the agency acts and develops knowledge and understanding of the various threats and opportunities the environment creates. In addition to environmental sensitivity, the strategic function can promote mission sensitivity among board members (Howe, 1997). Board members obtain considerable exposure to the agency mission as a principal organizational policy by engaging in extended or even brief dialogues about whether a mission should be reaffirmed, modified, or extensively change.

As noted previously, the strategic function contrasts sharply with the adaptive function. It also contrasts with the three other board functions. Whereas the strategic function focuses on the identification of opportunity in the present situation of the agency and acting on this opportunity, it does not necessarily mean that the agency will actually try to generate change in this environment through social action and service innovation (the generative function). The strategic function, through its focus on the here-and-now situation of the agency, may not prioritize the preservation of the founding values, beliefs, and ethical commitments of the agency (the ancestral function). Even though strategic management in human services often calls on other groups and people to offer input into agency strategy, strategy formulation and management is essentially an elite process requiring the board as the strategic apex to actually decide on agency strategy. The elite character of strategic management may actually circumvent participation from other stakeholder groups (the civil function) like lower level staff and consumers.

Overdevelopment of the strategic function within the board may result in some unwanted effects. First, this function can give an opportunistic character to the board. The board may abandon or relax its traditions and its founding values to take advantage of new opportunities within the environment. It may align itself with one population and then change this alignment during the next strategy cycle. Second, this function may result in mission drift. The board actually allows new opportunities to define the mission of the agency, rather than looking closely at what needs exist within a community and selecting those needs the board and the agency as a whole is best able to address and resolve successfully. Third, this function may result in the agency being unsuccessful because core competencies are not relevant to the opportunities the board has chosen to pursue. And, finally, the potentially opportunistic quality of the strategic function may create a feeling among agency personnel that change is undirected and overwhelming. They may lose an essential feeling of purpose, stability, and continuity.

Civil Function

This function may not seem obvious to many board members but it is quite relevant to the manner in which the board develops and performs. Community and public service organizations are basically nonprofit entities recognized under the federal tax code for the distinctive contribution they make to the well-being of communities and society. In recognition of this distinctive contribution they are given a special status within the tax code. In addition, as I note in chapter 1, the public sector has transferred a considerable number of public and quasi-public responsibilities to these organizations, thereby establishing them as extensions of government (Gilbert, 1983; Osborne, 1988). Many people who have pronounced social needs and experience serious social problems, as well as many communities requiring various public and cultural services, depend on these nonprofit organizations to help them, sustain them, or serve them (O'Neill, 1989).

The civil function recognizes that the nonprofit agency is indeed a public entity even though it is incorporated as a private organization (Lappe & Du Bois, 1994). It is an extension of government through privatization and contractual relations, created to provide public benefits. Nonprofits often respond to citizens who depend on them for justice, care, treatment, service, and enrichment (Ostrom & Davis, 1993).

The purpose of the civil function is to offer opportunities for citizens to become involved and to participate in addressing community needs as well as the needs of specific populations who require social benefits. The community and public service organization is one apparatus that offers citizens opportunities for involvement and participation, often in addressing some of the most critical and complex problems citizens and communities face (Gaillard, 1996; McLagan & Nel, 1997). As an expression of our democratic culture, community and public service organizations can offer citizens opportunities for participation and involvement and help organize various groups in the community to address the needs and problems the agency seeks to resolve (Lewis, 1991). These opportunities for participation and involvement are natural extensions of volunteerism that bring many people to board service.

The civil function of the board values participation and involvement. The function recognizes that it takes many people filling many different roles to contribute not only to the governance of the agency as a democratic institution, but also to making an impact on the need or problem the agency seeks to fulfill or resolve. This value also raises the issue of "who owns" community and public service organizations. They certainly are not owned by the chief executive officers. Board members do not own them either even though a metaphor of ownership may be contrived (Carver & Carver, 1997).

Ownership is more abstract—it cannot be assigned to any one individual or any one group. Ownership is in a sense social or public given the reality that many different entities and interests—public, quasi-public, and private—provide the resources to sustain the agency. Ownership is also social or public given the reality that many agencies exist because of a motivation on part of our communities and our society to create social justice. Agency services and benefits are offered to people who experience deprivation, discrimination, and diminished status. These services and benefits are offered to meet needs that other institutions (for example, the market) cannot or will not meet. Ownership is assigned to the community service board by the community and by society.

Participation and involvement within the board and the agency are themselves part of this service or benefit structure (Hodgkinson, Lyman, et al., 1989). The agency's board has a limited size, as prescribed by articles of incorporation or by-laws, and consequently it cannot accomodate all people, perspectives, and interests. Yet the complexity of the needs or problems, and the need to formulate equitable and fair responses to them, require a broader framework of participation and involvement. It is the civil function that reminds the board that it is indeed a public organization, and it is the civil function that reminds the board of the necessity and importance of extending its reach, its own perspective, and its own understanding through the involvement and participation of citizens. Involvement through board planning and evaluation activities, community forums, service on board committees and task forces, advisory structures and policy study groups, and special interest groups are some of the means that the board can extend its reach into the community and into various stakeholder groups.

The civil function brings the board into contact with those people, groups, and organizations who possess a strong "stake" or interest in the work of the community and public service agency and in the needs or problems addressed by the agency. The civil function enables the board to capture these perspectives and involves the people, group, and organizations that possess these perspectives to participate in the shaping of organizational policy, practices, and action. The democratic value of the civil function suggests that the community or public service organization has a public responsibility as an organizational citizen to enable people, groups, and other organizations to get involved in the work of the board. The civil function seeks to broaden and sustain this involvement and seeks to ensure that the voices of those people and groups who are not heard—often because of discrimination or lack of power—do indeed gain a hearing within the board.

The civil function means that the board is not an elite entity that is closed off to the community. It reframes accountability from accounting exclusively for funds and responsibilities to contractual entities to accounting for involvement and the inclusion of different perspectives and voices in agency policy making. Unlike the adaptive function it stresses that funders and donors do not have the exclusive say in shaping how the agency performs and practices. Compared with the strategic function, the civil function identifies strategy formation as a community and pluralistic process, rather than an elite process. Compared with the ancestral function, it recognizes that it takes a number of allies to achieve the founding vision of the agency. It is essential to the generative function because it assists the agency to build and sustain networks with various groups to formulate a community vision of and community ownership for the work and impact of the agency.

The civil function demonstrates the board's commitment to democratic process. It also is a recognition on the part of the board that it cannot internalize within such a relatively small group all of the perspectives, feelings, and views that are essential to good organizational policy making. However, the civil function over-developed can create some serious problems for the board. Too broad a scope of involvement and participation may overload the board with information and data. Such a broad scope may introduce too many perspectives, and by virtue of this create conflict that a board may find insurmountable. Some groups may begin to compete with others while other groups may want representation merely to monitor the agency and refuse to become truly involved in the work of the board. The purpose of the civil function is to promote participation and involvement, particularly among those stakeholders who often go unheard. The civil function enables the board of the community and public service agency to act on its responsibilities as an organizational citizen and to contribute to democratic culture. It is not a watchdog function and need not be developed as such.

Generative Function

The future orientation of the board is captured within the generative function. This function recognizes the important role the board serves in anticipating the future of the community or public service agency and in preparing for this future through the development of resources and the preparation of the organization so that it can be successful in meeting future challenges (Grace, 1997b). The generative function also involves the board's recognition that it does not have to only adapt to its policy, resource, and geographic environments. The board and agency can serve in leadership roles to create the changes that will enable the agency, and its partners, to make an impact on the problem or need the organization seeks to resolve (Burton & Moran, 1995).

The generative function, therefore, requires the board to think about its future and the future of the problem or need it addresses and to identify its leadership role in creating change or in establishing favorable conditions for change (Ackoff, 1991). The purpose of the generative function is to generate change not in the self-interest of the community or public service organization, but in the interest of making an impact on problem and need. The generative function requires the board to chart this change, which invariably involves the monitoring and analysis of external conditions or environment. But the eye of the board is on the future (LaMarsh, 1995). A board executing its responsibilities within the generative function, however, does not look for opportunities merely to position the agency. It focuses on how the agency can become an important influence in changing the circumstances of the community, population, or individuals whose betterment is reflected in the agency's vision (Chappell, 1993). This is indeed a leadership role (Nanus, 1992). And it is intentional. Myles Horton (1998) in the development of the Highlander Center illustrates this intentional effort and its implications for the agency and its board:

> We were all student leaders and activists before we started Highlander, so we brought that into the beginnings of Highlander. Later on the civil rights movement came along, and that came into Highlander and colored a lot of things. We deliberately set out to be involved in civil rights, and that brought changes in the process. It actually changed the composition of the staff. We had more black people. It changed the composition of the board. Movements change what goes on and how things are organized. (Horton & Freire, 1990, p. 178)

The generative function is executed by the board gaining an understanding of best practices or the state of the art within the field or problem area in which the agency operates. The board does not master these practices (because this is really the responsibility of agency personnel) but, rather, increases its knowledge base and understanding of what these practices are. This means that the board gains an understanding of the substance of high-quality practice and can offer leadership to the community and to the agency in identifying and installing these practices and ensuring that they are used on behalf of the populations served by the organization.

The generative function offers a framework within which the agency can engage in research and development—that is, engage in those processes that are essential to converting good knowledge into good practice. The generative function, where well implemented, can result in the board taking leadership in encouraging the use of best practices, refining what is meant by service quality, and establishing within the agency expectations that the organization will model these best practices through its services and programs. The generative function values innovation and the modeling of best practice within the community.

Unlike the strategic function that focuses on opportunities, the generative function encourages foresight and innovation leadership on part of the board. And, unlike the adaptive function, it requires the board to be dissatisfied with the current state of practice and its funding. It defines as an essential feature of board business the search for innovation and for those practices and approaches to service that will make its vision of service effectiveness a reality (West, 1992).

The generative function can complement the ancestral function by building service innovation on the sense of mission, purpose, values, and passion that are often present when a community and public service agency is first organized. It can also complement the civil function by offering to those individuals, groups, and organizations who collaborate with the board in advancing the well-being of a community or a population substantive tasks and responsibilities involving the identification of best practices and their use by the agency.

Overdevelopment of the generative function may make the board unfocused and too future oriented. The board may be too preoccupied with the future to look at the present performance and functioning of the agency or to address the strategic position of the agency within the community. Like the other four functions, the generative function offers something distinctive to the board and to the development of how the board functions. Without it, the board may not examine how it will generate those changes essential to the realization of agency vision. But the effort invested in the generative function should be weighed against the attention the other four functions require of the board.

Ancestral Function

The core values of the ancestral function involve continuity and integrity. Community and public service agencies are distinctive as organizations because frequently people who feel passionately about an issue, a problem, or a need initiate these agencies. They are concerned that a need is not being fulfilled within a community (such as cultural enrichment) or that an opportunity is not available to a specific group of people (recreation for youths). They may be concerned that a problem is not being addressed and is seriously jeopardizing the well-being of people (such as substance abuse). Or they may be concerned that a particular group—their well-being or even survival—is in jeopardy (such as people with serious mental illness).

The people who come together initially to form the community or public service organization are its founders. They bring their own concerns, values, objectives, aims, and visions and combine these with others within the board system to initiate the actual organization (Schein, 1983). This initial group can have a profound and enduring effect on the formation of the community or public service organization even if the board works in the shadow of the agency executive (Carver, 1992). The board can infuse the agency with hopes, dreams, and high expectations. It can establish the initial policy framework of the agency and install values that structure the services and opportunities available through the agency.

According to Schein (1992), the founders establish the basic belief structure of the agency. Newcomers are oriented to this belief structure and they are progressively socialized into it. First- and second-generations of newcomers may have firsthand contact with these founders and become very aware of what their beliefs, values, and aspirations are for the agency and for the problem or need they are enfranchised to address. As these founders move out of the agency, they do not take their beliefs or values with them (Schein, 1992). By then, these beliefs and values are well integrated into the agency and are expressed as part of its organizational culture. Subsequent generations become less aware of the founders' values and beliefs. Nonetheless, these beliefs and values likely influence members of subsequent generations even though they may not be fully conscious of them. These individuals are less conscious of those "founding" ideas that frame what the agency should do and how it should undertake its work but the ideas and values can be present shaping the behavior and actions of organizational members.

The ancestral function reminds the board that it is not a group or structure that is fixed in time. The current board is the beneficiary of members who came before it—of those organizational ancestors who founded and shaped the agency to serve a purpose, a mission, and to pursue its work in a specific way. Certainly, subsequent boards can reject these perspectives; it is remarkable how many boards do not do this but attempt to achieve some continuity by building on past ideas, concepts, values, perspectives, and practices. The ancestral function requires the board to undertake its work on a reflective basis: to reflect on why and perhaps how the agency was founded and what it stands for in the current environment. The ancestral function also requires the board to anticipate its own role as a steward of the future agency and of the future board.

This function is conservative just as the generative function is very liberal. It seeks to conserve those values and positions that have stood the test of time and that offer the agency style, character, and resilience. Change is not necessarily bad, from this perspective, but, rather, the need for change is to be appraised according to the traditions of the agency.

Decision making is not necessarily easy for the board that engages in the ancestral function. Although the adaptive and strategic functions require the agency to look outside of itself into its policy environment, and although the civil function requires the board to attend to external stakeholders, the ancestral function requires the board to examine itself internally—to examine its own traditions, own history, and own founding. Decisions are appraised in terms of their potential negative or positive impact on the "enduring character" of the community and public service organization (Adams, 1998).

Animating board dialogue are questions of integrity. What is the impact of these events, issues, or decisions on who we are? How do we stay true to the values of our founders? Should we stay true to the values of our founders? Is substantial change needed at this time? Questions such as these are critical ones. By answering them, the board shapes the very character of the agency. The ancestral function is another check and balance on the opportunism that can invade a board and that can threaten its integrity. The strategic function, and even the adaptive function, can raise opportunism as a threat to agency governance, but the reflection potentially introduced by the ancestral function can offset the development of an opportunistic perspective within the board. The ancestral function is also a check and balance on moving too far afield that can be a result of the overdevelopment of the generative function within the board. It is also a check and balance on the civil function in which the other groups may demand that the agency become something it is not.

Overdevelopment or overuse of the ancestral function can be problematic for the board. The values and beliefs of founders may be used as arguments to avoid substantial change when the organization must face challenges to its viability or relevance. The values and beliefs of founders may be used as arguments to avoid the adoption of best practices and related service technologies. In other words, the ancestral function can go too far in shaping the character and performance of the board. It can introduce traditionalism and defensiveness toward change into board deliberation, and can potentially erect barriers to self-renewal.

Organizational Governance and the Multiple Functions of the Board

These five functions taken collectively form the governance structure of the board. By *governance,* I refer to the manner in which the board as a principal structure of the community or public service agency shapes and influences the performance and behavior of the actual agency. This influence is a product of the individual and combined effects of the functions discussed previously.

Figure 4-1 offers a pictorial representation of these functions. Table 4-1 arrays for each of the functions its value base, its aims and desired outcomes, and the developmental implications the function holds for the board. I have carefully considered the position of each function within the board as a system, and I have intentionally placed the ancestral function at the center to indicate that the values of continuity and integrity are pivotal in influencing the character of the agency. Indeed, it is my perspective that, of the five functions, it is the ancestral function that requires board members to address the identity of the agency and what values need to be preserved, particularly during periods of crisis and acute environmental change. The other four functions are aligned in a circle around the ancestral function to indicate that they need to be integrated with the identity of the organization.

As with any system of governance, the board struggles with actualizing each value set identified within a function while simultaneously addressing the challenges, contradictions, or conflicts that each function can produce within the board and within the agency. It is the purpose of board governance to exercise these functions in influencing the performance and behavior of the agency. It is an understatement to say that this kind of influence is easy because the functions taken collectively reflect just how complex board governance is and can be.

The board functions themselves influence the manner in which the board conducts its business and executes its governance responsibilities. The jobs of board members can be dramatically influenced by the use of each of these functions. Although each function incorporates a distinctive set of values and aims, together they channel the way board members think about the agency and how they choose to think about board performance:

FIGURE 4-1: Functional Dimensions of the Community Service Board

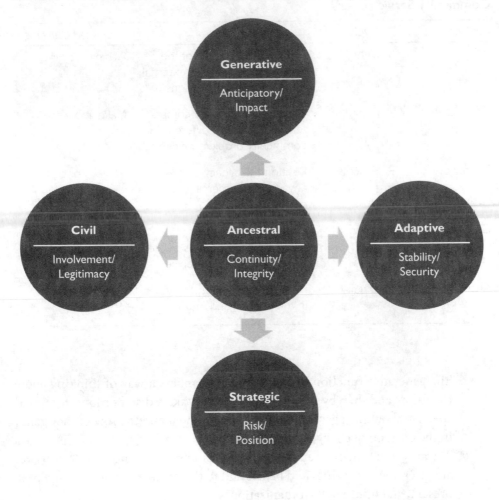

- The adaptive function can offer board members a short-term and practical frame of reference and focus the attention of board members on the wants, needs, and priorities and preferences of external funders, donors, and regulators.
- The strategic function can also offer board members a short-term frame of reference, but one that is heavily influenced by the search for opportunity and by the desire to position the agency within its environment.
- The civil function can offer board members a way of thinking about the agency as part of a broader community and as part of a broader set of networks formed by stakeholder interests.

TABLE 4-1: Overview of the Functional Dimension of the Community Service Board

Function Area	Value	Aim	Desired Outcome
Adaptive	Stability	Maintain the stability of the agency by adapting to external performance expectations	Achieve security
Generative	Anticipation	Create future agency competencies to make a difference in community problem or need	Make impact
Strategic	Risk Taking	Position the agency by taking advantage of emerging opportunities	Achieve position
Civil	Involvement	Serve as a conduit for the participation of various publics, stakeholders, constituencies	Achieve legitimacy
Ancestral	Continuity	Maintain strong founding values in the present and future	Achieve integrity

■ The generative function can offer board members a way of thinking about the future and thereby requires the board to take a distal or long-term perspective about the agency within its environment and the role of the agency in the creation of change within its community niche.

■ The ancestral function can sensitize board members to the need to consider and preserve core values and beliefs and to their role in integrating the past, present, and future of the organization.

In any system of governance we can see these functions acted out or acted on. Rigid adherence to prescriptive procedures for the use of these functions is not necessary. That will only limit the inventiveness of the board and prevent it from creating its own distinctive way of operating on the basis of its sense of duty and responsibility toward the agency's purpose and mission.

Conclusion

I would not be surprised to see some controversy about these various functions existing within any community service board. Board development is not only complex, but also controversial with the risk that considerable conflict can emerge within the board as the members undertake the development of these various functions. Typically, however, I have seen many boards simply overdevelop one function, such as the adaptive, thereby making the board strong in one area (for example, adapting to the agency's policy environment) while truncating its development in other key areas.

Perhaps the strongest community service board I have ever witnessed was a board of a national fraternity. The board's strength came from its successful efforts to balance carefully all of the functions within the context of its board structure and to integrate these functions through a deep commitment to the development of the board as a group. Certainly, one of its principal advantages was that all members were bound together by the traditions of the fraternity and the commitments they had made to the board during early adulthood. Service on the board was strengthened by a strong symbolic system that underscored the importance of the fraternity and its perpetuation in a most challenging environment in which fraternities were increasingly under fire within higher education.

The board was able to integrate the functions of adaptation, strategy, generativity, civility, and ancestry through the recruitment and retention of members who represented these functional perspectives and roles in their board. Several board members represented the ancestral function of the board. They were the oldest members who had the advantage of history and had witnessed the changes in the fraternity coincident with changes in society and higher education. These members understood the founding values and beliefs of the fraternity as an institution and were able to raise fundamental issues about the protection of these values as other board members reflected on, debated, and pondered critical policy questions.

Generative board members added to the mix a distinct perspective on where the fraternity was going and how the board could steward a successful future. These members talked about resource development, membership development, and the need for the fraternity to undertake critical leadership roles on campus. Adaptive board members raised issues pertaining to accountability emerging out of changing demographics, the need for fraternities to be seen as good citizens on campus, and the need to engage in risk management pertaining to incidents of alcohol consumption, drug use, and poor academic performance.

The board members advocating civility spoke of expanding the scope of involvement in the fraternity through inclusion of university faculty, new relationships with parents and families, and the involvement of students enrolled in secondary schools. Those board members embracing a strategic perspective focused on taking advantage of a "new environment" through the creation of academic retention programs, outreach to nontraditional students, and the marketing of membership benefits in the fraternity.

No one board member captured all of the reality facing this fraternity. Nonetheless, the comprehensive representation of these various functional perspectives among board members resulted in a rich plan for the perpetuation of the fraternity by preserving the essential identity of the organization while seeking to become viable in an environment of higher education that was changing substantially.

Questions for Board Discussion

1. Are there board members who serve the adaptive function within the board? Who are these members and what do they do on behalf of the board to enable the community service agency to adapt to its environment? What outcomes have these members produced on behalf of the agency and board?

2. Who are the board members who serve the strategic function within the board? What activities do they engage in that you consider being strategic? What outcomes have they produced on behalf of the agency and board?

3. To what extent does the current board engage in the civil function? Are there board members who serve this function? How do they undertake their work in this area? What outcomes have they produced on behalf of the agency and the board?

4. Are there "generative" board members who focus on the future of the community service agency? Who are these members and what does their future orientation do on behalf of the board and the agency?

5. Who are the board members who bring the ancestral function of the board into focus? What values do they represent and how do they reinforce these values? Have they produced any outcomes for the agency and for the board?

6. Does the agency mesh these various functions into a system of governance? Are some functions overemphasized while others are not addressed? What is the style of governance of the board on the basis of the functions that are the strongest?

7. What developmental needs does this chapter illuminate for the board? How will the board act on these needs?

■ 5 ■

Performance Dimension

We have charted a course of action regarding board development that is quite challenging. At our retreat we identified the board's institutional commitments and how the board can function as a high-performance system. This work was energized by our basic commitment to making the arts a viable part of the educational system of our community. We defined this broadly and included not only the education of our children but also the education of the community's young adults, families, and elders. Now we need to get down to some more basic board development challenges. How do we strengthen our performance? To answer this question, I will focus on the committee's two year plan to build board membership, improve the group climate of the board, enlarge the scope of the board's structure, strengthen the board's network, and increase productivity. Let me get started . . .

The two dimensions discussed previously focus the attention of the board and its members on forming the identity of both the board and the agency as well as on crafting the governance functions in which the board will engage. Using the institutional and functional dimensions to understand board development directs the energies of the board into answering critical questions that can dramatically influence how the community or public service agency will undertake its work and make an impact on the problem or need it is chartered to address. These two dimensions involve questions like these: Who are we? What do we stand for? Why have we come together as a board? And how will we function to govern the board?

The third dimension is probably the most concrete, practical, and traditional dimension of board development. The performance dimension requires the board to address how it will actually organize to undertake its work. It is concrete in that it requires the board to think through and to establish ways of executing its institutional and functional dimensions. It is practical because this dimension requires

67

the board to establish the actual structures and processes that enable it to under-take its work. And it is traditional because this is the form of board development that readily comes to mind of many board members.

How does the board actually conduct its business?

This critical dimension deals with the "working" aspects of the board and how it transforms the institutional and functional dimensions into actual work, per-formance, and products. The performance dimension moves the board out of the broad and perhaps idealistic perspectives needed to establish its institutional and functional frame of reference and directs the board into struggling with the actual performance of the board and its members.

Without this dimension the board risks the loss of legitimacy through the cre-ation of a chasm between what it aspires to achieve—as captured by the institutional and functional dimensions—and what it actually achieves. However, by develop-ing the performance function without developing the institutional or functional dimensions, the board may lapse into a false productiveness in which it produces work without much meaning attached to it. Within the model these dimensions join to link organizational meaning to actual board performance.

Like the other two dimensions, the performance dimension is complex and composed of at least six elements that together form a milieu within which the board executes its institutional and functional responsibilities of governance. These six elements are (1) membership, (2) group life, (3) structure, (4) network, (5) task, and (6) product. It is the purpose of this chapter to elaborate these various elements and as a result build the reader's understanding of the performance dimension of the board.

Board Membership

The board is a collection of members who affiliate voluntarily with the agency to serve in leadership positions. People may come to board membership for a num-ber of different reasons, and it is not unusual to find great variation in their moti-vations. Some board members become involved because it is good for business or because employing organizations require or encourage such service. Or board members may merely want recognition by the agency and the community while others may want to establish relationships with people who are active in their com-munities. Other board members may become involved because they are search-ing for a service outlet for their skills and talents or they want a greater sense of meaning than what they find in their work or profession. They may feel that board membership and agency service is an extension of their professional mission, such as when physicians, nurses, accountants, social workers, or professors enlist in a board to extend their professional knowledge and abilities to an agency as a form of public service. They may be motivated by more humanistic concerns. Some board members are motivated by the actual social problem or social need addressed by the community and public service agency. They see themselves as advocates.

The membership element does require some insight on the part of agency leaders about the motivation of people who come to serve on the board (Charan, 1998). The motivational aspects of board membership require boards to identify why people want to join the board and what they expect to get out of it. It is critical for agency leaders to understand that they are not merely recruiting people to fulfill the needs of the agency or organization, they are also recruiting people whose own needs must be fulfilled or addressed. Like any social system, to sustain the performance of the group, the needs of its members must be met (Bolman & Deal, 1997).

This element recognizes the importance of fulfilling people's needs and of providing the opportunities they personally seek through the board system (Bolman & Deal, 1997). However, it may also be assumed by agency leaders that these motivations may not be stable or rigid but may actually change over time, especially as board members gain a better sense of the agency and an understanding of the social problem or need that the agency seeks to address. Well-organized and high-performing boards can exert a tremendous influence over the values and motivations of their members through education, training, socialization, and exposure to the work of the agency (Schein, 1992). A person coming to board service to make better connections may subsequently gain a keen insight into the social problem the community and public service agency addresses and may begin to identify with the people who struggle with this problem. Motivation of people to join boards demonstrates how self-interest can contribute to collective or social interest (Mitroff, 1989).

The membership element also focuses the attention of the board on the kinds of skills, competencies, perspectives, and characteristics brought to the board by its members. Certainly, many board members are recruited for their technical skills, such as in finance and accounting, human resources, information technology, fund raising, public relations and marketing, and other managerial or administrative areas. These represent the "hard" skills of board members and the needs of the agency in these areas typically influence the recruitment of people to the board. Second, in addition to these hard skills, there is the recruitment of people who have connections or who are well positioned in areas of the community—in industry, commerce, education, and service—that are of institutional or strategic value to the community and public service agency (Charan, 1998).

The "positioned" member brings different assets to the board than the "skilled" member. The positioned member may have influence, connections, and linkages with other key people and it is this member who may have better access to important political leaders, corporate executives, and entities or people who control monetary or other resources needed by the agency (Charan, 1998). Overrepresentation of these kinds of members on the board may make it too opportunistic and too political, but, nonetheless, such members are vital to board development and functioning.

Special or desired perspectives and characteristics of members may be overlooked as important aspects of board membership. Skilled or positioned members may represent elite structures of the community like the corporate business sector. Overrecruitment of these members may not only bias the perspectives brought to the board by these members, but also limit their contributions to the institutional or functional dimensions of the board. Skilled finance professionals who are motivated to join a board of an agency serving people with disabilities because of a community service requirement established by their corporations may have limited or no knowledge of the needs of the people served by the organization. Indeed, their business frame of reference may limit the establishment of a valid and inspiring organizational purpose if there is a preoccupation with financial matters alone.

Other members are needed who bring to board service the essential perspectives, or demographic characteristics, needed to frame an institutional purpose that is relevant and meaningful (Zander, 1993). These members may include consumers themselves—especially people served by the agency—or their family members, loved ones, or advocates. These people may not bring specific skills or position to the board. However, they likely bring an essential passion and concern for the people served by the agency, a commitment to work tirelessly on behalf of the people served by the agency, and a challenging vision about what the agency can achieve on behalf of the people served. The passion and energy brought to the board by these members may be based on anger, dissatisfaction, and disaffection with the status quo and they may be quite challenging to the agency as a whole as well as to other board members (Dybwad & Bersani, 1996). They may create some conflict of perspective within the board. It is critical for the board to expect this kind of conflict to arise and to use it in a proactive manner to create a challenging institutional framework for the agency (Zander, 1993).

Diversity is another factor to which membership development must be sensitive. The involvement of community elites through the recruitment of highly skilled professionals and well-positioned people, as well as the involvement of highly motivated consumers, may mean that the board does not reflect the mainstream characteristics of the community. Membership development can incorporate diversity through the purposeful recruitment of people who share demographic characteristics with the target population and the intentional recruitment of people who share demographic characteristics with principal minority groups within the service population (Berquist, 1993). It is likely that community and public service organizations serve people who are members of minority groups because it is these groups that are overrepresented among service populations and in certain social problem areas. A pronounced demographic mismatch between the board and the service population may mean that the board is unable to understand the needs and perspectives of the people served and may, in turn, fail to create relevant policy and make well-informed decisions.

The membership element of the performance dimension helps board and agency leaders to think about the relationship of board membership to the development of agency identity and purpose as well as to the execution of the board's governance functions (Zander, 1993). It also forms an important foundation of board performance because it is the knowledge and skills, community position, perspectives, and demographic characteristics that will influence the vitality of the board. Indeed, the vitality of the board is based on a number of membership considerations used purposefully to shape who serves on the board and identify why their service is needed by the agency. This purposeful or intentional balancing and intermixing of board membership qualities—based on the needs of the community and public service agency—offers the board the opportunity to develop its own style and character. It is this style and character gained largely from membership qualities that in turn could influence tremendously the development of the community and public service agency.

Group Life of the Board

This element of the performance dimension requires the board to understand itself as a social system that is formed by interconnecting bonds among the members of the board (Zander, 1993). Board performance cannot be merely composed of the individual contributions of each board member. Certainly, the board will benefit from gifted and well-motivated members who make outstanding contributions as individuals to the board and to the agency. However, to perform effectively, board members must come together as a group and to work together on mutually defined and agreed-on aims, goals, and products (Duca, 1996).

Developing a strong and supportive group life is a considerable challenge in light of a membership development approach that favors diversity. A diverse membership means that board members will come from many different walks of life and with many different motivations for joining the board. They will come with different skill packages and have different positions within the social structure of the community. They can come with different perspectives and with different demographic characteristics. As noted previously, this diversity holds the promise of vitality if and only if these members can join together around a shared vision and purpose as well as a shared set of goals.

To perform as a group, the board must develop competencies to become a group (Stoesz & Raber, 1997). Important here are three qualities involving (1) norms that build support among members and create positive human relations within the board, (2) informal approaches to conflict resolution that support the board's execution of its working agenda, and (3) development of a sense of group cohesion and identity (Zander, 1993). I have found from much of my board work a pronounced limitation on the part of many boards. Rarely do board members find time to get to know each other as people, as professionals and workers coming from different walks of life and as individuals with hopes and aspirations for themselves, their families, and their communities. Building support within the board requires this kind of personalized knowledge among board members. This knowledge can help create bonds of friendship and collaboration. And this knowledge can help others understand the perspectives, attitudes, and worldview of a particular board member. Time invested in getting to know one another can foster positive human relations and can help the board to create a "give-and-take" culture in which people are willing to listen and to negotiate (Bolman & Deal, 1997).

Norms that govern or influence how board members will work together emerge out of group life and are often a function of the interpersonal ties board members have created among one another and the amount of time they spend together in groups working collaboratively on tasks and issues. Basic norms supporting positive interaction are critical to effective board performance. Examples of norms involve the expectation that people will share their perspectives openly in front of the group, people can and will openly disagree, no one person can dominate the sessions of the board, and that decisions are a group product achieved through careful deliberation among members.

An essential set of norms involves conflict resolution (Zander, 1993). Effective boards make critical decisions the substance of which can have profound implications for the development of the community and public service agency. An effective board makes these critical decisions in a timely, diplomatic, and, perhaps even, democratic manner. Thus, it is not unusual for boards to experience considerable conflict that can potentially result in some board members deciding to leave the board or some members psychologically removing themselves from the board by skipping meetings or by distancing themselves from deliberations during a meeting. Some board members may even adopt acrimonious relationships with other members.

This kind of conflict is expected, and the more critical the work of the board, the more likely it will emerge. Norms pertaining to conflict resolution need to emerge within the group life of the board and can involve the conscious discussion periodically among board members about how conflict can be expressed and what the board will do to reduce it or resolve it. Ways of resolving conflict within the effective board are numerous. Among them are

- using an external facilitator to mediate conflict,
- calling special sessions of the board to discuss and resolve conflicts,
- undertaking outreach to specific board members to bring them back into the life of the group, and
- institutionalizing within the board minority perspectives and opinions that are routinely reviewed by the board as a whole as a check and balance on the "tyranny of the majority."

The best approach to conflict resolution, however, from my own experience as a board member and as a consultant to boards, involves strong and enduring positive human relations among board members. These relations are built on previous opportunities to get to know one another through board-sponsored events that involve socialization, celebration, and education among board members. The most fragile and conflict-sensitive board is the one that has not developed interpersonal bonds among its members. The board most ready to make productive use of conflict in its deliberations is that board in which members have formed positive and enduring relationships based on personal knowledge and personal understanding of the other members.

In other words, board development does indeed involve the intentional pursuit of cohesion among board members from which positive norms can develop and become stronger. These kinds of norms are not necessarily cast in writing. They are formed during the course of board deliberations—during meetings, retreats, and evaluation sessions in which board members openly discuss how they relate to one another and how they want to relate to one another. They are also influenced by the board's development of its own identity.

Certainly the institutional dimension can influence very positively the formation and strengthening of group life because this dimension requires the board to come to grips with the agency's own purpose and identity as well as with the board's purpose and identity (Ward, 1997). Forging among group members a formal sense of identity requires involvement in working sessions and meetings. It is this productive involvement that can in turn produce group cohesion and group identity. In other words, members get to know one another when they spend time together productively and successfully. Productive group life emerges when the time invested by board members leads to an understanding among them of how to work together in productive ways.

Board Structure

How the board structures itself is another element that is critical to its performance. We can think of board structure as those parts or components that enable the board to execute its functions and to achieve its short- and long-term objectives. The structural element focuses the attention of board members on thinking about the collection of parts or components through which the board actually undertakes its work and creates products.

A key to understanding board structure lies in identifying the scope of the overall structure of the board. Scope refers to the area covered by the board's structure and consequently involves the relative complexity or simplicity of structure. Imagine a board with a very narrow scope. It focuses its work and its performance only on planning a budget and monitoring the budget. With requisite information from the agency financial officer, budgetary planning and special fiscal analyses undertaken by agency staff, and annual external audits, the board's scope is quite limited. Thus, the actual structure of the board is quite limited or simplistic.

Alternatively, imagine a board the scope of which is quite broad. The board seeks to create very important outcomes on behalf of the people served by the agency and undertakes its institutional responsibility by protecting critical values, husbanding and developing agency resources, positioning the agency, involving the community, and generating changes in practice so that the agency will model best practices. To undertake work of this scope the board needs considerable skill and expertise, a number of highly motivated members and allies, and considerable information. This kind of scope demands complex structure.

The functional dimension influences the scope of board structure. Five functions are identified in chapter 4 and in conjunction with the identity work required of the institutional dimension the scope of the board can result potentially in an elaborate board structure. The adaptive function requires the board to undertake monitoring of performance and financial requirements demanded by external sources while the strategic function requires the board to establish a relevant and valid strategic planning process, planning cycle, and written plan. The civil function requires the board to involve representatives from various stakeholder and community groups in the process of governance while the generative function requires the board to establish a momentum and a framework supporting best practices and model programs. The ancestral function requires the board to promote continuity and integration of the agency around historically relevant values, beliefs, and principles.

These five functions suggest that the board has a number of quite relevant responsibilities to package and to allocate to various substructures. Depending on the board's style and the manner in which it has decided to undertake its work, the structural design of the board can be undertaken in a variety of ways (Stoesz & Raber, 1997). For example, the strategic planning, long-range planning, community involvement, and systems change work can be delegated by the board to a variety of mechanisms staffed in various ways. Below are principal mechanisms that a board can use to define and execute the scope of its work.

Use of a Seasonal Cycle by the Board as a Whole

A board may undertake a portion of its work as a "committee of the whole," but use a seasonal cycle to manage the actual work (Berquist, 1993). A strategic planning cycle for one board can involve two years with the first year devoted to undertaking key planning activities while another part of the year is devoted to monitoring and evaluating implementation that results in either updating the plan or formulating a new plan. Individual board members undertake responsibilities for strategic planning on a one time ad hoc basis and these informal roles are updated and perhaps reassigned in subsequent cycles of planning.

Use of Standing Committees

A board may undertake a great deal of its work through the formation of standing committees that have specific charters, goals, and responsibilities. The board makes explicit decisions—typically through its by-laws—about the packaging of responsibilities, their assignment to specific committees, and the formalization of member roles in relationship to the responsibilities of board committees. The scope of board functions, the grouping of responsibilities, and the assignment of responsibilities to actual committee structures influence the number of board committees. For example, responsibilities for all planning—including strategic, long range, capital, contingency or retrenchment, and financial—may be delegated to a board standing committee on planning. Or these various responsibilities may be broken out by time frame: crisis planning, strategic planning, and long-range planning. Table 5-1 lists some of the possible "responsibility packages" a board may identify as within its scope. It is useful as a self-assessment tool concerning what responsibilities a board wants to undertake.

Those enduring responsibilities, especially ones that need to be undertaken on a repetitive or ongoing basis, are good candidates for assignment to an actual standing committee. The establishment of a standing committee also requires the identification of formal roles for leading these structures and for executing the work of the various committees. Therefore, the formation of standing committees influences the formalization of board structure.

Use of Task Forces

These structures are temporary and ad hoc formed on the basis of immediate and short-range needs of the board. Task forces are useful when the board seeks to create a needed product, identify decision options, and resolve a dilemma or respond to an urgent or crisis need. The use of task forces alongside standing committees offers boards flexible options for assigning work and offers options for balancing bureaucratic or routine structure (committees) with ad hoc or temporary work (task forces).

A task force may come into being because of a significant need (for example, to address how a board enters the business of fund raising or the creation of an endowment) or because of a significant controversy (for example, the board needs a policy on the prevention of sexual harassment). The task force may undertake its work under the leadership of board members in conjunction with other participants who are invited to participate because of their skill, expertise, motivation, or

TABLE 5-1: "Responsibility Packages" that Can Influence Board Structure

Responsibility	Example Activity
Board development	Membership recruitment
	Succession planning
	Role assignments
	Orientation and board education
	Performance evaluation of board members
	Self-evaluation of board performance
Agenda management	Ongoing identification of issues
	Linkage of agenda to agency strategy
	Translation of issues into agenda items
	Tracking of accomplishments
Corporate planning	Capital planning
	Contingency planning
	Long-range planning
	Development of agency vision
Executive development	Performance monitoring
	Performance evaluation
	Professional development
	Compensation, rewards
	Succession planning
Social responsibility	Community development
	Corporate responsibility
	Corporate citizenship
Budgeting	Budget cycle
	Budgetary oversight
	Financial contingencies
Evaluation	Mission evaluation
	Evaluation of agency vision
	Monitoring of corporate outcomes
	Monitoring of key market indicators
Resource development	Fund development
	Endowment oversight
Image management	Oversight of public relations campaigns
	Oversight of corporate brands and logos
Policy management	Policy planning
	Policy implementation
	Policy evaluation
	Policy change

position within the community but who are not formal board members. After the work is executed and a product is delivered to the board the task force dissolves.

Alternatively, the task force may actually transfer its product or work into a standing committee or the task force itself may become a standing committee, something that may actually occur in fairly new agencies or in agencies that undergo self-renewal. The following examples reflect the transition of a task force into a standing committee:

- A task force assigned to prepare personnel policies for the agency becomes the standing committee on personnel.
- A task force assigned to investigate insurance coverage and benefits for the agency becomes the standing committee on risk management.
- A task force assigned to plan a board sponsored fund raiser becomes the standing committee on resource development.
- A task force assigned to generate corporate vision becomes the standing committee on long-range planning and institutional development.
- A task force assigned to address barriers to diversity both within the board and within the agency becomes a standing committee on human resource development.

Use of Advisory Groups

These groups can become an essential feature of board structure when the board requires input concerning new directions, needs, service populations, technologies, and practices. Often, boards face great uncertainty about mission, vision, and purpose. An agency, for example, that becomes very effective in helping people with serious mental illness to find, get, and keep employment may be approached by funders and advocates for poor people trying to transition out of welfare. Should the agency begin to serve this population? Should the agency serve other populations like people with developmental disabilities or neurological problems? The board may lack the actual expertise to make these decisions without additional information and input.

Advisory groups to the board that are specifically chartered to advise the board on an ongoing basis regarding emergent community needs and populations may enable the board to obtain the requisite information. These groups are advisory in that they are not making decisions on behalf of the board. Nor is the information or recommendations they offer binding on the board. These advisory structures may be permanent. They are not established as task forces charged to address a time-limited issue. The advisory structures are in a sense standing structures because they offer the board ongoing input and information. They may fluctuate in permanency. Unlike task forces, however, they are not short-term in duration but rather may last for some time as long as they remain relevant to the board.

These groups are especially important to the board that prioritizes its civil and generative functions. Advisory groups are excellent means for obtaining input on needs, issues, and concerns voiced by members of populations, advocates, and citizens who may not have representatives on the board. They offer the board a means for extending its reach into the community and in generating knowledge and information about best practices and emergent technologies, thereby enabling an agency to establish itself as a model or as a vanguard within a given community (Duca, 1996).

In the early history of head injury rehabilitation in a particular community, I had the opportunity to observe a board of a newly forming parent advocacy group creatively use advisory groups to complement its policy, service, and issue advocacy on behalf of people who had sustained traumatic head injury. The board, dominated by parents who were very committed to the advancement of services and rights for this population, recognized that it required additional input from other "stakeholders" to advance the cause of the organization. It established a professional advisory group to offer information and insight into best practices and a consumer advisory group that offered information and insight on the perspectives of people who had sustained head injuries. A third advisory group on minority affairs helped the parent advocacy group to craft sound organizational policies on promoting the involvement of underrepresented members of diverse communities in the organization's advocacy work and in the formulation of its agenda.

These three groups often came together with the board of the organization to plan strategy and to educate board members about best practices, consumer perspectives, and minority concerns. Most important, the three groups offered the board a trial setting in which potential candidates could be evaluated for membership on the actual board. The groups also expanded the number of people who were being prepared as advocates for people and families who were coping with the personal, social, and medical consequences of traumatic head injury.

Expanding Involvement in the Board

Standing committees, task forces, and advisory groups can be used as a structural strategy for expanding the potential membership pool of the board. The board as a membership body does not have to be confined to those people who are formally recruited to the board as official members. These various board structures expand the scope of board participation. These structures enable the board to expand the scope of involvement from those people who may not be ready for board service to those people who may not want to participate in the formal board, but who nonetheless want to make contributions in a specific or limited area. The structure of the board itself is a means to expand involvement of a range of people who can contribute to the work of the board without formal membership.

These various ways of structuring the board reveal that board structure is not cast in stone (Stoesz & Raber, 1997). Nor can one prescribe a specific structure. The board as a whole must decide on its own structure on the basis of its own needs, its own style, and its own functions. Through the choices the board makes about undertaking work through the board as a whole, standing committees, task forces, advisory groups, or a combination of these, the board is defining its configuration and how it performs. By recognizing these various mechanisms for encouraging the participation of people who are not necessarily members of the formal board, the board is expanding the human energy available to it to complete its work. In other words, board members may lead these various structural alternatives but their own membership may actually expand the functional boundaries of the board as a system.

In addition, it is difficult to establish the actual size of the board. The by-laws typically incorporate a statement about the size of the board but this language typically does not identify the rationale governing the size. It is probably accurate to assert that size is a product of the scope of the work of the board. The more simplistic the structure, the fewer members the board will need. The more complex the structure, the more board members the board will need. Complex structure requires board members to serve in formal and informal roles. Would a board create task forces or advisory groups without board members as chairs? Most likely not.

The linkage between these structures and the parent board is vital and it is the board member serving as chair, leader, or senior member who will ensure continuity, integrity, and consistency of purpose and intent. Thus, board size must be established in relationship to scope, which in turn will influence the number of mechanisms and the types of mechanisms the board uses to undertake its work. In this sense, the board is an ad hoc–racy—it seeks a structure and size that fit its scope. And scope is influenced by the board's conception of its purpose. Without making deliberate decisions about its scope, a board will have a difficult time finding a suitable structure.

Board Network

So far we have considered the membership, group life, and structure of the board. Yet these features of the board as a performance system are internal to the board and influence how it is organized. The board network offers a different portrayal of the board. It is composed of a number of interrelated linkages that connect the board and the agency externally to other groups, people, and organizations as well as resources. These interconnections offer the board opportunities to transact business and commerce with others, to obtain resources, and to establish the identity of the community and public service agency within its environment.

One way of looking at the board network is as a social network. Board members bring an array of business, commercial, social, political, and interpersonal contacts with them to the board (Zander, 1993). These social networks may prove to be invaluable because they can connect the board through the board member to important, if not critical, resources such as awareness of what the agency is trying to do, other skills and competencies, equipment, and political support. For example, a board new to fund raising was able to link into an array of experts in this area through a board member who recently retired as a professional fundraiser. Through this board member's own social network composed of relationships developed and strengthened over a 35-year career, this board was able to mobilize the fund-raising talent of an entire community on behalf of the agency.

Some board members may not be comfortable in accessing their social networks on behalf of the board. They may feel that this intrudes too much into their personal lives. They may not want to obligate a friend or a colleague. Or they may not trust the competence of the agency to make good use of the relationship. Yet it is important for the board as a whole to gain some understanding of its members' social networks and it is equally important for the board not to expect that a board member will put these networks to work on behalf of the board. The social networks of board members do stand as one resource that should be carefully considered by the board within the constraints of the individual preferences of board members (Grace, 1997b).

The board also represents an institutional network. The board members as a group can possess important institutional linkages within the community that can span almost every sector. Systematic board development may have resulted in the purposeful selection of board members to represent specific sectors of the community like higher education, local and state government, certain professions, large corporations, small business, consumer advocacy groups, media and public relations, principal industries, social and health services, and the arts.

The institutional network may be diversified or specific sectors of the community may be selected on the basis of the needs of the agency and its purpose, aims, and goals. A performing arts organization that seeks to offer accessible theater on the basis of an outreach model to populations that normally would not be exposed to theater requires relationships with a variety of institutions in the community to execute its mission. This mission is facilitated in part through a board development strategy that strengthens the institutional network of the board. Board members who represent those institutions serving these populations are purposefully recruited to board service so that the agency is better able to link with relevant populations. The board's membership includes representatives from various disability communities, nursing and health care providers, the aging community, and neighborhood organizations in low-income areas. Board members in this case are boundary spanners. They represent one way the organization links access to the performing arts to other institutional sectors within the community (Bergquist, 1993).

Board developers can easily overlook the institutional network of the board. Board developers may think more in terms of a potential member's social network because they are concerned with the personal standing and influence of the member. The community institution represented by the board member may in fact be a more important board development factor. Such a board member can bring a wealth of understanding of a particular institutional sector to the board and offer other board members knowledge and understanding of how to connect the organization to the resources available within this sector (McMaster, 1996). In this context, information and its infusion into the board become an important benefit of the purposeful development of the institutional network of the board (Stoesz & Raber, 1997).

Finally, the board represents a resource network for the community and public service agency (Grace, 1997b). The linkages board members possess through their social and institutional networks are conduits through which these members can identify and locate potential resources. As noted above, the board member who was willing to contact his or her community of fund raisers on behalf of the agency reflects the kind of cache of skills that a board can potentially mobilize. Board members can be conduits through which equipment and tools can be acquired, buildings and services secured, and dollars obtained.

Often the recruitment of board members is undertaken with a utilitarian objective in mind. They are recruited because they can muster specific resources like money within a community. As a driving force for recruitment this is probably opportunistic and shortsighted. The threat here is that the board becomes a group of well-connected people or perhaps elites who can make key telephone calls on behalf of the agency and secure needed funds. Certainly, these are important people for a board to recruit, but this kind of recruitment must not obscure the reality that people from all walks of life can bring an array of resources to board service. Consumers of agency services, who are asked to serve on the board because of their first-person experience with a service system, dedication to their own recovery, and dedication to the recovery of their peers, can serve as a significant resource to the board and agency. Such people can bring timely information about consumer perspectives and sentiments to the board that probably no other member can. They can contact consumers when input is needed for grant proposals. And perhaps they can easily solicit input from consumers about agency direction, mission, and performance.

The network of the board need not be an elite structure. It should be carefully articulated from social, institutional, and resource perspectives. The agency's purpose and aims can influence the development of this network. Its development can offer the logic for membership recruitment. Well-conceived membership development can result in the creation of social, institutional, and resource networks that contribute to the vitality and viability of the community and public service agency.

Board and the Performance of Tasks

The distinction between a working and policy board is trivial. All boards are "working boards" in the sense that board members as individuals and the board as a whole have duties to execute and responsibilities to fulfill (Charan, 1998). Some of these tasks are formally assigned whereas others are assigned through informal expectations. The former evolve out of the actual formal role of the board member and the structure of the board whereas the latter evolve out of the individual talents, interests, and energy brought to board service by members.

The formalization of tasks within the board is very important because it is this formalization that anchors the member to the board and to his or her formal responsibilities (Zander, 1993). Although board membership is voluntary, it is still a job within the agency and like any job specific expectations must be established and monitored. Without this formalization, the board may lose the ability to channel the energy of board members and to ensure that the board as a whole is productive. And without this formalization the board may not be able to improve its actual performance.

The tasks of the board are informed by its mission and its goal set, the purpose of which is identifying what it intends to achieve on behalf of the agency it sponsors and governs. The mission establishes the boundaries of the board and defines the kind of work it will undertake. This mission can be developed at an annual board retreat and can be used as a framework for the goal set of the board. This goal set, in conjunction with the board mission, defines what the board will achieve during a given period. These goals are not tightly drawn with rigid deadlines and measurable outcomes. They are merely end statements that offer the board some direction, gives individual board members an idea of what is needed from them, and offers standing committees and task forces an understanding of what the board wants to achieve and the role they may play in this achievement. Board goals that are coordinated with the overarching agency goals offer a means of integrating board performance with agency performance and this coordination underscores that all principal systems—including the board—make important contributions to agency performance.

There are several tools that can be useful to fostering the formation and completion of tasks within the board. These involve the board service contract, board job description, the committee or task force work plan, and the board evaluation protocol.

Board Service Contract

This simple contract defines those basic expectations the board has of its members and offers a way for board members as individuals to identify the contributions they can make or are willing to make to the board. The contract can identify expec tations concerning attendance, minimal time commitments, and minimal assign- ments. The contract can identify the specific objectives that the board member will pursue on behalf of the board and agency. Table 5-2 offers an example of this kind of board member contract. It shows what is expected of a board member who has been recruited to an agency that serves people with epilepsy over a two-year period, including attendance and committee work. The board member has agreed to serve on the health policy committee. As a physician, she will offer board members her expertise, knowledge, and understanding of neurology and the medical manage- ment of epilepsy and of managed health care.

As a physician advocate within the community, the board member selects three objectives that she as an individual will pursue within the board:

1. to help the agency create linkages within the health care and pharmaceutical industry to expand the emergency pharmacy program,
2. to offer board members training and education on the psychosocial and medical aspects of epilepsy and the state of the art in the treatment of people with epilepsy, and
3. to help the agency formulate an advocacy agenda to improve primary health care of people with epilepsy.

These objectives are consistent with the institutional character of this agency. It does not limit its attention to the medical aspects of epilepsy, but has established as its purpose the need to address the social, economic, personal, and medical consequences of epilepsy through service innovation, advocacy, and community support. The physician advocate was recruited not only for the expertise and com- mitment she exemplifies as a medical professional in the field of epilepsy, but also because she adds to the institutional network of the board. Thus, the contract shows the intersection of a member's tasks with member characteristics and insti- tutional network.

Board Job Description

The board job description complements the board structure. Such a job description is formulated for all formal roles designated by the board to support its work and the achievement of its goals. The job description formalizes the job or position of the board officer. In addition, it is especially important for those individuals who chair formally designated board committees and for those who chair task forces.

TABLE 5-2: The Association for Services to People with Epilepsy Expectations of Board Members

TO: Mary Jaeger, MD
        Assistant Clinical Professor of Neurology
        School of Medicine
        State University

FROM: David Perkins, Chair
        Board of Trustees
        The Association for Services to People with Epilepsy

The Association for Services to People with Epilepsy recognizes the great contributions each board member makes to the success of the agency. The agency recognizes that the time and energy each board member commits is a gift to the organization, and the administrators and staff members of the agency are grateful for these contributions. In particular, the board is most appreciative of your commitment to service on the association's board and we look forward to a productive relationship. You have been selected because of your nationally recognized expertise in neurology as well as your commitment to facilitating the health of people struggling with epilepsy. In consultation with the board development committee and your board mentor, we have identified three major contributions you can make to the board. These are:

1. To assist the agency to make linkages with health care resources and pharmaceutical companies in order to expand the emergency pharmacy program.
2. To assist the board to expand its knowledge of the psychosocial and medical aspects of epilepsy as well as the state of the art in the community support and treatment of people coping with epilepsy; and
3. To assist the agency to formulate an advocacy agenda to improve primary health care of people coping with epilepsy.

You have agreed to fulfill the following expectations while a member of the association's board:

1. The board expects you to participate in and complete the five-hour board member orientation program.
2. The board expects that you will be present for all scheduled quarterly meetings. Since the board holds its major meetings on a quarterly basis consistent attendance is crucial to the completion of board business.
3. The board expects your attendance at the board retreat, which requires a full day commitment, and the annual meeting, which involves the board's acceptance of the annual budget and the annual plan of agency work.
4. The board expects that you will stay current with the principal issues facing the board by reading documents and materials disseminated during the periods between quarterly meetings.
5. The board expects you to serve on the agency's health care policy committee and bring to this committee your extensive expertise in epilepsy.

The board and the agency will support your achievement of these expectations by:

1. Ensuring that you receive only pertinent and relevant information from the agency.
2. Ensuring that all board meetings start and stop on time.
3. Refraining from asking you to become involved in activities that are not consistent with the purpose of your board service.

The association thanks you for your involvement. The members of the board welcome you to board service.

For the board officer, the job description identifies the purpose of the position and the key responsibilities on part of the officer. The job description can also identify the principal outcomes of the position and the principal products the position is expected to produce. For the chair of a committee or task force, the job description identifies the charter, purpose, and aims of the body. The job description then identifies relevant responsibilities pertaining to membership of the body, including the scope of membership, convening the members, monitoring performance, reporting to the board, and the delivery of expected products. The job description defines the boundaries of important key leadership positions and requires the board to identify what is expected of these positions. It also identifies the role relationship between the chair of the committee and agency personnel who staff the committee.

Table 5-3 illustrates a board's job description for the chair of its health policy committee. The job description defines the purpose and scope of this committee, and its aims and expected outcomes. The responsibilities of the chair are identified in terms of how the work of the committee will contribute to the performance of both the board and the agency. And it identifies specific products the board desires from the committee.

Work Plan

The board committee or task force is responsible for filing the work plan. This brief plan identifies the purpose and goals of the committee and translates these into performance objectives and related tasks and activities. The plan is somewhat formal but only enough to give direction to the committee or task force. The development of the plan is undertaken by the board as a whole but the committee or task force chair has the responsibility of ensuring its completion and use as a guide to task completion. Oversight by the board itself—typically through the executive committee—ensures the completion of the plans and their relevance to the overall mission and goals of the board.

Board Product

The product of the board's work is likely the most important element of board performance. *Product* is the root of *productivity,* and it establishes the contribution that the board makes to the agency it sponsors and stewards and, ultimately, the impact the organization makes on the social issue or need it is chartered to address. Board development incorporating the other five dimensions examined in this chapter (membership, group life, structure, network, and task) creates a context in which board productivity and resulting products are more likely to be adequate and appropriate to the overall direction and purpose of the community service agency. However, how can we conceive of these products? What products are essential to a well functioning community service board?

TABLE 5-3: Job Description: Chair, Health Policy Committee, Association for Services to People with Epilepsy

Charter and Principal Aims of the Health Policy Committee

The Health Policy Committee is an agency wide standing committee that includes board members, agency staff members, recipients, and community members committed to improving the responsiveness of health policy and health services for people coping with epilepsy. The charter of the committee is to assist the agency to implement its health advocacy agenda that is formulated annually as part of the association's comprehensive work plan. Its aims are to: (1) identify the unfulfilled health needs of people coping with epilepsy and document these unfulfilled needs; (2) promote effective primary health care of people coping with epilepsy; and (3) identify innovative policy and programmatic initiatives that the association can undertake to improve health care provision to people coping with epilepsy.

Principal Responsibilities of the Committee Chair

The chair ensures that there is full participation of the association's various constituencies in the committee including agency staff members, representatives of nonprofit health providers, recipients and recipient advocates, and relevant providers of human and social services. The chair will work closely with the membership of the committee to formulate an annual working plan using the association's annual advocacy agenda as a framework. The committee will meet frequently enough to ensure that progress is made on the working plan.

The chair is responsible for making timely reports to the board, typically at its quarterly meetings and for ensuring that the committee offers input on health policy and services to the association's annual work plan.

Principal Outcomes of the Committee

The chair will work with the committee to achieve four outcomes in the area of health policy and services. These are:

1. Increase the awareness of legislators of barriers to adequate medication by low-income people who are coping with epilepsy.

2. Provide testimony at state and local legislative bodies on the need for accessible emergency pharmaceutical programs for people who are coping with epilepsy.

3. Document for state policy makers the unmet primary health care needs among people coping with epilepsy, particularly people with other disabilities or who are below the poverty line.

4. In collaboration with administrative staff, ensure the currency and dissemination of the association's white paper on "Epilepsy and Health Care: Progress and Need" that documents the unmet health needs among members of the epilepsy community.

I can highlight four critical board products on the basis of my practice experience in the development of the boards of community service agencies. I do not go into these products at length because they are discussed elsewhere in this volume. I do offer an overview of each one to remind readers that the effectiveness of community service boards is based in their performance (that is, in what they actually do on behalf of the agency). And the ultimate impact of these boards on the social issues or needs that society charters them to address lies in the relevance and meaningfulness of their products.

The four essential products, from my perspective, are (1) aspirations, (2) expectations, (3) plans, and (4) critical decisions. A board that focuses on these products will emerge as a strong and high-performing board. Like the other elements of the performance dimension, the board product helps the agency align a principal organizational system with what it ultimately wants to achieve in relationship to a social issue or social need.

Aspirations

An aspiration can be construed as a strong desire for achievement. Throughout this volume, I highlight the importance of these aspirations for establishing the themes, tone, and context shaping the form and content of community service. I note the critical role the community service agency possesses in addressing social equity and in the distribution of social benefits to those members of society who are often deprived or who are in urgent need of social support and assistance. I also raise aspirations as the motivators encouraging citizens to join a community service board, and to engage voluntarily in action to address a social issue or a social need.

Aspirations as a board product remind the members of a community service board that they are in the business of articulating organizational identity and meaning. The aspirations of a community service board will be visible in its own expectations of itself expressed in a document like the board development mission statement. Also, these aspirations are often found in the articulation of critical values by board members regarding the manner in which the agency offers community service and the kind of impact this service should make on the lives of citizens who use the services the agency offers. Community service boards often produce concrete products to capture these aspirations, such as a vision statement, an organizational mission, a set of principles guiding the conduct of the agency, and a statement of duty that articulates what "value" the agency will produce for the community.

Ultimately, in the context of organizational character, board members as principal leaders of the agency, hold the responsibility for articulating these aspirations and for delegating their actualization to the organizational leadership of the agency, most notably the executive director. Certainly, other internal and external actors will bring their own individual aspirations to the agency. However, a dominant set of aspirations is essential to the institutional formation of the community service organization as a permanent, established, and stable force in community life. Thus, these institutional aspirations—their formation and their use—are critical products that the community service board cannot overlook.

Expectations

At some point in its development, the community service agency will require a coherent set of policies that guide the organization in its everyday work, that help it to respond to environmental contingencies, and that inform personnel of the agency what "ought" to be done and achieved. Other writers on boards have identified frameworks useful to the development of these policies (Carver, 1992; Carver & Carver, 1997). I will defer to these frameworks, and as a consequence, I will not address board policy making other than to articulate the notion that policies extend from a critical product of the community service board, that is, the expectations the board establishes for the performance and effectiveness of the agency itself.

Expectations can be seen as an extension of aspirations. Certainly, as the community service board articulates what it desires for the agency in relationship to the production of value for the community or for a group of community members, it will bring to bear its own aspirations in the establishment of expectations. Expectations suggest anticipation of some kind of social good or some kind of ultimate benefit. However, expectations are not merely a set of aspirations the board transforms to frame and guide the agency. Indeed, generally community service boards operate within complex policy and transactional environments in which the field of expectations is often dense, to say the least. The density of this field is influenced, if not determined, by the number of stakeholders and the power of these stakeholders to exert expectations on the nature and form of agency performance and impact. Stakeholders represent federated funders like the United Way; policymakers at local, state, and national levels; public bureaucracies that contract with the agency; accreditation and regulatory agents; consumers; donors; and the general public all can be influential candidates for determining the expectation set in which an agency performs community service.

Thus, if organizational policy is an extension of expectations, it is certainly an act of "productive" governance for a board to come to grips with these multiple expectations, as well as its own aspirations and the aspirations of its members, and to form intelligent and meaningful policy. The political nature of boards cannot be discounted because ultimately their policy making "allocates values" in a manner that may satisfy some and disappoint others. The establishment of these expectations and satisfying a board may engage in to maintain its own aspirations in light of a strong forced field of potentially countervailing forces can create high levels of ambiguity, conflict, and complexity within community service boards. The resolution of these tensions often produces organizational policy. In other words, policy making is not a simple, technical act within boards. It is very much a political process involving deliberation, lobbying, reflection, and debate.

Ensuring that the agency is not consumed or co-opted by these multiple expectations may be one of the most important roles of the board. In its search for integrity, a community service board must evaluate the development and use of policy against both aspirations and expectations to create policy statements that protect the institutional substance of the agency (Selznick, 1992). There is certainly a strain between aspirations as essential agency values and the field of expectations within which the agency must perform. Thus, the clarification of expectations, the framing of expectations, and the prioritization of expectations form a critical product of board work.

Plans

There are multiple plans any community service agency must prepare, from strategic to operational ones. I find that the community service boards I work with either do not plan or plan too much. Rather than delegating the preparation of core organizational plans to the executive director, one community service board requires that it offer input and approval of all plans within the agency, including those within major programs. Another community service board chooses not to engage in any kind of planning, and members, as a result, are typically unaware of the direction the agency is heading and the critical choices that must be made to steer the agency in a direction the board desires.

As Ackoff (1991) emphasizes, "plan or be planned for." Although this motto may rally a board to plan, it does not answer the substantive question of what a board should produce as a plan. The executive leaders of a community service board should likely produce all of the plans that are essential to the short-term performance of the agency, and that are relevant to maintaining the short-term focus of the agency. The business of the community service board is institutional in nature, and in relationship to planning, this means that the board is responsible for the long-term development of the community service agency.

It is difficult to place a strict parameter around the duration of long term. Suffice it to say that it is anywhere that is within the cognitive comfort zone of the board as a whole. This comfort zone may be established by the relative degree of change occurring within the environment of the agency. Turbulent resource, policy, and regulatory environments may suggest to the community service board that a planning horizon of five years is too ambitious, or perhaps merely unrealistic. A more placid environment may suggest that the "long view," as P. Schwartz (1991) calls it, is more justifiable. Nonetheless, it is up to each board to establish this time frame and to exercise its planning responsibility within this frame of reference.

Substantively, the community service board is most interested in long-term plans that establish the end state of the organization (Ackoff, 1991). Ends planning requires the board to contemplate the environment of the social problem or social need it must address, and then to anticipate the major changes the agency anticipates to take place within the time frame the board stipulates as the time horizon. This environmental sensitivity, as Ackoff (1991) notes, helps the board to reexamine key assumptions about the role of the agency in addressing the social problem or need. And it helps the board to evaluate and reconsider how aspirations, expectations, and values of the agency may change in this future state. Ends planning is consistent with the institutional responsibility of the community service board, the principal organizational system whose responsibility it is to consider the identity, meaning, and social role of the agency.

The board incorporates the degree and form of change as basic assumptions into ends planning and considers alternative scenarios of potential agency development (Olsen & Eadie, 1982). These potential "ends" can be evaluated on the basis of multiple preferences held by board members, and a new vision of the agency can be articulated from a chosen end state (Ackoff, 1991).

The board can incorporate into this process environmental scans, social indicators, data regarding social trends and developments useful to the establishment, naming, and articulation of various scenarios. Of equal importance, the board can tap into emerging aspirations, expectations, and value sets to consider the ultimate direction of the agency as it moves toward the time horizon it establishes as meaningful.

Some boards use the performance dimension of board development to establish a framework that naturally produces and reevaluates institutional plans or ends plans. The articulation of board involvement, the establishment of task forces and committees, the work of individual board members, and the tasks executed by the board on an incremental basis may feed data continuously into the institutional plan.

An advocacy organization that uses the arts to advance the support of people coping with HIV/AIDS maintains an up-to-date institutional plan on an ongoing basis through the hosting of an AIDS futures conference once a year. Toward the end of each year, every board committee and task force prepares a set of observations about the future of AIDS based on the knowledge each board-sponsored body acquired during the year. These sets of observations are then organized by a small task force of board, agency personnel, service recipients, and community activists into a larger document entitled "This Year in AIDS: Implications for Our Future in the Community Support of the People We Serve." The agency invites over 100 people to a "day of reflection" during which the major issues are framed, reframed, and deliberated by small focus groups.

The conference leaders then summarize the findings, and present them to the board for consideration and resolution. The board then works with the material in appraising its impact on the agency's vision, aims, and principal directions. After the board concludes this appraisal, the agency "long-range ends plan" is revised usually incrementally, although at least once this process resulted in the establishment of a new agency direction focusing on the support of people with AIDS who are returning to the workforce.

The plan as board product highlights the critical role of the community service board in preparing for the future of the agency. This responsibility illustrates in action the institutional dimension of board development (see chapter 3). Through ends planning, the community service board considers at critical junctures the identity of the agency through a consideration of the agency's environment, the nature of community service, and tracking and responding to change.

Critical Decisions

This product is less tangible than the others and likely will not result in written guidelines or specific documents. Nonetheless, the decisions community service boards make when they meet will have a major impact on the shape, functioning, and integrity of the agencies they sponsor. I refer to these decisions as critical because the community service board that functions well does not interfere with the domain of other organizational actors and the decisions that are rightfully theirs to make as defined by agency or organizational policy.

Critical decisions are those that shape the community service agency as an institution. By *institution,* I refer to the agency as a collection of values that establishes the organization as a meaningful, stable, and highly regarded aspect of community life. To bring about the other products (that is, aspirations, policies, and plans) the community service board must make critical decisions concerning the identity of the agency and concerning its priorities, sense of community service, and critical outcomes.

Critical decisions also are made at important developmental points in the agency's lifespan. For example, hiring an executive director is a critical decision that certainly will influence the institutional framework of the agency. The selection of an accreditation source may also constitute a critical decision that possesses lifespan significance for the agency as will the purchase or construction of a building. Perhaps the productivity of a board can be measured in terms of the importance of the decisions it makes and the substance and consequences of these decisions. The absence of these decisions may alert the board that its productivity is inadequate. Preoccupation with lower order decisions may apprise the board that it is usurping the role of the executive leadership of the agency. Or decisions that result in a weak institutional structure may suggest to the board that it is not producing the kind of outcomes the agency needs to establish itself in the community.

My observations of boards suggest that a viable avenue of board development resides in the craft of making significant and important decisions in a manner that builds the institutional standing of the agency in the community. One board refuses to address issues created by the agency's dependency on one source for its operating funds. Another agency will not make decisions about the long-term development of the agency. A third board does not think through its agenda in terms of the critical decisions it must make and the disposition of these decisions in a timely and effective manner. All of these boards face developmental challenges. And these developmental challenges lie in the manner in which they make decisions regarding their respective agencies as community institutions.

Conclusion

There are many elements to board performance and, consequently, there is much to organize to develop the performance of a community service board. Each element of the performance dimension adds something distinctive to the achievement of the board's own performance, and that establishes the community service board as a resource to the agency it sponsors and stewards. The membership element of board performance reminds us that the demographic, background, personal, and experiential qualities of board members are relevant to performance, and do matter. Recruitment of key people who come with a range of motivations, resources, and characteristics can influence, sometimes dramatically, the commitment and energy of a particular board. Good people, however, are not enough as the element of group life shows. The community service board must function ultimately as a group. Board members must interconnect, form relationships, and establish a personal investment in one another to conduct the business of the board and to perform in a manner that contributes to the effectiveness of the community service agency.

Structure requires the board to be deliberate and thoughtful about how it will organize its work, and to establish and execute an agenda that strengthens the agency as a community institution. Certainly, each board will make its own decisions about structure. Some boards will choose not to create an elaborate or formal structure whereas another board will see relevance in the establishment of committees, task forces, and advisory groups. Structure will flow out of the board's sense of identity and its conception of what it wants to contribute to the agency. Structural decisions will interact with the scope of involvement the community service board establishes. Some boards will establish very strict and formal boundaries allowing only those who are formally selected for membership to participate in the business of the board. Other boards will discover opportunities in the elaboration of board involvement and participation, tactically using this involvement to co-opt, include other perspectives, and screen people for potential membership. Again, like with the other elements, the scope of board involvement is up to each board to make on the basis of its own conception of performance.

Yet it is important for members of community service boards to recognize that their boards are not closed systems. Linking with other community groups, organizations, and institutions is one strategy for the community service board to become more sensitive to its environment and to interact with its environment through new and different venues. The board network and the social networks of members offer community service agencies access to resources, to policy systems, and to advocacy.

Board development that takes a performance orientation must combine and link membership, group life, structure, involvement, and network into a functioning board that executes relevant tasks and brings about meaningful products. Ultimately, it is task and product that define the community service board, particularly when performance is evaluated against the extent to which the agency elevates its status within its respective community. Task reminds board members that they need to be doing something tangible in service to the agency while product reminds members that this service does not really intrude into the everyday life of the agency.

Questions for Board Discussion

1. Given the vision of the agency, and the vision of board performance, does the current board have the right number and mix of board members? Are the right kind of assets and skills represented among current board members?
2. Are there a sufficient number of board members who bring passion, inspiration, and excitement to the work of the board?
3. Is diversity important to the current board? How will the board act on diversity to develop this dimension if it is deemed important?
4. Are there positive human relations within the board? Are there informal approaches to support cohesion, socialize members, and offer opportunities for members to get to know one another as people?
5. Is there a strong sense of peer support within the board? Do people support one another even if there is conflict or disagreement? Is conflict and disagreement considered by board members to be acceptable in light of the complexity of board decision making?
6. Is there a structure that fits the purpose, vision, and responsibilities of the current board? What are the strengths and limitations of the current structure?

7. How does the board make use of a seasonal cycle of planning? How does the board make use of standing committees? How does the board make use of task forces? How does the board make use of advisory committees or structures?

8. Does the board intentionally expand involvement of agency staff, community members, and people who have special expertise in the work of the board?

9. How does the board create various networks to link the agency to community resources, power structures, opportunities, and new funding sources? Is this network building intentional or is it something that is left up to an individual board member?

10. How does the board support individual board members to complete tasks and to engage in productive board work? Are board members clear about these tasks and their responsibilities?

11. Has your agency defined the critical products for which the board is responsible? What are these? Is the board clear about the products it is responsible for?

12. What developmental needs does this chapter illuminate for the board? How will the board act on these needs?

■6■

Lifespan Dimension

Two Board Members Reflect on the Past

Joe: When I came on to the board it was dominated by people who founded this agency. They spent a considerable amount of time talking about purpose, mission, and focus. Now, the agency seems to be going down hill and the board doesn't feel like it can do much about it.

Sally: Perhaps we need to come to grips with this reality. Some of our funders have shared their concerns with me. They think that time has passed us by. The agency hasn't changed with the times.

Joe: It certainly isn't like it was, that is, in the past. Board members were really involved then, even willing to dig into their own pockets to support the start-up of the first program.

Sally: Things have changed! We can barely get a quorum now.

Board development is not static. Each stage of agency development or change brings with it substantive challenges to the board, and to the development of the board (Bonner, 1993). Indeed, board development is quite a dynamic idea if we place the development of the board into a context of organizational lifespan. Community service organizations, like any other type of organization, move through phases of development and each of these phases has implications for how the board organizes, the tasks the board works on, and the theme for board development (W. R. Scott, 1987).

I identify four phases of board development that are also relevant to the development of the agencies boards sponsor. The first phase can be described as the "founding" of the agency. The agency during this phase crystallizes and comes into existence. It is most likely a fledging agency that probably is facing numerous developmental challenges to perpetuate itself (Bergquist, 1993). But perpetuation is not certain, and the leadership of the agency, particularly its board, must be prepared to establish the agency and to build a foundation that will support the agency's development. Thus, the board itself must create an institutional identity and deploy this identity to establish agency legitimacy and relevance (Bergquist, 1993).

The second phase can be described as "growth and maturation." The successful agency, if it occupies a favorable niche in its community, will begin to expand—financially, organizationally, and perhaps programmatically. Various stakeholders may ask the agency to expand services for the people the agency serves, or it may be asked to create a more complex array of programs. The growing and maturing agency presents developmental challenges to the board. It most likely will need to enhance its own performance and to become more productive and effective as the policy making component of the organization. Growth and maturation may threaten core values and cause the agency to drift from its original mandate, founding beliefs, and commitments (R. H. Hall, 1987). The board must be prepared to protect, reaffirm, or change the agency's institutional framework while creating and enhancing a performance framework that strengthens the board and the agency.

"Stabilization," the third phase of organizational development, finds the board in a crisis of relevance. Routinization of agency performance and work may give a false confidence to the board that all is well and the agency is stable. The board may drift from its own commitment to development and allow routine procedures to steer its work. The board may begin to ignore its fundamental commitments, its founding values, and even what is occurring in its environment that can threaten the adaptation of the agency. It may, most of all, overlook the need to steward the agency and to prepare the agency for an unpredictable future.

The fourth phase can be identified as "decline and renewal." The agency may experience a loss of relevance and a decline in performance. New leadership will be required, one that is generative and one that moves the agency toward renewal. Decline may mean death of the agency, and a board may decide to shut its doors (Adizes, 1988). However, most boards that I have observed in this phase do not want to take this extreme action. Usually too much is at stake. Renewal, however, requires the board to undertake a demanding board development agenda, one that will invigorate or reinvigorate the board as the principal leadership system of the agency.

Thus, in the context of this chapter, board development involves the lifespan development of the board as a system. This development is closely linked to the organizational development of the agency. It requires the board to understand what developmental stage the agency is in, the challenges to board development inherent in each stage, and the aims of board development within the context of a given stage.

Board Development in the Founding Stage

Excitement most likely characterizes the founding stage. Board members hold the status as founders whose vision and motivation bring about the formation of a new community service organization. Although some board members may be attracted to the fledging agency after it has been initiated, it is not unusual that a number of board members are the people who possessed the original idea about the need for community service. They take it on themselves to translate this need into action through the founding of the actual agency (Zander, 1985).

I have seen in action many "founding" boards. They seem to defy logic at times. There is probably no material reason for the members of these boards to coalesce into a force to found an organization devoted to community service. Yet most of these boards are deeply motivated to do so. And they typically bring energy, purpose, and a sense of urgency that something must be done to address a particular need or a social problem (Zander, 1985). Take, for example, family members who come together to form an agency offering community-based rehabilitation options to people with severe head injury; the citizens who bring into being an organization devoted to advancing the performing arts; the human service professionals who ban together to create a new social support system for people coping with epilepsy; or the survivors of domestic violence who create a grassroots advocacy organization for victims of violence. These individuals often begin with few if any tangible resources. They do bring intangible resources to bear on the problem, including their own commitment, reputations, and concern.

The members of founding boards can be passionately committed to a cause. They are willing to devote time, energy, ingenuity, and innovation to this cause. It is not unusual for these boards to be small because the personal commitment and direct action they demonstrate are rarely present in the community. This small number of people forms a cadre or the nucleus of a larger board that forms around them.

These boards often possess an uncompromising sense of mission. They likely infuse the initial lifespan stage of the agency with strong momentum. The roots of the institutional dimension are seen most visibly in this stage as the board begins to give some basic organization to itself and to the agency it governs. The agenda of the board is dominated by a number of institution-building activities (Selznick, 1957). The founding board offers a sense of purpose based on a conception of how a social problem or need should be addressed by the fledging agency. In other words, these boards conceive the basic definitions that coordinate the effort of the agency, including what is meant by community service (Schein, 1992).

Structurally, the founding board is usually simple. The roles of members are not highly differentiated. Members are not likely to be organized into discrete committee structures. This structural simplicity enables the founding board to become a coherent group and to undertake tasks and responsibilities within a generalist as compared to a specialist framework. Outside consultants and technical assistants may be brought into the board to help it complete its more technical tasks and responsibilities requiring financial, legal, and organizational expertise (Stoesz & Raber, 1997).

The board of the founding phase of agency development identifies and encodes the critical values or beliefs of the agency. Such boards undertake the basic identity work of the agency, and they integrate this identity into the basic framework and policies of the community service agency. For example, a founding board may recruit the first executive director of the agency. The board shapes the institutional identity of the agency by appointing a director who brings into the organization the requisite beliefs, perspectives, and values the board feels are consistent with this identity.

The founding board is likely involved in the initial development of the resources needed to launch the agency. Board members may be directly involved in fund raising campaigns, community appeals, grant development, or contract negotiation. Success in these activities can weld board members to the administration of the agency, perhaps too closely. Some founding members may identify with the agency so strongly that they cross the fine line that demarcates governance and administration. These members may find it difficult to let go of the more hands-on responsibilities of operating the agency.

But the dilemma here is inherent to the founding stage. With so few people involved in the founding enterprise, and without a formal staff, who is to do the initial work involved in launching the agency? Most founding members want and expect to get involved. Yet when it comes time to back off, some founding board members may find it difficult to do so.

The members of the founding board serve as the ancestors of the community service agency. Their motivation, conception of problem or need, beliefs, values, and perspectives can live on in the agency as subsequent generations unknowingly are socialized into the framework that these founding members have left behind (Denhardt, 1981; Schein, 1992). The founding board members are culture builders. It is important for its members to recognize the critical role they play in crafting the initial institutional framework of the community service agency (Denhardt, 1981). Their role is not to be taken lightly. They are more than figureheads. Their energy, passion, commitment, and enthusiasm help form the substance of agency culture.

There are three principal challenges to board development during the founding stage. First, the board must successfully form the nucleus of the agency. This means that the founding members must form a coherent group committed to advancing the agency, rather than merely an idiosyncratic conception of their own cause (Zander, 1993). The founding members must work together as a small group making critical decisions about the initial establishment of the community service agency (Zander, 1985). Infighting, interpersonal conflict, and the emergence of factions must be reduced in service to the creation of the agency. Cooperation and collaboration must be achieved for the group to be successful.

The second challenge is more instrumental. The founding board must engage in two sets of tasks simultaneously. It must begin to formalize the basic institutional features of the agency, particularly the identity formed through the board's conception of community service. And it must begin to engage in those pragmatic tasks that will ensure the initial survival and subsequent viability of the agency, including the recruitment of key staff, the establishment of facility, the mustering of resources, and the initial identification of appropriate social markets.

The third challenge may be the most critical one in relationship to the advancement of the agency. The founding board must prepare for its "creative destruction" in preparation for the development of a board that will likely include other people who bring to board service the requisite networks, technical skills, and roles needed to ensure future organizational success. The founding board may emerge as such a strongly coherent and integrated group that its members have difficulty in actually contemplating and engaging in change. The founding board must yield to a future board the members of which do not likely possess those initial affective qualities of passion, enthusiasm, and excitement that were so important to the creation of the agency. The founding board must begin to work on board development, something that may be difficult given all of the personal commitment and contributions made by these ancestral members.

Board Development in the Growth and Maturation Stage

As the agency grows and matures, new challenges face the community service board. Successful establishment of the community service agency creates a market niche for the organization. And success within this niche will bring it more and more attention by potential funders. Particularly in this time of privatization and public–nonprofit collaborations, an agency may find new resource and service opportunities in the public sector. The agency may expand its products and services to address more comprehensively the social problem or need it has been founded to address. The arts organization originally founded to bring theater to the community may expand into other areas of the performing arts. The agency that offers housing to people living with HIV/AIDS may expand to offer vocational and work opportunities and social supports for independent living.

Growth and maturation may be induced by heightened demand brought on by new public sector opportunities or new resource opportunities. The community service agency may seek out these resources on the basis of an intentional plan of expansion and development. Or these opportunities induce the agency to grow in a market-driven but unplanned manner.

Growth and development challenge the board in this stage. The agency itself must make decisions about whether it will grow and develop and how it will do so. There are institutional decisions to be made about agency identity, the basic meaning of community service, and the reputation of the organization within its community. Questions regarding resource development and the administrative capacity to expand services and products will also likely emerge as challenges. Formalization of policies and procedures will become increasingly important as the agency experiences heightened oversight by public, foundation, and private funding sources (Houle, 1997).

Funding sources will require accreditation, certification, and licensure. Consequently, the agency will find a need to establish and strengthen basic organizational systems, including human resource management, program evaluation, information systems, and financial reporting (Gray et al., 1998). Expansion of programs, services, and products will create new organizational structures and new forms of supervision, teamwork, and perhaps even a differentiation of the agency along divisional lines (Galbraith, Lawler, et al., 1993).

The community service board of an agency experiencing growth and maturation will feel the pressure of these changes. The founding board probably was concerned more with ideas than with its basic structure. The community service board experiencing growth and maturation will become increasingly focused on decisions pertaining to resource development and marketing, strategy, organizational change, and organizational accountability. Pressure to differentiate the board will become strong during this period. The community service board will begin to think about board development in three ways:

1. structural change involving the creation of committees to manage the demands placed on the agency by its environment,
2. policy development that will guide the agency during the course of growth and maturation, and
3. information management involving the translation of data into indicators that enables the board to monitor and execute decisions about organizational performance.

Unlike the founding board concerned with establishing the basic meaning and framework of the community service agency, the board of this stage focuses on its structure. The identity work completed by the founding board becomes formalized in the growth and maturation board through structure, policy, and information (Carver, 1992).

The simple structure of the founding board gives way to a more differentiated and formal structure. The environmental pressures on the community service board encourage this differentiation. The board begins to focus on the performance dimension giving consideration to the committees, task forces, and other groupings needed to fulfill a more complex governance task than what was required of the board in its founding stage. As the board's size increases, an executive committee likely will be formed. By-laws will offer a formal role to this committee as it offers oversight to other board committees like finance, human resources, program, resource development, and long-range planning. These standing committees each may have their own set of working plans coordinated by an overarching strategic organizational plan.

A diversity of committees requires membership and an increased board size. The focus of board development moves from institutional to performance considerations. Board leaders see the necessity for more board members; thus, it is natural for the community service board to expand in size. The agency begins to search for these members often unsystematically and often in competition with other community service agencies that also require additional members.

Founding boards can resist this formalization and the expansion or proliferation of committees it produces. Founding boards actually may be suspect of growth and maturation and yearn to remain small and informal. But many community service agencies cannot resist environmental pressure, particularly if the market niche they fill is favored by public and private funding sources. The community service board of the growth and maturation stage works in a less idealistic atmosphere and must respond to the many demands placed on the agency by virtue of the accountabilities or requirements of various funding sources. Indeed, the eclipse of idealism in this stage may pose the most significant challenge to the board. The community service board may drift away from its founding ideals and become opportunistic in character and behavior. Strategy may replace vision.

Environmental demands and the formalization that results from environmental pressures means that policymaking increasingly becomes a responsibility of the community service board. The community service board of the growth and maturation stage further strengthens the board's governance role. Policymaking is one approach the board uses to respond to its environment. The community service organization is growing beyond the direct reach of the board. Interactions between board and agency in the growth and maturation stage are less personal than they were in the founding stage. Board members may not have direct involvement in the life of the agency and board members may have a remote understanding of what the agency does.

Policymaking ostensibly fills this void. The gulf between the board and the agency may be reduced from the perspective of board members by framing, implementing, and evaluating policies that are useful to governance. Three types of policies emerge as governance tools. First, identity policies help define the meaning of the agency and its role in the community. Framing purpose, vision, goals, and aims is the purpose of this kind of policy. Second, formalized plans such as organizational strategy, financial development, and resource development explicate the direction of the community service agency. And third, organizational system policies define the scope and substance of major areas of the agency like personnel, financial management, and marketing.

Policymaking is legitimized by the world outside of the community service agency. Funding sources and other external stakeholders, like licensing or accreditation bodies, instigate this kind of board responsibility (Mitroff, 1989). This is appropriate. The public should be confident that the agency operates in an accountable manner. But the board in the growth and maturation stage does risk overstepping its governance role and becoming overly involved in administration. One of the most challenging competencies involved in effective board work is for the members of the community service board to learn how to frame effective policies that truly guide the performance of the agency (Carver & Carver, 1997).

Information management is a third aspect of board development in the growth and maturation stage. Expansion of marketing, administrative, and service activities leads to a virtual explosion in data. Regulators external to the agency require this data and induce new forms of reporting and accountability. It is not unusual for the board to feel overwhelmed by this explosion. And it is not unusual for the board to be puzzled about how to make use of these data.

Expansion of external reporting, the explosion of data, and the expansion of the size and scope of the organization push the community service board to reconcile data and reporting with its own values. The board learns that many external entities exist to define for the agency what is "right" performance. But ultimately, it is up to the board to define this and to oversee the performance of the agency in relationship to its own sense of purpose, vision, and mission. The community service board begins to align its institutional and performance dimensions. Data is converted into board information when the board identifies what it values. The board uses existing data to create performance indicators that reflect the values of the organization. Board-level information may come in the form of report cards, performance reports, or outcome management reports. The form, though, is not as important as what these reports communicate to the board about institutional performance. The board uses information to govern. *To govern*, here, means whether the agency achieves what the board expects of it given the institutional framework defined by the board. The board monitors whether the agency achieves those outcomes that are considered to be important, whether the agency offers services in a manner consistent with organizational vision, and whether community service is undertaken according to how it is defined by the board (Weick, 1995).

Thus, in the growth and maturation stage, structure, policy, and information become the substance of board development. It is inevitable that the community service agency will become more formalized (Adizes, 1988). And the board must be prepared for this eventuality. The issue is no longer whether the board should have a formal structure, explicit policies, and structured performance indicators. It is, rather, how the board will make use of these tools to add value to the performance of the agency.

The risk in this stage lies in the board's abandonment of institutional development in the face of strong environmental forces that define the direction and substance of community service for the board and the agency (Mitroff, 1989). The agency risks co-optation here in which the values of external funding sources and regulators replace those of the agency. In the process of formalization, it is important for the board to be mindful of its institutional heritage as well as its vision and mission. It is imperative that the board not overlook or lose its sense of purpose or vision in the process of formalization. The historical nucleus of the agency is the founding board. And the current board must be mindful of why the agency was founded in the first place.

Board Development in the Stabilization Stage

Heralding the stabilization stage is an apparent slowdown in the growth of the community service agency. In actual agency situations, growth may slow over a period of time. This slowdown may alarm agency leaders who become preoccupied by continued and unabated growth, and who equate success with this state of affairs. However, opportunities come with stabilization. This stage offers community service agencies opportunities for self-reflection and a reconsideration of the direction and vision of the agency. It offers an agency opportunities to look within and to consolidate the changes that came with the previous growth of the organization.

Board members can ignore the challenges and opportunities inherent in the stabilization stage. The challenge is to recognize this stage as a real state in the lifespan of the agency. Leaders may overlook this period and fail to recognize that it is crucial to begin the consolidation process. Early indicators of decline may be apparent in stabilization. For example, for one community service agency, stabilization occurred after a period of excessive growth in which the organization was unable to satisfy its principal funding sources. These funding sources did not reduce or cut funding; they merely stopped the growth of the business until the agency proved that it could perform in the desired manner. The stabilization stage was induced externally for this organization, and the agency was unprepared for it.

I have seen other community service agencies, ones more oriented to their own self-development, actually slow down the process of growth to take advantage of the self-induced stage of stabilization. These agencies recognize the potential crisis of relevance the agency can experience when it grows at a tremendous rate in terms of scope and volume of service, but key organizational systems do not keep pace with this growth. The stabilization stage allows the organization to address this crisis or the potential of it.

Internal and external dissatisfaction with the agency and its practices and outcomes can signal this crisis. Internal dissatisfaction can come in the form of staff members who argue that they are under considerable levels of performance stress but feel that the quality of their work is suffering. Yet productivity is not declining. Also, internal dissatisfaction may come from consumers who argue that they are not getting the service or supports they need in a timely manner or with a loss of quality. External dissatisfaction may come from purchasers or funding sources who are not pleased with performance and its outcomes.

Board development in the stabilization stage creates a number of challenges for the community service board. The board cannot fall into a placid style of governance in which it merely follows through with its own set of procedures without monitoring agency performance. Stabilization heightens the responsibility of the board to oversee performance and to foster higher levels of performance by the agency. During this stage, the board becomes even more conscious of its information management competencies. It becomes more conscious of the indicators of performance and it learns how to use these in the process of setting or resetting expectations concerning the agencies' contributions to community service. Board development within this stage means that the board refines these indicators and adopts vigilance in its use in the process of board decision making. Of course, two of the most potent actions the board can take involve the review of existing expectations and their revision. A third potent action the board can take is to ensure that the agency obtains the resources it needs to execute these expectations. The stabilization stage offers the board a period in which this review can be undertaken and in which appropriate plans can be formulated (Grace, 1997a).

Institutionally, the board's conception of the quality of performance and the use of this conception to guide the agency are important board development outcomes in this stage. This activity can help agency personnel and consumers to become more conscious of what the agency seeks to do and how it seeks to perform. Ideas concerning quality can become more important to agency personnel when they understand the importance placed on it by the board itself. Board development in the stabilization stage requires the board as a whole to return to basic, founding ideas to reaffirm them or redefine them. Defining quality, establishing basic quality policies, and evaluating quality may be the most beneficial acts of board governance in this stage (Juran, 1992).

Board development in the stabilization stage incorporates the theme of preparedness for the future effective execution of agency performance. It is a plateau in which the board can return to working on fundamental ideas and deploying these within the context of the themes of organizational consolidation of the changes that were realized during the growth stage. The development of quality management and evaluation systems is also important in this stage (Gray et al., 1998).

Indeed, the board may find that it is in the business of leading quality. The board becomes more focused on what quality means to the successful execution by the agency of its performance and ultimately its vision (Juran, 1992). And it becomes vigilant in monitoring the achievement of quality. The stabilization stage may see the introduction by the board of policies on quality management, program review, and program evaluation. The board may incorporate indicators of organizational quality into its standard reporting systems. And it may require the chief executive officer to formulate organizational plans that address the achievement of higher levels of quality within the agency. In this stage, success becomes equated with the achievement of quality, rather than with the expansion of the scope of the agency or the volume of agency services.

A focus on quality in this stage of organizational development also can be applied to the development of the board. Any successful program of quality management requires the agency board to put this into practice within the board itself. Board development, therefore, incorporates continuous quality management. The board becomes effective in the improvement of its own practices, structure, productivity, and outcomes. Success here models for the agency as a whole the importance of quality. Application of quality management to the board's work illustrates that agency quality policies apply to all systems of the organization.

Board Development in the Decline or Renewal Stage

Some agencies may fail in either growth or stabilization. Decline may set in, and the agency find itself in a serious crisis of survival. Decline is a serious situation for any organization. It is particularly serious for a community service agency. Several factors can influence the onset of decline. The agency may become too dependent on a single funding source and ignore the need to create a diversity of funding possibilities. An agency may allow its performance to decline dramatically and to allow poor quality to drive away its external support. Or an agency may simply fail to plan for its future and fail to anticipate change in the social problem or need it was founded to address, or in the technologies or policies relating to this problem or need.

An agency in decline also means that a board is in decline. Indeed, the community service board should look inward when the agency it is to steward is not successful and a crisis of survival becomes real. Organizational decline indicates that the board has failed to execute its core responsibilities of governance. The board likely failed to execute its institutional responsibilities. As a consequence, the agency drifts from its mission, and its vision and purpose do not animate continuous change. Also likely is the absence of purposeful board development leading to the availability of a leadership mix representing strategic, generative, ancestral, adaptive, and civil functions. And it is likely that the board has failed to perform in a manner that supports organizational success.

Symptoms of decline within the board are clearly visible. It is difficult for a board to secure a quorum. Board membership declines, and it is difficult to recruit new and energetic members. Board committees fail to meet or they meet sporadically. Committees may actually disappear. The board is unable to pursue a relevant agenda. Board productivity declines. Administrative leadership of the agency can be alarmed. Executive staff complains that the board is inert. Staff is alarmed at the declining leadership of the board.

The decline of the board raises questions about whether the agency should continue. There may be discussion about closing the agency's doors. Funding sources, donors, and other sources of community support may no longer see the agency as relevant. The internal atmosphere of the agency changes as staff recognizes that the agency does not have a viable future.

Board development is absolutely a frontline strategy for the prevention of agency decline. Such decline is certainly not inevitable. An astute board considers its own development to be essential to fostering a solid and viable organizational future. However, at the point a board admits that the community service agency is in dramatic decline only two choices can be made. They are obvious choices: Does the agency close? Or does the board engage in renewal in partnership with the agency and the community?

Renewal can be an exciting period for the board, the agency, and the community. The challenge of renewal comes at a time of crisis and suspense. There is considerable risk. The board leading the renewal process will need to coordinate much activity. Indeed, this stage in the lifespan of the community service agency may recapitulate the founding stage as a handful of board members join together to recreate the agency and to bring back a sense of purpose, vision, and mission. The board in the renewal stage is likely to be small because a number of members most likely have abandoned their board service. The renewal board must reinitiate the institutional work of the board, revisiting key issues that relate to organizational viability, including basic definitions of community service, institutional purpose, and values. The functional dimension of the board most likely needs to be rejuvenated by identifying and recruiting members who bring strategic, civil, adaptive, generative, and ancestral knowledge and competencies to board service. The board will have to renew its by-laws and establish a structure that enables it to navigate the challenges of renewal. Linkages between the board and the organizational staff will need to be strengthened during this stage. And linkages between the board and external stakeholders must be strengthened.

As in the founding stage, the board engaged in renewal is a working body. It is characterized by hands on activities in service to salvaging the community service agency. The board members will face cynicism and skepticism. They will face considerable disbelief both internally and externally about the probability of success.

Thus, the board in this stage will be focused on legitimization of itself and the community service agency. It is likely that the board will become a strong, coherent group like the board that initiated the agency's founding. The five properties of board development discussed in chapter 2 will become important enabling conditions supporting the work of renewal. Board members will have to bring to their service the qualities of energy to devote to renewal—an end state they value and are motivated to achieve—a strong belief system concerning community service, a commitment to improvement, and a commitment to learning. Boards in decline that seek renewal and rejuvenation must assess whether these qualities are available to them. Their absence suggests that renewal will only fail.

Conclusion

This chapter offers a perspective on the development of the community service board over a series of lifespan stages. These stages illustrate the complexity of board development as the community service board moves from founding or initiation through growth and maturation to stabilization and then to decline or renewal. The nature of board development varies somewhat across these stages with each stage placing different demands on the board and, as a consequence, requiring the execution of different tasks and activities. Nonetheless, each stage requires the community service board to be conscious of how it develops along the functional, performance, and institutional dimensions.

The institutional dimension emerges within each stage as perhaps the most critical to the board's development. This dimension brings into focus the board's responsibilities of governance and how board development requires a clear sense of organizational meaning, purpose, and values that are actually used by board members to govern the community service agency (Pascarella & Frohman, 1989). The institutional dimension influences viability and communicates the public character of the community service agency (Selznick, 1957). And it is the institutional dimension that communicates integrity. It serves as a manner in which internal and external stakeholders can evaluate the action of the agency.

Naturally, from a lifespan perspective, board development is never complete, and if it is treated as "done," then the community service agency and the board that governs it risk decline. The lifespan perspective suggests the importance of continuity, the purposeful management of change, and the infusion of energy into the development of a community service board. A lifespan perspective can make renewal an ongoing property of the board that recognizes its most important contribution as residing in the preparation of the community service agency for its future emergence as a community institution.

Questions for Board Discussion

1. What phase of the board lifespan best describes your board? What is your rationale for this choice?
2. For those boards in the founding stage, what is the "irrational" element that motivates the work of board members to bring into existence a new community service organization?
3. For those boards in the founding stage, what critical values are board members acting on? How do these critical values shape the purpose of the

new agency? How do these values make the agency distinctive compared to other community service agencies that currently exist?

4. For the boards in the growth and maturation phase, what is the need or logic for the growth of the community service agency? How does this growth serve the community in a better way?

5. What tasks must your board fulfill to negotiate the stage of growth and maturation?

6. How will the board look and behave in the growth and maturation phase?

7. For those boards negotiating the stage of stabilization, what principal challenges does the board face? How will the board meet these challenges successfully? What is the board's stabilization strategy?

8. For those boards in a stage of decline, what are the indicators of "serious trouble" facing the board? How should the board address these indicators?

9. What is the board's strategy for renewal in the decline stage? What is the board's vision of renewal and how will this vision influence the manner in which the board conducts its work?

10. For those boards early in their lifespan, how should they prepare for the subsequent stages? What is the board's strategy to negotiate each stage successfully? How will the board avoid the stage of decline? How will the board maintain a spirit of continuous renewal in its work?

11. What developmental needs does this chapter illuminate for the board? How will the board act to address these needs?

Developing Board Identity

Successfully meeting the initial challenges of board development is the overriding theme of the two chapters composing this section. These chapters are especially relevant to new boards that are seeking to get started in community service work, and are typically in the founding stage of organizational development. Although these chapters address some basic challenges, and are most relevant to relatively new boards, more seasoned and mature boards may want to revisit these challenges, particularly if they find themselves in the stages of decline and renewal.

These chapters taken together remind us that the governance work of community service agencies requires a framework of identity and character that supports performance, productivity, and outcome. It is important to remind ourselves that the only reason a community service agency exists is to render service with this service linked to the achievement of some kind of valued positive difference in the lives of citizens and their communities. Without this positive difference, organizational meaning and character are likely lost, and legitimacy can evaporate.

The two chapters address some basic responsibilities that all boards interested in their legitimacy and in their development must execute. Chapter 7 deals with the basic institutional question of "who we are." The board development challenge comes in the form of defining purpose and expectations, and appreciating and valuing the distinctiveness of the community service agency. Chapter 8 builds on this basic identity by focusing on the role of vision and the establishment of agency direction by the board. Both chapters have implications for thinking about a board's commitment to outcome—that is, the board's devotion to making positive and relevant differences in the lives of people and in the lives of human communities. Board identity is fundamental to the ability to identify ultimate agency outcomes by board members.

The chapters in this section are more concrete representations or reflections of the chapters composing section 2. They are incorporated into the book to stimulate among board members discussions of the overarching agency framework that supports agency performance. If the board does not define this framework, who will?

■ 7 ■

Understanding "Who We Are"

A Segment from the Address of the Board Chair to the Annual Meeting of Friendship House

> This past year has been one of growth and change. Very honestly, a new policy environment in which traditional funders adopted new ways of doing business created this change. We did not merely adapt to them. Yes, we responded to these changes in constructive ways but we did not and have not overlooked the reason we serve this community. The agency remains true to its purpose and the board recognizes the necessity of maintaining this vigilance about our purpose and focus. We are the only agency that serves the children of women who are incarcerated in prisons and jails. No other agency in this community offers this kind of support. Our purpose is to help women cope constructively with this overwhelming life experience and to prepare themselves for the time when they return to their families to begin anew. We do this in a supportive and proactive manner. This is who we are. Incarceration of women brings to light dramatically many of the injustices the women we serve experience in life. Contemporary society says punish these women. We say "offer a hand of friendship and of support." This makes us distinctive. We cannot forget this.

A basic premise of board development is that boards and their members must know the organization they lead. Boards cannot merely know about the funding streams and the budgetary resources of the agency. They must come to know about the work of the actual agency (McMaster, 1996). The fundamental qualities the board must know about are the purpose of the agency, the expectations the agency holds for its performance, and the ways that the agency is distinctive. Purpose, performance expectations, and organizational distinctiveness define both the agency and the board and offer the organization a sense of its own identity (Weick, 1995).

In their stewardship of the community service agency, board members will often revisit purpose, expectations, and distinctiveness (Gauthier, 1995). It can be argued that they become so intimately involved with these qualities that the board becomes responsible for their formation, their perpetuation, and their use in the execution of critical policy decisions. Agency purpose, performance expectations, and a clear sense of organizational distinctiveness become critical tools to the board in its own development and in the execution of its governance. They become principal reference points that can organize the identity of the board and its development efforts.

This chapter frames these three qualities as principal responsibilities of the board. The board develops itself by developing and protecting the purpose, expectations, and distinctiveness of the community service agency (Selznick, 1957). Thus, if the board is to undertake its work effectively, it must have a good understanding of and commitment to strengthening the identity of the agency as a whole.

Role of Board Education In Formulating the Purpose of Community Service

The community service agency has been founded to address a specific purpose. I frame purpose as emanating from the problem the agency seeks to address and the impact it seeks to make on this problem. Purpose is more than mission because it requires the agency to reflect on how it conceives of the problem it seeks to address. For the community service agency devoted to helping people coping with HIV/AIDS to live independently, safely, and productively, the "problem" and the resulting purpose is qualitatively different than for the agency that is committed to addressing the medical consequences of this disease. The community service agency devoted to involving children with disabilities in the arts has a different conception of problem and purpose than the agency seeking to involve members of the general community in the arts.

The formulation of purpose results in board members achieving enlightenment. Board members understand the social problem or need they seek to address, and they come to understand the role of the agency in making an impact on this problem or need. Developing board knowledge about the social problem or need requires it to engage in a continuing process of self-directed board education that is designed purposefully to help board members to increase their awareness of the problem or need area in which they are working (Morris, 1995). The enlightenment that is sought through this process will be evident when board members consider the fundamental purpose guiding the community service agency, and the impact the agency can make on the local dimensions and characteristics of the problem.

The clarification of purpose is linked to the education of board members (Cunningham, 1994; Thompson, 1995). A continuous process of board education will find its expression through a number of board-adopted strategies.

Strategy 1: Education as a Precursor to the Formulation of Purpose

The board of the community service agency adopts an expectation underscoring the importance of this education to each board member, and the board formalizes this expectation by making it a part of the "job description" of each board member (Morris, 1995). Indeed, participation in continuous education, much of which focuses on clarifying the purpose of the agency, is a principal responsibility of a board member. By assigning a standard of performance to education, this expectation becomes explicit within the board. For example, one board established the following standard: Board members invest 5 percent of their service time in educational activities designed to increase their understanding of the social problem or need the agency seeks to address. The educational program also enlightens board members about the social movement that has formed in response to this problem, and the state of the art that has come about to respond to this problem or need.

Strategy 2: Adoption of a Core Curriculum that Addresses Purpose

The board adopts a core curriculum. This curriculum is implemented on a continuous basis. The continuous offer of education ensures that members are receiving timely and continuous input concerning the status of the social problem the agency seeks to address and the impact of the agency's work on this problem, particularly in terms of how people benefit from the agency's work. The curriculum is designed to achieve four objectives with the aim of enlightening board members about the challenges faced by the people the agency is serving:

1. Increase the understanding of board members of the actual social problem and social issues, factors, and forces that create the needs faced by the people served by the agency.
2. Increase the understanding of board members of state of the art practices adopted within the problem area or field within which the agency is working and "models in action" involving the practices that have been implemented by specific agencies, and that are valued within the field.
3. Increase the understanding of board members of the needs and issues faced by the people served by the community service agency, and the living conditions they face on a daily basis.
4. Increase the understanding among board members of the capacities of the agency's local community to address the needs of people served by the agency, especially in key areas of daily support, including education, cultural enrichment, employment, housing, training, health care, mental health care, mobility, and social support.

Strategy 3:Vigilance about Board Knowledge Development

The board must maintain vigilance about its own knowledge development (Sparrow, 1998). To do so successfully, the board appoints a member to serve as an educational leader who works closely with agency staff and people served in designing a continuous process of board education. The educational leader of the board ensures that the core curriculum is developed, a schedule is created for implementation, and the education is delivered in a feasible and consistent manner.

Implications of Board Education for Purpose

It is up to the board as a whole to deliberate on the implications of its education for its purpose. For example, after participation in several sessions examining the emergence of recovery as a new aim of psychiatric rehabilitation, a board of a community service agency working with people identified as seriously mentally ill may decide to shift its purpose. It decides to shift its purpose from one that is dedicated to addressing the medical consequences of serious mental illness to one that is dedicated to promoting recovery. Open discussions and deliberations concerning organizational purpose that follow educational sessions may take place among board members as a group. Or retreats organized specifically to integrate board education with the search for organizational purpose may take place at intervals during the year.

Consideration of agency purpose may emerge when board members, sensitized to what is known about serious mental illness as a social problem, examine actual needs data obtained from people served by the agency. These data may suggest a purpose to the board that is given meaning by the educational material offered to its members. Relatively simple statements offered by board members may capture an agency's purpose:

- ▦ "Our purpose is to combat the social isolation that is so prevalent among the people we serve."
- ▦ "Our purpose is to help people establish a career direction, and to move ahead in a career."
- ▦ "Our purpose is to help people work in the community as much as they want."
- ▦ "Our purpose is to help people purchase homes, and to hold onto these homes."
- ▦ "Our purpose is to help people start their own businesses."

The importance of these statements is found in their metaphorical value (Bethanis, 1995): what Bennis (1993a) refers to as the "collectively held image" of what the agency should do in its community and of what the agency can become.

Understanding purpose is a precursor to the formulation of vision. Purpose is the desired end or result and it signifies resolve, determination, and resolution among board members. It is a critical decision that perhaps is basic to the realization of board and organizational cohesion (Ryan, 1995). It does not, however, come out of a vacuum. There is no set purpose for any community service agency. Establishing this purpose, making sense out of it, and giving it symbolic value is up to the agency's leadership (Brown, 1995). This is why the formulation of purpose is a responsibility of the board because it is the principal policy structure of the agency.

The embodiment of purpose will emerge out of ongoing board education. The loss of purpose occurs when the board as a principal system of organizational governance loses its sense of what is important. When this occurs, it means that the board does not fully understand that aspect of the social problem or that aspect of community need the agency seeks to address.

Purpose, problem, and need are interrelated. They are closely linked to the education of board members and to their enlightenment. But the dynamic nature of the agency's environment requires a board to maintain over time an enlightened awareness of these three things:

1. the social problem the agency addresses,
2. the social movement that has emerged within society to respond to the problem or need, and
3. the state of the art that has emerged to make an impact on the problem or need.

Continuous board education is one key to ensuring the ongoing viability of purpose, and the periodic consideration of purpose by the board as a whole. It is a principal board development strategy to forge consensus on the substantive nature of the work of the community service agency.

Role of the Board in Identifying Performance Expectancies and Core Beliefs

Expectations about performance are important influences on behavior within any organization. They are powerful in shaping the performance and effectiveness of individuals and groups. Expectancies and the beliefs they communicate can set the tone of performance, and can serve as a framework of what people want to see happen. In a sense, expectancies are things we look forward to, or perhaps more strongly, things we want or expect to happen through our work within organizations.

Expectancies are crucial in any field of community service, primarily because many of the community expectancies that surround people who are coping with serious social problems are so negative. These expectancies can be communicated in the form of negative stereotypes and negative attitudes. People coping with HIV/AIDS can confront very real negative expectancies communicated in the form of discrimination and stigma. People coping with serious mental illness can experience negative expectancies in the form of fear communicated by people who are profoundly ignorant about these illnesses. People with developmental disabilities may be seen within the general community as poor candidates for cultural enrichment and involvement in art education. Expectancies suggesting that people will not work, cannot perform well in independent living, or cannot "recover" establish a very negative set that can turn into self-fulfilling prophecies.

Positive expectancies are crucial to fostering the development of people. They are especially important to the people who hold service roles in community service agencies. I have seen too many agencies downgrade the status and contributions of people in key service roles, and fail to identify the supports service personnel need to perform in exemplary and effective ways. Indeed, a positive set of expectancies addressing the performance of people fulfilling service roles may be essential to promoting effective agency performance.

The members of high-performance organizational systems carefully consider and frame their expectations of the agency, of the community in which the agency transacts business, and of the people who conduct the business of the community service agency (J. Hall, 1980). These expectancies are often framed as beliefs that are encoded into organizational charters and serve as a framework for the creation of other organizational products, such as policies and procedures, staff development programs, and consumer satisfaction surveys (Falsey, 1989).

Because organizational beliefs will vary by the purpose and mission of the agency, its context, and history, it is difficult to prescribe the actual content of these statements. Many of these statements, however, incorporate beliefs about the social problem the agency seeks to impact. And they incorporate the role of the organization in the community; the people who receive help, assistance, and services from the agency; the people who offer assistance and service; and the community in which the organization is embedded.

The board of one community service agency uses a "Charter of Agency Beliefs" that establishes an organizational framework guiding the work of the board and the agency. Board members see this as a critical document that flows from its understanding of the social problem of serious mental illness, and that establishes an agencywide statement useful in guiding the work of all organizational members.

The 14 Core Beliefs of Sagammon Center

Our Beliefs about Serious Mental Illness

Although serious mental illness is likely a medical illness, its consequences are profoundly social, interpersonal, and cultural. We expect all members of the Sagammon Center to approach mental illness as a social problem with many dimensions, and to reduce the negative social consequences of this problem.

Serious mental illness does not have to dominate the lives of people who experience this problem. We do not conceive of serious mental illness as a chronic condition resulting in dysfunction but as a situation that can create barriers. People who obtain compassionate support can successfully negotiate these barriers. This success in turn will help strengthen and empower people. We expect that people can undertake a journey of recovery, and develop in ways they define as personally meaningful and valued.

Our Beliefs about the Role of Sagammon Center in Its Community

We expect that Sagammon Center will demonstrate to the community that people with serious mental illness can develop successfully, and become active citizens in our community.

We expect that recovery will serve as a framework guiding the work of the center, and the substance of our rehabilitation activity. Recovery is both process and product. As a process, it means focusing on strengths and human development. As a product, it means achieving life outcomes that are personally meaningful and valued by the people we serve.

Rehabilitation at Sagammon will be driven by a vision of each person we serve that is a product of a careful dialogue among the person and the members of the support system who are selected by the person served.

We expect Sagammon to make important contributions to the quality of life in our community. These contributions will make an impact on social support, human services, the nurturing of our ecology, and the safety of our immediate neighborhood.

Our Beliefs about the People We Serve

We expect the people we serve to define recovery in very personal and individualistic ways requiring our center to create flexible and personalized systems of support.

We expect the people we serve to assume responsibility, with support from the members and staff of the center, for defining recovery for themselves, and for establishing a personally meaningful and valued direction.

We expect the people we serve to be critical of the center's efforts to serve and support them, and to raise their concerns about the quality of rehabilitation supports in which they participate.

Our Beliefs about the People Who Offer Service

We expect our staff to offer the most proactive and effective rehabilitation service possible, and we recognize that this can only be achieved when staff members are offered meaningful skill development opportunities, effective administrative supports, and personally valued rewards.

We expect our staff to thrive as service providers when they understand what is expected of them, when they assist the center to establish standards of performance, and when they can offer critical input to the center concerning the quality and effectiveness of organizational performance.

Fostering recovery requires collaborative relationships among staff and consumers. We expect that all staff will take leadership in fostering collaboration among the members of their own teams as well as with the members of other agency teams.

Our Beliefs about Our Community

We expect our local community to welcome us, and to undertake activities that enhance the quality of life of our neighborhood. We expect our community to recognize us as good citizens.

We expect our local community to treat people with serious mental illness in dignified and respectful ways, to respect the human and civil rights of the people we serve, and to offer access to essential resources like housing, employment, and leisure activities.

Sagammon's board developed this statement of 14 beliefs in conjunction with administrators, staff members, and people served by the agency. The board sought the input of internal stakeholders to ensure that it undertook the creation of a key organizational document in an inclusive manner (Kofman & Senge, 1995). Recovery, as a core idea within the document, was identified and promoted by the people served who advocated for its inclusion as a concept that requires a personalized approach to rehabilitation.

The center enjoyed several benefits from the developmental activity the board invested in this document. First, it formulated a set of beliefs and expectations, consistent with the state of the art in psychiatric rehabilitation, one that offered to the agency a framework of performance (Dubois, 1993). Second, the board did not dominate the process but, rather, initiated and led it. The inclusion of staff and consumers increased the legitimacy of the board's leadership. Third, the inclusion of staff and consumers offered the board direct input concerning the aspirations, hopes, and expectations agency members have of the center, of the community, and of each other. And, fourth, the board formulated a critical organizational tool useful to the creation, refinement, and appraisal of agency policies, procedures, and decisions.

The board was able to formulate this statement of beliefs because of its commitment to its own education within the field of psychiatric rehabilitation (Kofman & Senge, 1995). Board members benefited from the discussions regarding agency purpose that took place for approximately 15 minutes after every training event. Staff members from all agency levels and consumers themselves serve as trainers and workshop leaders for the board. This had the effect of reducing the social distance that often exists between board members and other agency members. It also offered board members an opportunity to obtain firsthand input and perspectives from the people who actually do the work of rehabilitation and from those people who are beneficiaries of this work. This is an example of board development in action because it shows how the understanding of the board is enhanced through educational experiences and how this knowledge development can lead to the formulation of a key organizational policy (Sparrow, 1998).

Role of the Board in Defining Agency Distinctiveness

Purpose and expectancies require the board of the community service agency to consider the identity of the organization. Board members must address questions of identity such as "Who are we?" and "What do we believe in?" At some point in the history of the agency these questions will require answers. Perhaps they will emerge during a period of crisis, when doubt emerges, and internal and external stakeholders question the basic underpinnings of the agency. Or perhaps board members will address these questions as a routine part of their governance work.

Understanding organizational distinctiveness relates to purpose and beliefs and it can be appreciated as part of the character or identity framework of the community service agency (Bennis, 1993a). It raises another question that can be considered an essential feature of the governance work of the board: "What makes us unique?" The significance of this question lies in its obverse: "Are we just another organization with nothing that makes us different?" I have found that many community service agencies overlook their distinctiveness, and what defines them as unique contributors to local efforts designed to improve the quality of life within their respective communities.

Without a clear sense of organizational distinctiveness, board members may make decisions that undermine the uniqueness of the agency, especially during periods of stress or crisis. Failing to appreciate organizational distinctiveness may lead board members to make decisions that jeopardize the essential character of the agency. And without appreciating distinctiveness, the board may lose the opportunity to identify a set of values or characteristics useful in evaluating change in the agency's environment, considering new programmatic initiatives and new policies, and in making judgments concerning the implications of a change in purpose and direction of the agency.

In a sense, addressing distinctiveness is an extension of the board's educational efforts. It requires board members to examine the task environment of the agency. The task environment consists of those organizations, agencies, and groups with which the community service agency does daily business, and perhaps with which the agency competes for resources, recognition, and support. Gaining an understanding of agency distinctiveness requires the board to compare itself with other agencies to judge its own relative strengths, assets, uniqueness, and special features. This comparison identifies the position of the agency within the local community, and offers board members an understanding of the niche the agency has crafted for itself. The niche may be quite broad, or it may be quite narrow. However, it is important for board members to understand the overall community position of the agency as a basis for creating better policies, and for making better decisions.

Comparative analysis (some may see this more as competitive analysis) will require the board to undertake a number of tasks:

- It must define the constellation of organizations and agencies with which the community service agency is to be compared. Board members can gain some scope by using their sense of agency purpose to identify the work of the community service agency, and to select agencies or organizations that are undertaking similar work.
- It must identify relevant criteria that will guide comparative analysis. These criteria can include reputation, purpose and mission, where services are offered (for example, in the community versus facility based), how people are selected to participate in service, the technologies used, and the level of innovation. Criteria are not set in stone. Board members can select those that appear to be most meaningful to the agency, and to the realization of agency purpose.
- It must obtain the data necessary to conduct the comparative analysis, and to identify what makes the agency distinctive within its community. Most likely board members will not engage in data gathering or analysis. This is something that agency personnel can undertake. Indeed, agency personnel may have more access to the needed data, and to the perceptions agency members have of the other organizations that are included in the comparative analysis. Staff can prepare a brief memo summarizing the relative strengths and unique qualities of the agency compared to other agencies in its local community.

An understanding of the agency's distinctiveness will increase the enlightenment of board members, an important developmental outcome (Morris, 1995). This is just one outcome, however, but one that nonetheless justifies the investment of board energy in putting this foundation into place. A second outcome is the knowledge board members gain about what to protect, and about what to preserve, especially during periods of crisis, retrenchment, and growth (Hirschhorn et al., 1983). A third outcome is found in the formalization of a document that contains those qualities that make the community service agency distinctive within its community. One board did this to create a frame of reference useful in appraising decisions it made particularly concerning the agency's future development. Here is its product:

The Distinctiveness of the Stewart Agency

As part of our governance work, the members of the board of the Stewart Agency (a pseudonym) identified what makes us unique and distinctive in serving people within our community who struggle with HIV and AIDS. We identified our unique qualities by comparing ourselves to six other agencies serving the HIV/AIDS community. Here is what we discovered about Stewart Agency:

1. Although there are three agencies offering residential options within our community, we are the only agency that is supporting the housing choices of people. We have a strong commitment to personal choice. We focus on helping people to organize the supports they want in order to be successful in searching for, selecting, and keeping their housing.
2. We are committed to helping people to establish permanent homes in regular communities. We have a commitment to inclusion and to community support. These philosophical orientations guide our practice and this makes us distinctive.
3. The agency's board is composed of people who are experts in the field of housing and in the delivery of social services. Represented on our board are experts in real estate, estate planning, housing rights, outreach to consumers, housing development, self help, housing repair, and mortgage banking.
4. Our staff has created a unique synergy through the integration of community support and housing, and through the adoption of a philosophy of client-driven housing services and supports.
5. We define our "client" broadly to include people coping with HIV and AIDS, landlords, neighborhoods, and the real estate community.
6. We offer many flexible supports to consumers directly, and to landlords and to housing developers as our clients. Loan programs, technical assistance, advocacy, in-home services, and self-help opportunities are offered to the people we serve.
7. Although many of the people we serve are seriously ill, we do not focus on AIDS and HIV as an illness. The agency is more concerned about "handicappism," and the housing discrimination that occurs against people coping with HIV and AIDS. This makes us distinctive since many of our fellow agencies emphasize illness and dysfunction.
8. We are a small agency, without facilities per se, unlike all of the agencies to which we compared ourselves. We do not see a value in having our own facilities, but only in obtaining housing that will support the development of the people we serve.

During a stressful period when financial pressures appeared to threaten the permanency of the agency, Stewart was approached by a local mental health system to open several alternative residential facilities that were basically group-housing programs. Some board members advocated for the agency to enter this area, seeing this opportunity as a means to offset financial problems.

The board as a whole used its statement of distinctiveness to examine whether the agency should move in a new direction, one that would materially and substantially redefine its fundamental purpose. The board made a key decision to retain its founding purpose even through this created a host of financial issues the board needed to address in a relatively short time period. Staff concurred with this decision. They saw other agencies in the community as having the capacity to create and offer group residential care. What Stewart was committed to achieving in the community was distinctive, indeed so novel that it was a challenge to sustain financially.

The work of Stewart's board enabled the agency to become cognizant of its identity and of its character. The work answered all three of the questions posed at the beginning: (1) "Who are we?" (2) "What do we believe?" (3) "What makes us special and unique?" The work enabled the board to differentiate the agency from others in the community and to understand what makes it stand out from other organizations. The work enabled the board to address a question of policy that could threaten the distinctiveness of the agency and ultimately compromise its special purpose within the community.

By undertaking this work, a board should be able to identify what gives the agency a distinctive character within the community. When the board understands this distinctiveness collectively, it gains a richer image of what makes the agency unique and important in the community. This understanding can in turn strengthen the board's role as guardian and advocate of the essential character of the community service agency. The board is more apt to nurture and develop this unique identity through its policy leadership and stewardship when it collectively appreciates and values organizational distinctiveness.

Conclusion

Gaining an understanding of "who we are" offers the board an opportunity to develop its identity in conjunction with the identity of the community service agency. This understanding enables the board to formulate its purpose and to identify what must be achieved through community service in relationship to a social problem or a community need. It offers the board an opportunity to identify core expectations and to develop a framework for its own performance and the performance of the agency as a whole; and it offers the board the opportunity to appreciate its own distinctiveness and the uniqueness of the agency.

In formulating, refining, and using agency purpose, expectations and beliefs, and distinctiveness the board's development intersects with the development of the community service agency as a whole. This work offers the agency a common language in which staff members and leaders can articulate the substance and importance of the agency's work (Bethanis, 1995). When board members as a collective understand the substance and importance of organizational purpose, then they have truly achieved an important developmental milestone (Pascarella & Frohman, 1989).

Questions for Board Development

1. What strategies will the board undertake to develop a sense of identity among board members?
2. How does the board address continuing board education as an identity-building strategy? Will the board have a strong or weak program of continuing board education? What is the content of the board's curriculum?
3. What is your board's statement of purpose? What is your board's statement of performance expectations for the board and for the agency? What are the core beliefs of the board concerning the agency's production of value for the people it serves, for the community it serves, and for the people who offer service?
4. How does the board define its distinctiveness and the distinctiveness of the agency? How does the board ensure that the agency will continue to be distinctive within the community it serves?
5. What developmental needs does this chapter illuminate for the board? How will the board act on these needs?

■ 8 ■

Identifying "Where We Are Going"

Questions Asked by New Board Members during Orientation

> *John:* What is the agency trying to do in the next five years? I mean, where does it want to be and why is this important for the people it serves?

> *Cindy:* I have a similar question. I know it is hard to look into the future, but what difference does the agency make or try to make in the lives of the people it serves?

> *Sam:* I haven't seen a vision statement. I've seen a mission statement. But there doesn't appear to be a rich statement about the intended benefits the agency seeks to make in the lives of the people the agency serves. Is there a vision statement?

> *Facilitator:* Well, I'm glad you are asking these questions. I can't really answer them yet because we are only now creating this vision.

Purpose may not be graphic enough to inspire action, or to define the "image" of the desired destination (or ultimate outcome) of the agency. Purpose certainly points an organization in an initial direction, but it does not richly portray the desired or possible end state sought by the agency (Egan, 1985).

One of the most powerful products of the work of the board is found in the organizational vision. The vision is an extension of the board's conception of agency identity that emerges from the identification of purpose, beliefs, and distinctiveness (Egan, 1993). It offers the board and the agency an inspiring statement of a future state that the agency wants to bring about on behalf of the people or community the agency serves. Board members can choose to frame the vision in the context of organizational success. It can illustrate how the agency prospers and grows. Yet this only serves the agency's self-interest and misses the true purpose of the vision.

A more relevant frame of reference for the vision lies in the perspective of the people served by the agency. Articulating the vision from the perspective of the ultimate beneficiaries of the agency's work offers a graphic understanding of what difference the agency will make in the lives of the people making use of agency services and supports. A vision may read like a story. Indeed, it tells a story about the anticipated improvements brought about in people's lives. The vision is compelling (Bennis & Nanus, 1985). It can invigorate action. And it begins to explain why the agency exists.

The board struggles with a basic question: What ultimate positive differences does this agency seek to effect in the lives of people? What positive difference does this agency seek to effect in the life of the community? With vision, the agency can inspire action at all levels of the agency (SANNO, 1992). Without vision, the agency risks malaise (Tweed, 1990). With a vision that only speaks to the agency's growth, the organization risks opportunism.

Ingredients of a Vision Statement

Both Nanus (1992) and P. Schwartz (1991) identify the essential ingredients of a vision. A vision must inspire. It must be feasible, and it must portray a new reality of a preferred end state. Often vision statements are abbreviated: "We will offer an outstanding arts program to children and adolescents"; "We will create a great recreational program"; or "We will have cultural enrichment available to everyone in our community." This brevity is not so bad. It communicates an idea with some economy.

Yet the vision may lose something if it is kept only in an abbreviated form. People often come to service on a community board to be challenged in bringing about a better situation or life for citizens who need the benefits of a community service agency. Seeing the agency make dramatic changes in people's lives is found by board members to be the most inspiring aspect of their work. These board members are likely to be inspired by a vision that really does speak to how people will benefit from the agency and how their situations could be changed for the better. Brevity may simply fail to capture the richness identified by various stakeholders as they tell stories about what they wish the community service agency will achieve in action (H. Gardner, 1995). A more detailed elaboration of the agency's vision may be very worthwhile. It enables board members to ponder in depth what they wish for the community service agency. It offers the board an opportunity to offer a rich conception of how and why community service occurs and the impact that community service can have on real lives.

A more elaborate vision enables board members to give some depth to those critical values they want the agency to embody (Selznick, 1957). Formulation of the vision offers board members an opportunity to dialogue about purpose and to translate this purpose into a story of the future: a story that can serve to inspire the work of the board, mobilize energy of the organization, and gain the support of the community (H. Gardner, 1995).

Framing the Vision

Too often, board members fail to consider the future of the people served by the agency, and what they want the agency to look like in some future state if the community agency is to achieve this impact. Vision work requires the board to invest time in the future. It requires the board to consider emergent trends that can create change in the problem or need area in which the agency works, and to consider how the identity and character of the agency will be expressed in some future state through the eyes of the users of agency services. Vision work is not wasted time. It is, however, a time for board members to play with ideas, with forces, with assumptions. A vision is not set in stone. It is a powerful tool for helping the board create an understanding of the value the agency seeks to add to the lives of the people it serves, and to the community within which the agency does its work.

The reading of a vision statement should be a pleasurable experience. It captures the aesthetics of the agency (Ackoff, 1991, 1994). It is framed in positive terms, and illustrates how the lives of people who make use of the agency are improved by the efforts of the agency. One should be able to identify critical values the agency seeks to embody, and to identify the embodiment of agency purpose (Selznick, 1957) or the social cause the agency addresses (Handy, 1995). The vision statement should bring alive the distinctiveness of the community service agency. It can do this by giving voice to the people served by the agency, by crafting a narrative that highlights how consumers or clients see success, that amplifies the perspectives of people who often may not be heard by board members.

Example of the Vision Statement

Here is a vision that encompasses most of these attributes. It was written by a small team of three board members who offered planning leadership to the board as a whole. The small team incorporated three different perspectives: a business person who wanted to engage in community service, a consumer advocate who worked to improve life circumstances of people struggling with mental illness, and an entrepreneur who was also a family member of a client of the agency. The formulation of the vision followed the board's completion of a vigorous educational program that enabled its membership to understand serious mental illness as a social problem, the social movement that has emerged to address this problem, and the state of the art in serving people dealing with psychiatric disabilities.

The board members felt that this educational program helped them to appraise the status of their environment, and to frame their purpose (which is to help people to use social supports that help them to be successful in living, learning, and working in their community). Thus, they felt that their vision was founded on good data. And these data were used to craft a story using the perspectives of the people they sought to serve:

I come to the clubhouse on a regular basis. At first I was reluctant to come. I thought it was just another day treatment program I've attended where people simply did not have any expectations of you. I did not realize how wrong I had been. The clubhouse is in a very nice location. It is right on the bus line and it is easy to get to from my apartment. Before my first day, several people from the club came to seem me, and asked whether I needed some help figuring out how to get to the club. They came with open arms, with a welcome basket full of goodies. They helped me to learn about the clubhouse and how to get there. They even made sure that I would have a personal tour.

The clubhouse is not a mental health facility. People who come to it are members, and they are expected to make important contributions to running it. People who originally created this place gave a lot of thought to the building. There is a lot of light, small places where I can work alone, big places where groups can gather, a bunch of computers, and a very, very nice kitchen. It is open every day of the week, during the evenings, on weekends, and on holidays.

The clubhouse has small station wagons that are driven by members to reach out to other members, shop for the club, and help members to get work. Also, the club is helping members to rent homes and apartments in the local area. And it is helping people make employment connections, get ready for interviews, and participate in what is called transitional employment. The clubhouse has members who are artists, musicians, athletes, poets, scholars, and experts at crafts. We share these gifts with a local adult education program and we have a connection with the art museum that is putting the work of some of our members on display.

Next week I will start work. Well, some trial-work. I do not want to go to work full time yet. But I want to think about working again. I've talked to one of my mentors—someone who works with computers for a car company. The clubhouse has matched me with her. She is making arrangements for me to visit her at work and to see what she does with computers. The clubhouse is also helping me to participate in community college classes. I'm looking into a computer course, and a faculty member at the college who teaches this course is meeting with me to tell me about it. The clubhouse offers me plenty of opportunities. I don't feel like I'm mentally ill. I feel like a regular person who is starting to live on her own, the way I want to.

Vision as a Board Product

I helped this team to craft this vision. But board members controlled the parameters of the vision. More important, however, the information that serves as the building blocks of this story came from the board interacting with essential stake-holders (especially people served by the agency). The vision was created through organizational and community dialogue that centered on what social needs the clubhouse should meet and how they will be met.

Board members were energized and inspired by the vision, but felt somewhat challenged by the great accountability they felt in making it a reality. The vision was crafted in 1992. The board in partnership with agency personnel, the people served by the agency, and key community leaders fulfilled the vision in 1996. The current tension at the board level is healthy. Board members are challenged by the need to create a new vision guiding the work of their organization. Or they feel a profound loss of relevance, according to these members.

All ingredients essential to a good vision are embodied within this statement. The purpose of the agency is communicated through the eyes of the storyteller; the clubhouse helps people to make choices about independent living and then supports them in the successful achievement of these choices. I see critical values expressed in the characteristics of the facility, the use of time, the inclusion of diverse supports, the cooperation with other community resources, and the efforts invested in helping members to make use of the community. The vision underscores that the clubhouse is part of a network of other community institutions (Handy, 1989). It does not stand alone in the "mind" of the board.

But is the vision compelling? Feedback from consumers and from staff was very positive, and people indicated their excitement about participating in the preparation of the vision. Focus groups of consumers and staff reviewed the vision statement at different times during its formulation. Dissemination of the statement to the agency's membership resulted in feedback from the staff and consumers that was very favorable. They found it to be inspirational but incomplete. The authors, according to staff and consumers, failed to identify transportation in the first draft. The inclusion of the material on transportation "bubbled up" from below. Members and staff communicated the expectations that station wagons would be available to support involvement in the community. This may seem like a minor addition, but for members it demonstrated the board's commitment to the values of mobility, accessibility, and community inclusion.

Utility of the Vision to the Board

For board members, the vision is a reference point for their success, and the success of the agency. It offers a board a reference point to judge the effectiveness of its stewardship. It offers a framework guiding the work of administrative leaders of the organization. The board can use it to judge whether the administrative leadership of the agency is moving in the right direction, and doing the right things to bring the vision into reality. And the board can use it in collaboration with the chief executive officer to identify environmental forces frustrating or compromising the achievement of the vision. It can also be incorporated into strategic planning to identify and choose those strategies that are found to be useful in achieving specific aspects of the vision.

In formulating the vision, the idea and contribution of board education emerges again. The crafting of a useful vision requires board members to obtain a rich understanding of what the agency is trying to create, and of the future it is trying to bring about. Vision planning and board education can be linked so the vision is a product of the board's program of continuous education. But vision work does add another responsibility to the job description of board members because their stewardship of the organization requires them to consider and project the future of the agency. Putting vision planning into place and keeping it going may require the appointment of a vision leader (Jackson, 1995), a board member responsible for keeping the board on track in its formulation of a compelling vision.

Linking the Vision to Agency Development

Vision is a destination. And this destination lies on a distant horizon. One does not arrive at this destination unless there is a journey. The board's leadership role is not complete after it crafts a vision. It must ensure that the community service agency uses this vision, that progress is made to the desired destination, and that progress is monitored. Momentum is achieved when the community service agency makes systematic progress toward this vision (SANNO, 1992). Yet achieving this momentum is complex and requires the community service agency to engage in a learning process that is not linear.

The community service agency develops along platforms. I invoke the term *platform* intentionally. Think of a platform as a rising above the level of an adjacent area, perhaps a floor, or landing. People walk along one platform and then must step up to a landing to move toward their destination. Multiple platforms can constitute a journey along which the community service agency is traveling toward its vision. Although it is difficult to anticipate all of these platforms, intentional planning of them can help the board project those platforms that the agency needs to complete to achieve its vision.

Intentional development means that the board is anticipating those platforms that will bring it closer to the achievement of its vision. Through the identification of organizational platforms the board recognizes that movement toward the vision is critical, that it must be done intentionally and systematically, and that the attainment of vision does not occur in the short term. However, movement along an intentional platform can result in "a step up" to a higher level of agency performance. Intentional development means systematic progress undertaken by the community service agency to achieve its vision of a better quality of life for the people it serves.

You, the reader, may want to refer to the vision adopted by the clubhouse described earlier. After carefully crafting its vision, the board identified four platforms, all of which can be linked to one another, and all of which mean that the agency is working purposefully to achieve a higher level of performance—to rise from one platform to another. Platforms are linked sequentially. Although they may overlap, accomplishment of these platforms take the agency from one level of performance to another. They move the agency toward its vision. For this psychiatric rehabilitation agency, the intentional platforms spanned a period from 1992 to 1996. The four platforms follow below.

Theme of Platform 1: Making a Home

This platform encompasses those elements of the vision that speak to finding a facility that reflects the core values of the agency, and that promotes the accessibility of the clubhouse to its membership through a desirable location, peer outreach, friendly visiting, and social marketing to members from members. It includes building a membership representative of the community in which the clubhouse is embedded. The platform also encompasses the structuring of internal arrangements and physical characteristics of the club to offer the spatial arrangements, amenities, aesthetics, and qualities valued by founders and members.

Theme of Platform 2: Expanding Participation of Members in the Community

This platform encompasses those elements of the vision that underscore the importance of the clubhouse becoming part of the community, and that enable members to have supportive and personally rewarding involvement in the community. Establishing relationships with key community institutions (such as the community college), expanding opportunities for club members within these community institutions, and supporting members to make use of these opportunities through the enhancement of community mobility characterize this platform. In addition, involving community members in the club, serving as a resource to the community, and improving the quality of life of the immediate community are other aims within this platform.

Theme of Platform 3: Becoming Participants in the World of Work

This platform focuses on those qualities of the vision that speak to the vocational development and employment of clubhouse members. The creation of linkages to potential employers and the recruitment of people in the community who will serve as mentors are vital aspects of this platform. Other essential qualities covered by this platform are the creation of a viable transitional employment program, including transportation supports; participation in postsecondary training or education, including the provision of supports necessary to the achievement of success in education; and career development opportunities.

Theme of Platform 4: Supporting the Housing Choices of Our Members

This platform focuses on the housing dimension of the vision. The clubhouse is concerned with the development of housing resources within the local community, and the establishment of supports that will enable people to make housing choices, and to maintain homes successfully. There are a number of programmatic outcomes of this platform that enable the clubhouse to realize aspects of its vision:

- the creation of a housing registry and information system staffed by a housing coordinator,
- a loan program to support access to apartments,
- a chore and home maintenance outreach program,
- the forging of relationships with banks and real estate professionals, and
- the purchase of several homes by the clubhouse.

The four platforms ensure that the clubhouse board has thought through its own development within a long-range time frame, and that it has specified an intentional movement through the time frame in which the organizational vision is to be achieved. Each platform contains a theme that gives a developmental and task focus to the clubhouse. Each platform suggests critical results that are required to move the clubhouse forward (Handy, 1994). The content of each platform is descriptive and identifies what needs to be achieved to perform within the theme of a particular platform. Each platform can be benchmarked according to critical outcomes or milestones that must be achieved. This enables the board to develop its own information system and to monitor the progress the agency is making toward the realization of its vision. The board of the clubhouse formulated the following benchmarks for each platform.

Platform 1: Making a Home

- Accessible location
- A facility that communicates dignity and worth of members
- A facility that adds value to a neighborhood
- A facility that offers suitable space and equipment
- Facility qualities that are aesthetically pleasing to members

■ Membership development undertaken with substantial involvement of members
■ A growing and diverse membership

Platform 2: Expanding Participation in the Community

■ Members of the clubhouse are using the community college, YMCA, adult education, and art museum.
■ The club membership has physical mobility in the community.
■ Participation of members in community development projects external to the clubhouse
■ A growing involvement of members in community activities

Platform 3: Becoming Participants in the World of Work

■ An advisory panel of employers who attend meetings and who create employment opportunities
■ A mentoring program that successfully matches members with corporate, business, or technical mentors
■ A state-of-the-art transitional employment program used by a growing number of members
■ Involvement in postsecondary education by a growing number of members
■ Career planning and development used by a growing number of members

Platform 4: Supporting Housing Choices

■ Housing information system
■ A housing coordinator
■ A housing support program integrating chore, nutritional, and home maintenance services
■ Purchase of three homes by the club
■ A growing number of members who have found housing of their own choosing through the clubhouse

Some boards, perhaps many, will delegate the responsibility for the establishment of these platforms to the chief executive officer. This may reduce the involvement of board members in planning the achievement of the agency's vision. This can reduce the appreciation board members have for the challenges the organization faces in its development.

Collaboration between the board and chief executive officer and other staff leaders is certainly desired (Handy, 1995). This can be undertaken within the context of the agency's board planning committee that can adopt the tripartite responsibility of formulating the agency's vision, translating this vision into relevant platforms, and identifying the benchmarks that compose each platform.

Investment of time and energy in the formulation of the essential platforms is time well spent by board members. This investment offers board members a first-hand understanding of how the agency needs to perform to make progress toward its future end state. It offers the board a specific set of performance expectations that can be delegated to the chief executive officer. And it offers the board a framework within which its own performance and the performance of the chief executive officer can be more clearly evaluated.

Linking the Vision and Platforms to Consumer-Driven Milestones

The platforms establish a means for the board of the community service agency to chart its own course, and to define the journey it will take toward the agency vision. It is within these platforms that the agency identifies the milestones that will demarcate the journey it is taking. A board of a community service agency that is committed to achieving a bold and challenging vision in service to the resolution of a community problem or the fulfillment of community need will find interest in framing milestone accomplishments from the perspectives of the people it serves. It is these individuals who possess the need. And it is these individuals who look to the community service agency for support, services, and opportunities. Thus, it is wise to frame these milestones using the frame of reference of the people who are served.

To ensure that the agency would make a positive impact on the people served, the board leading the clubhouse adopted four milestones the achievement of which are the markers or milestones of the performance and effectiveness of the agency. The achievement of these milestones represents important movement toward the vision of the clubhouse. The agency frames the milestones as achievements that add value to the lives of users and members. For example, the clubhouse formulated its four milestones from the perspectives of its members, people struggling with serious mental illness:

■ Milestone 1: Our members find the clubhouse facility aesthetically pleasing, accessible, and personally useful. The basic supports the clubhouse offers to our members are seen by them as contributing to the quality of their lives.

■ Milestone 2: Many of our members are involved in community activities through clubhouse-sponsored events. The members find them to be meaningful and relevant to the improvement of the quality of their lives.

■ Milestone 3: There are several different vocational development and community employment options that members find to be valuable, and these options are used frequently by a majority of clubhouse members. The employment of members, as evidenced by hours worked, and duration of work increases. Members see these options as contributing to the quality of their lives.

■ Milestone 4: There is a pool of housing alternatives from which our members can choose. Members report that their housing, and the assistance they receive to get and keep their housing, contribute to the quality of their lives.

Board Information System

These milestones are products of the work undertaken within each platform. They represent the board's sense of vision, and the translation of this vision into substantive indicators of organizational performance. Every milestone serves as a short term mission, and their relevance is found in their linkage to organizational identity. They represent what the agency means by community service. These products reflect the board's commitment to performance as found in its aspirations and expectations. This is a board that seeks to improve the quality of life of people coping with serious mental illness. All four milestones of the clubhouse are relevant to the attainment of quality of life when we think of this outcome in terms of its constituent elements of social relationships, meaningful involvement, housing quality, and involvement in productive activity. The milestones point the clubhouse in the right direction.

The framing of the milestones is also an important consideration. These milestones are framed from the perspective of consumers. And they require the board to monitor the satisfaction of the agency's users with the services and supports they receive from the community service agency. Using milestones in this manner keeps board members in touch with the agency's performance and makes them sensitive to the perspectives of a major constituency or stakeholder group: the recipients of community support.

These milestones also help to demystify the board information system. Obtaining, processing, and using information, especially information pertaining to critical achievements, products, and outcomes, are essential to board development. The board must not only identify focused milestones, but also develop and use an information system that captures the perspective of key constituencies about whether the agency achieves these milestones. The development of such an information system requires the board to plan for the enhancement of its information and evaluation capacities.

Conclusion

The board's clarification of how it will achieve its mission, the journey it will take in its enterprise of community service, may be one of the most fundamental steps the agency will take to achieve its purpose, beliefs, and core principles. This clarification helps the board to monitor whether the institutional ends of the agency are being achieved on an ongoing basis. And this clarification places the board into a role not necessarily of oversight and enforcement, but, rather, of policy management in which board members identify issues, barriers, and challenges to bringing as much of the agency's vision into reality as possible.

Information about performance flows from making up one's mind about what is important. Previously, in chapter 5, the idea of identifying what is important to a community service board becomes a key product in which aspirations, expectations, plans, and critical decisions shape and form the agency. Information requires valuing, and it is the role of the community service board to identify these values so that information about performance can be created and used to steer the journey toward an organizational vision of community service.

Questions for Board Discussion

1. What is the substantive vision your board holds for the community service agency in terms of how people who need the services of the agency will benefit from these? In other words, what is the agency's vision of client-driven service?

2. How will the board develop this vision and maintain its relevance and vitality? How will the board ensure that the vision incorporates the spirit of purpose, performance expectancies, and core beliefs?

3. How will the board deploy this vision to the people served by the agency? To the community? To the personnel of the agency?

4. How will the board make use of the vision in its deliberations and in its committee and task force work?

5. How will the board make use of the vision in the advancement of the agency's work and in preparing the agency for its future?

6. What developmental needs does this chapter illuminate for the board? How will the board act on these needs?

SUPPORTING BOARD DEVELOPMENT

Taking action to develop the board is the theme of this section. The four chapters that compose this section examine practical supports for undertaking and actualizing board development within the community service agency. Chapter 9 presents the idea of the board development mission. Chapter 10 discusses the board development committee as a primary support for the progressive improvement of the community service board. Five responsibilities of this committee are offered:

1. perpetuating the board through new membership development,
2. improving the performance and effectiveness of the board as a whole,
3. building the knowledge base of the board and its members,
4. developing and fostering board leadership, and
5. planning and monitoring board development outcomes.

Chapter 11 examines board leadership in supporting board development. Leadership is broadly construed to include various types: transformational, task, transactional, and situational. The first type is devoted to assisting the board to transform itself and the agency by moving it closer to its vision. Task leadership is more narrow and focused involving the execution by relevant board members of specific board tasks essential to board development. The third form—transactional leadership—involves board members in forming and sustaining critical internal relationships as well as relationships with important external stakeholders and organizations. Situational leadership helps the board and agency to navigate crisis and urgencies. The integration of all four forms—means that the board is better able to perform. It can foster its vision (transformational). It can get work done that is essential to board and agency development (task) and it can manage important external political and policy relationships (transactional). And the board can address immediate threats to the agency (situational). Compared to a board that does not have this pool of people and roles on which it can rely, the board that develops its leadership will be better able to foster community service and the development of the agency it sponsors.

Fostering the development of the interface between board and agency is the theme of chapter 12. I have included this theme because of my recognition in a number of consultation projects with community service agencies that this interface is vital to overall organizational performance but is often ignored or neglected by board and agency leaders. The fostering and strengthening of this form of development brings us back to a consideration of an ongoing challenge—that of creating a coherent sense of institutional identity among the board and agency members.

More practical considerations are also discussed involving staff roles in the board system, supporting staff involvement in the board, and board–executive relationships. Several conditions are identified and discussed that offer community service boards a rationale supporting the need to pay attention and to develop this interface intentionally. "Supporting board development" reveals the intentional work that community service boards can undertake to make ongoing and progressive improvement of the board system feasible and productive.

■ 9 ■

Board Development Mission

A Complaint by a Board Member

We get together each year to plan. And we plan. And we plan. It seems that the planning is somewhat ritualistic. We focus on the agency and what the agency needs to achieve in the next year. Frankly, I want us to focus on how we are to develop. Felix, the CEO, can take care of the agency planning. We need to work with him to ascertain what the board needs to do from a development perspective in order to help the agency attain its goals or its vision. We—the board as a group—have not made a commitment to our own development. This lack of commitment is simply a handicap to this agency.

Role of the Board Development Mission

The board development mission solidifies the commitment of the board of the community service agency to the demanding process of board improvement and change. This internal mission statement complements the greater, more encompassing, mission of the agency, and articulates to the board, the agency, and to the community the board's recognition of the important role it plays in the advancement of the agency (Clifton & Dahms, 1993).

As an internal statement, the board development mission is a framework that directs the attention of board members to their social responsibility to advance the performance of the board in service to the agency, and ultimately in service to the community (Brinckerhoff, 1994). It is a reference point, a framework, and a source of inspiration for engaging in the process of board development.

This mission statement sets forth the spirit and purpose of board development and informs the substance of board development that is subsequently found in the board self-evaluation, the board development retreat, and the board development plan. The creation of the mission statement affirms that important if not critical aspects of board work lie in the improvement of the board as a system of organizational governance.

Previous chapters outline the importance of board stewardship to the effectiveness and subsequent viability of community service and to the agencies that perform this invaluable work. The prologue highlights and frames board development as stewardship: that the board steward is deeply rooted in the agency, and deeply committed to addressing a specific social concern, need, or outcome. The board development mission further articulates this stewardship and can help a board to create the collective commitment the agency requires to advance its work through the improvement and strengthening of the board.

The formation and preparation of the board development mission anticipates the cycle of board development. Its formation requires a consciousness among board members about the importance of board development. The preparation of the board development mission requires the board to commit itself to purpose and to create an expectation for improvement within the board itself. The board development mission also empowers the board and its members. It can make members affirm that the responsibility for development resides within the board.

The formation and preparation of the board development mission are increasingly important to those agencies that embrace total quality management or continuous improvement. Too often, quality improvement initiatives within organizations fail because those structures composing the top levels of organizations are unwilling to recognize their responsibility for improving their own performance and effectiveness, and are reluctant to act systematically to engage in this improvement. The idea that the board does not need to engage in quality improvement while the rest of the agency is required to is only a formula for the failure of any quality campaign. The board development mission can be treated as a commitment to quality improvement by the board itself and its use can model this commitment for the total agency (Handy, 1995). The statement says that every major system within the agency needs to be concerned about its own improvement and its own development.

This mission statement anchors the cycle of board development. It offers a sense of meaning to board members, and offers a rationale supporting the involvement of the board in its own development. The board development mission offers a reference point for any subsequent self-evaluation of board development and can drive the convening of the board development retreat. And it can frame the board development plan that emerges from this retreat. The board development mission makes the process of board development more disciplined and consistent and reinforces this process as an ongoing and necessary process of board work. Thus, the board development mission plays a crucial role in the process of any subsequent board development.

Five Basic Attributes of the Board Development Mission

The board development mission incorporates five qualities that give it form, substance, and meaning to the board. First of all, the mission statement underscores board development as a "principal responsibility of the board." Board development will not happen naturally or systematically if it is imposed from outside or if someone other than key board members force it on the board. Perhaps the worse instigator of board development is by accreditation requirements. Board development is a social responsibility. It is a natural outcome of the voluntary character of most community service organizations that emerges out of an ethos of service (Drucker, 1990). Often, community service agencies emerge out of felt needs. These needs coalesce into social movements, energized by citizen or collective action. People come together to address a concern or issue that is going unattended and that poses serious consequences for people and for communities if not addressed (Bettencourt, 1996). Board development is undertaken because it is seen as a need of the board. Board members recognize that the viability of the board will be jeopardized if it is not undertaken and, ultimately, the viability of the community service agency and its role in addressing major social concerns or social needs can be threatened. Thus, a second attribute of this mission statement lies in its identification of the "importance of board development" to the community service agency. The board development mission makes this a priority of board work.

The third attribute of this mission statement involves the "conceptualization of board development" by the board. Board development is a broad encompassing idea. It is complex and cannot be approached by a board in a formulaic manner. Board members and the board as a group invest creative thought into board development. It requires the board to define or conceptualize board development for its own purpose. Some boards may define board development only from an institutional perspective, highlighting the important role of the board in defining values, commitments, and vision of the community service agency. Other boards may focus more on the functional dimensions (for example, the role of the board in strategic planning) or from a performance standpoint (that is, organizing the work of the board). Some boards may define board development comprehensively along multiple dimensions. I cannot prescribe how a board should think about or engage in board development. But I can assert that it is up to each board to define this idea within the context of its board development mission.

A "set of broadly stated board development goals" is the fourth attribute of this mission statement. These goals can relate to (1) the strengthening of board performance, (2) the advancement of agency vision, (3) the stewardship of the agency into the future, and (4) the impact on the staff and performance of the agency.

These goals help board members to understand that board development relates to greater outcomes, and that the board is ultimately connected to the agency, and to the social concerns and needs that are the foundation of agency purpose.

The fifth attribute of the mission statement is found in "how the board intends to make board development routine practice." This aspect of the mission outlines the supports for board development within the board, and identifies events and activities that the board will undertake to ensure that board development occurs on a continuous basis.

Example of a Board Development Mission

Let me introduce a community service agency located in the midwestern United States. Its name is KIDS. Founded as an early childhood education program 20 years ago, KIDS has recently revised its vision to reflect a broad commitment to the development of young children within their families and their communities. The historic commitment of the agency is to children living in poverty or who experience limited income. It works with young children and their families below or near the poverty line.

The new vision has not changed this commitment. Indeed, people affiliate with the agency as funders, board members, administrators, and staff members because they are concerned with the negative effects poverty creates for children. These circumstances alarm them and, consequently, they want to do something about them. The change in vision comes at a time of new board and administrative leadership, which has worked vigorously to build a consensual but challenging sense of identity among the board, the administrative staff, and agency personnel.

This leadership supports the broadening of vision to encompass a family, community, and developmental approach to the "whole" child. The previous vision of early childhood education is incorporated into this new vision but this more recent statement is much bolder and challenging. It asserts that the children served by KIDS will progress into their adolescence better educated, safer, more healthy, more socially involved, and more nurtured than if they had not been involved with the agency.

Board development is a top agenda item of the new board president who has had lengthy discussions with board members about the importance of board development. There is now a consensus that the board has to engage in board development in a systematic, continuous, and self-directed manner. It is a natural outcome of the new challenges the agency faces created by the change of vision. No one required the agency to change its vision—it is an outcome of leadership. No one requires the board to engage in board development. But it is now seen as a necessity by board leadership to engage in the new vision quest successfully. The board development mission of KIDS follows.

The Board Development Mission At KIDS

The board members of KIDS, in keeping with its historic commitment to advancing the well-being and health of young children, accepts primary responsibility for the improvement and strengthening of the board. Board development is one strategy to meet the challenges created by an agency vision that seeks to foster the full development of young children growing up in poverty. The board takes pride in the purpose, vision, and mission of KIDS. And it takes pride in the commitment of the agency to the well-being of children in jeopardy. Now more than ever, it is important to create and shape a board that fosters the effectiveness of the agency in the development of young children experiencing poverty. The agency seeks to achieve those child, family, and community outcomes that support the full development of young children who find themselves due to no fault of their own or of their families coping with poverty.

We, the members of the board, commit ourselves with foresight, enthusiasm, and a sense of social responsibility to the advancement of the board. The members of the board commit themselves to the development of the agency's institutional identity, its functioning, and its performance recognizing that a sound board is fundamental to the advancement of a social purpose, vision, and mission as expressed in the work of KIDS. It is the purpose of the board to make a fundamental, positive difference in the performance of this agency. And it is up to this board to ensure that KIDS possesses the people, technology, organization, and relationships to advance the vision of young children who make the transition into adolescence with the assets of health, education, safety, and caring relationships.

The members of this board cannot contemplate an agency with a weak board, an uncaring board, and an uninvolved board. Alternatively, we envision an agency with a vital, committed, and energetic board that possesses the strengths and assets to advance the basic purpose of KIDS. Our board development mission is to ensure that these strengths and assets are in place, and are available to the service of young children, to the families and communities within which they live, and to the agency that seeks to advance their well-being.

The Concept of Board Development

The board of KIDS embraces a broad concept of board development. To have an effective board, the members must engage in board development along several dimensions. Board development means:

1. The institutional advancement of the board through the identification and articulation of the fundamental purpose of the agency, the

maintenance of a vision that expresses our values in action and that demonstrates the intended impact of agency services and programs on the well-being of the "whole" child. We will model creativity, enterprise, enthusiasm, and excitement in the advancement of the well-being of young children. The board seeks to create an atmosphere within which this positive sense of mission can grow and develop.

2. The improvement of the functioning of the board. This is found in the board's capacities to promote the effective administration and management of the agency. And it is found in the ability of the board to position the agency to behave strategically while mindful of its core values and commitments. The board will promote a broad scope of citizen involvement in the life of the board and agency, and to plan effectively for the resources, tools, personnel, and dollars the agency will need in the future.

3. The fostering of high performance within the board through intentional membership recruitment, member development, productive committees, a sound internal structure, external networking, and productive task completion.

4. Integration of the board's agenda of work with those of the agency to ensure relevance, timeliness, and effectiveness.

The Goals of Board Development

The mission of board development is to achieve five specific outcomes relating to agency performance:

1. We will foster a sense of responsibility within the board for the success of the agency, for agency personnel, and for the people served by the agency.

2. We will demonstrate a strong, enduring commitment to effectively addressing the social issues and needs this agency has been established to address. We will demonstrate a long-term commitment to addressing the social ills created by poverty and fulfilling the needs that will benefit the young children the agency serves.

3. We will ensure that the work of the agency makes substantial positive differences in the well-being of young children living in and coping with the ravages of poverty.

4. We will ensure that the agency has the resources it needs in order to advance its work and the work of its personnel.

5. We will ensure that the board possesses the competence to make possible the long-term viability of the agency.

Supporting Board Development

The board of KIDS, recognizing its fundamental importance to the agency, and to advancing the vision of the wholistic development of young children who prosper, will ensure that specific actions are taken to support the continuous improvement of the board and to the long-term development of board performance. There will be in place a current and relevant annual plan of board development that articulates how this mission will be executed in the work and deliberations of the board. This plan will be formulated through the conduct of an annual self-evaluation of board performance that looks at the progress of the board in relationship to specific board development objectives and outcomes. The findings of the self-evaluation will be interpreted and utilized at an annual board development retreat. This retreat will be attended by board members, new board members, key administrative personnel, and key community representatives who will work together to translate the findings of self-evaluation into a relevant board development theme and into specific aims, objectives, and actions supporting board development.

The board development plan will be written and will stand as a core document of the board. The board will adopt the plan after appraisal and appropriate revision. The board will form as a standing structure a board development committee the responsibility of which will be for the management of this plan. The committee will monitor the execution of the aims, objectives, and actions of the plan and the progress it makes. The board development committee also will be responsible for the identification of barriers and for working with the leadership of the board to resolve these barriers. The chair of the board development committee will update the board quarterly on the progress made and the barriers that must be addressed.

However, the full responsibility for board development lies with the executive committee of the board that will make use of the input of the board development committee to steer on a continuous basis the process of board development. To ensure that board development is a priority of board work, the chair of the board development committee will hold membership on the executive committee.

The executive committee will have the responsibility for ensuring that:

1. The report to the board made by the board president at each monthly board meeting addresses the status and progress of board development and will identify issues relating to the advancement of board development.
2. Board development is a standing item on the monthly agenda of the board and is discussed by board members as a priority item.

3. Appropriate meeting time is devoted to board development, including orientation, membership development, and board education.
4. Meeting time is devoted to the appraisal of board development and direction is given to the board development committee.

Conclusion

The board of KIDS recognizes the importance of board development to the advancement of the agency's vision and to supporting the work of the agency. The board exemplifies an awareness of the necessity to integrate the work of the board and the work of the agency. Implied in this board development mission is a context that favors this integration. It appears that the board president and the agency executive are working collaboratively to create organizational change starting with an updating if not total retooling of the vision guiding the organization (Eadie, 1997). The board president and agency executive engage in transformational leadership to begin to drive the change process into the board using board development as a basic tactic of change (Eadie, 1997).

The tone of the board development mission is somewhat idealistic if not romantic. It is a bold statement full of vision, dripping with values, and infused with basic assumptions that may not be realistic in other agencies. Nonetheless, the mission frames the importance of board development and the specific goals it seeks. In addition, the mission statement gives the idea of board development top priority within the board that is supported through explicit tactics to make board development a useful tool.

This board development mission reflects the five properties of board development outlined in chapter 2. Indeed, it is remarkable that this board, on paper at least, meets these five conditions quite well. The board has a high level of energy to invest in its development (property 1). This energy is likely a product of the commitment and social responsibility deeply felt among board members. And this commitment is translated into high aspirations for young children and for the outcome of service. It sounds like this is a board that possesses a strong commitment to young children and embraces a responsibility for them as an important group within the community. The emotional tone of the document is quite positive. It speaks to excitement and enthusiasm as enabling conditions of board work.

Property 2 is found in the board's clear conception of a highly valued end state. The board development mission makes use of the agency's vision, underscores the importance of this vision, and uses it throughout the statement to define what the board needs to achieve in its work. The vision converges on the well-being of young children coping with poverty, and the board development framework is informed by this vision. Related to this is property 3: The board has a strong belief system to steer its work. There are some fundamental beliefs about the nature of the agency's purpose and how the board relates to this purpose. Indeed, one can argue that the foundation of the board development mission is this belief system about young children and their well-being.

Property 4 is clearly incorporated into the board development mission: The board embraces and acts on continuous improvement. The mission is driven by the notion of continuous improvement. The mission statement suggests that board development is an ongoing process that needs to address institutional, functional, and performance-based development. In addition, the mission statement underscores the important role of the board in modeling the process of continuous improvement.

And, finally, property 5, the board is deeply committed to its own learning, is reflected in this statement. The mission statement suggests the need for board members to learn about the board and about the work of the agency. Boards devoted to this learning process will find that board development is a natural outcome of this work.

The board development mission is a pivotal tool for empowering the process of board improvement. Without such a statement, it will be difficult for any board to make its own development a central feature of board work. The likelihood of a board engaging in productive development increases as the board

1. articulates responsibility for its own improvement,
2. establishes board development as a priority,
3. makes explicit its basic concept of board development,
4. identifies relevant goals and outcomes, and
5. identifies meaningful supports and practices to make board development a focus of board work.

The completion of the board development mission statement is a major milestone for any board and deserves the great effort required to formulate it.

Questions for Board Discussion

1. Is the idea of a board development mission relevant to your board? Why is it relevant? Why is it not relevant?
2. For those board members who feel it is relevant, what is a board development mission that captures the direction your board is heading? What is the substance of such a mission statement?
3. How will your board execute its responsibility for board development? How does this responsibility link to the work of the agency?
4. What is the importance of board development to your agency? How will the agency benefit from a board committed to its own development?

5. How does your board conceptualize board development within the context of agency purpose and vision?
6. What set of board development goals will your board achieve?
7. What supports will your board organize to execute its board development mission?
8. What developmental needs does this chapter illuminate for the board? How will the board act on these needs?

■ 10 ■

Board Development Committee

Board Chair: I am very pleased! The board development committee really did its work. This is the first year that we have a great slate of candidates for board membership.

Board Vice President: The committee scanned the community and identified candidates who can meet our needs. For example, look at these two candidates who have experience in information technology. And here is a candidate who comes with ties to the financial sector.

Board Development Chair: The committee has developed a database of potential board members. In fact, the database isn't complete but it now numbers forty people. You have in your hands the eight people we screened as most suitable and appropriate to board membership at this time. After the nomination process is completed, the committee will begin identifying other people who can serve on our two task forces.

Board development requires a focus within the board as a system. With this focus, the board can more effectively make a commitment to its own development, plan its development in a systematic manner, and undertake and track those tasks and activities critical to its own development. Without such a fixed point of responsibility, the board may fail in its vigilance and allow responsibility for board development to slip away in light of the many challenging responsibilities a board faces.

It is probably typical of a board to establish a board nominations committee to oversee the identification of promising board members and to recommend these candidates to the board for membership. Given the broad definition and role assigned to board development in this book, a board nominations committee may be too narrow in scope to address the many aims and responsibilities of board development.

Community service boards often need to broaden the scope of board development to address a full range of board development activities and responsibilities. Some boards may not feel comfortable with this broad scope because they may find it too difficult to manage. Yet I have found those boards committed to high performance and whose properties favor high performance to be very amenable and interested in forming a board development committee of broad scope that goes well beyond the singular responsibility of nominations.

The scope of board development involves five core responsibilities. Certainly perpetuating the board through the identification and induction of new board members and participants is an essential responsibility (Duca, 1996). Yet beyond this responsibility lie four other critical ones involving improving the performance of the board and its effectiveness, building the knowledge base of the board and its members, developing board leadership, and planning and monitoring board development outcomes.

These responsibilities and related activities are discussed in this chapter as a means of placing the board development committee into the context of the larger board. The board development committee is perhaps the most critical structure within the board as a whole. It is this committee that reflects the board's commitment to its own improvement and advancement, and models for the board, for the agency, and most of all, for the community the proactivity required of an organization to advance its vision of community service.

Qualities of a Good Board Development Committee

There are basic qualities that are characteristic of a good board development committee, one that is committed to its mission of strengthening the board as a high-performance system. One essential quality is the committee's orientation to the developmental needs of the board. This committee and its members are knowledgeable of what the board needs to become more effective. It is knowledgeable of the types of members that are needed and what kind of assets and characteristics are needed in these members to advance the work of the board. In addition, the committee understands what the board needs to undertake to improve its performance and the knowledge members require to execute their responsibilities effectively. The board development committee understands the leadership needs of the board as a whole, and it understands what developmental outcomes the board must achieve to strengthen the board system.

Thus, it is likely that a "good" committee conducts needs assessments to identify what the board requires in the core areas of board development. The agency's vision offers the board development committee a reference point for these assessments. A good board development committee understands that all of its work is related to the advancement of this vision by identifying the developmental needs of the board and by helping the board to fulfill these needs.

The identification of the needs and fulfilling them means that the board development committee undertakes its work within the context of two time frames. First, the committee must work in the "here and now," identifying and fulfilling those developmental needs that are essential to the development of the board in the present. But the committee should not confine its vision of its own work to the present. It also needs to expand its focus and to engage in forward and anticipatory thinking about the future needs of the board as identified and defined by the board's vision for the agency and by the long range plans of the agency (Ackoff, 1991). This forward and anticipatory thinking means that the board development committee embraces the generative function of the board system. It begins to "look down the road"; to reflect on the kind of members and participants the board will need. The committee anticipates the knowledge that the board will need, the performance that will be required of it, and the leadership that will be required to guide the agency in the long run (McMaster, 1996).

These qualities mean that board development is not a limited undertaking. Nor is it merely undertaken periodically or on a onetime basis. A good board development committee is institutionalized within the structure of the board as a structural entity with ongoing responsibilities. It is made permanent. The board development committee possesses those values that are essential to development: continuous work, continuous improvement, and continuous examination of outcomes. The board development committee is likely a standing committee with a clear charter about its mission and purpose in relationship to the improvement of the board and the development of the board over time. As a standing committee of the board it has responsibilities for meeting regularly, for producing outcomes, for reporting its progress to the board as a whole, and for identifying and overcoming those issues or barriers that block its own productivity and performance. Any meeting agenda of the board allocates time to understanding the work of the board development committee and to prioritizing the work and outcomes of this committee.

The committee's work in the identification and assessment of board development needs, anticipating board development needs in the long run, and in undertaking continuous work is concretized through its planning function. A good board development committee has a clearly focused plan that can be communicated to the board as a whole and that is useful as a guide to the work of the committee and its members. A clear plan means that the board development committee understands its purpose and mission, the board's vision of the agency, the developmental needs of the board, the developmental outcomes it seeks to produce for the board, and the monitoring of these outcomes. The development plan reflects the substance of the committee's work and how the board as a whole conceives of board development.

Finally, a good board development committee is evaluative. The committee tracks its productivity and achievements and evaluates whether its level of effort is consistent with the development plan. It appraises achievements and products and judges whether these are suitable to the accomplishment of the development plan and the strengthening of the board. It evaluates its outcomes or bottom-line results to understand whether material or substantive benefits are produced for the board. In this case, the board development committee is interested in whether its work is actually strengthening the performance and effectiveness of the board.

A commitment to evaluation means that the board development committee values, collects, and uses data. It is very interested in how the board as a whole and its members appraises its work, and whether the board sees progress in its own development. Collecting data, therefore, from other board members, observing what occurs as a result of board development activities, and observing changes in the board system form a vital aspect of the board and committee's self-evaluative activity.

These qualities taken together certainly call for a board development committee that has a strong leadership role within the board as a whole. It may also mean that this committee is central to the work of the board and may be at the confluence of all work of the board. After all, the board cannot really perform without good and talented members, who are well organized, who possess the right knowledge, who perform and produce, and who lead the agency in the right direction. These are all board development outcomes and thereby reinforce the pivotal role board development plays in the life and work of the board.

Responsibilities of the Board Development Committee

There are five responsibilities of board development that form the purpose of the committee. I place these in outline form because each of these responsibilities is discussed in subsequent chapters of the book:

I. The board development committee is responsible for perpetuating the board through membership development. Chapter 13 summarizes these responsibilities in the context of anticipating board membership. This principal responsibility is composed of activities that involve the following:
    A. Identifying candidates who can make contributions to the advancement of the board's vision of the agency and for reaching out to candidates to assess their interest in board service
    B. Screening and recruiting specific candidates on the basis of criteria and values established by the committee and confirmed by the board as a whole

C. Selecting and inviting candidates to join the board after obtaining the consent of the board as a whole

D. Developing and maintaining a board candidate data bank that identifies potential board members on the basis of the current and anticipated needs of the board

II. Improving the performance, productivity, and effectiveness of the board is a responsibility that the board development committee shares with the board as a whole. Contributions by the board development committee include the following activities, some of which are further developed in other chapters (for example, chapter 16):

A. Coordinating the annual board self-evaluation in which the work and outcomes of the board are judged, the formal and informal structure and processes of the board are analyzed, and board development outcomes are identified and prioritized

B. Assisting the board to identify improvement aims and outcomes and identifying implications of improvement for subsequent board development

C. Communicating the board development agenda to the board as a whole, to the agency, and to the community on the basis of self-evaluation findings of board performance

D. Building board cohesion through social activities and events that enable board members to get to know one another and to build individual and group relationships (for example, the board development committee may take responsibility for the annual board retreat and incorporate into this event an opportunity for board members to get to know one another)

III. The board development committee assumes the principal responsibility for development of the knowledge base and understanding of all board members relating to the vision and work of the agency. As discussed in chapter 14, primary responsibilities here involve the following:

A. Ensuring that a preservice orientation program is in place for all new board members and participants and ensuring that these individuals receive a sound and comprehensive orientation to the community service agency

B. Ensuring that a continuous orientation process is in place for all board members and participants to keep them apprised of emerging and recent changes to vision, policies, procedures, and programs (the committee is responsible for ensuring that all members and participants receive a sound continuing orientation to the agency)

    C. Ensuring that a continuing education is in place for all board members and participants that equips them with the requisite knowledge to achieve the vision of the agency

    D. Anticipating the mentoring needs of new members and those members moving into leadership roles or roles of major board responsibility and making the arrangements within the agency or board to make this mentoring available

IV. The board development committee assumes responsibility for leadership development. The committee, as discussed in chapter 11,

    A. Identifies potential leaders within the board and works with the executive committee or board chairperson to identify those roles and structures in which these potential leaders can make a contribution to the board's vision of the agency

    B. Manages the nominations and elections process within the board to foster the placement of potential leaders into key board positions whether as committee or task force chairs, executive officers of the board, or as committee members

    C. Anticipates succession needs of the agency especially among executive officers of the board (the committee initiates in a timely manner the preparation and socialization of board members to fill critical leadership roles)

V. As discussed in chapter 18, the board development committee undertakes the responsibility for planning and monitoring board development outcomes by doing the following:

    A. Formulating the board development plan on an annual basis

    B. Keeping the board as a whole apprised of board development activities, achievements, and outcomes as well as barriers that are faced through relevant verbal and written reports

    C. Monitoring and evaluating board development outcomes and preparing an annual report on board development that anticipates the subsequent year's board development plan

These responsibilities do not need to be overwhelming for the board development committee. With staff support, streamlined work procedures, and brief but focused plans and reports, the committee can undertake its work and execute its five responsibilities in an expeditious manner. Certainly the support of agency staff becomes fundamental in the effective work of the board development committee.

As indicated by the discussion of board–executive and board–staff relationships in chapter 12, because of a synergy within the board development committee created through effective working relationships among board members and staff, the broad scope of responsibility can be handled productively. The board development committee, however, is a primary leadership component of the board and requires a chair and membership that are deeply committed to the realization of the board's vision of the agency.

Chair of the Board Development Committee and Committee Membership

As noted before, the board development committee may be one of the most active within the community service board. The leader of this committee should anticipate a very active agenda that changes seasonally as board development addresses the responsibilities of perpetuation, self-evaluation, training and education, leadership development, and creation of the board development plan. The chair understands these needs:

- to make board development happen as an ongoing process of improvement;
- to follow a seasonal agenda in which responsibilities, tasks, and activities are undertaken continuously so that the board does not find itself and the agency unprepared to address important challenges (Bergquist, 1993); and
- to maintain momentum within the committee so the board has new members, participants, and leaders who are available to undertake the policy and vision work of the board in an available, energetic, knowledgeable, and committed manner.

The board carefully chooses the chair of the board development committee. Because this is such an important committee to the overall success of the board, the chair should possess as many of the properties sought in the overall board. The chair is energetic and holds high aspirations for the performance of the agency. A strong understanding of and commitment to the board's vision of the agency on part of the board development chair offer a nexus between the purpose and responsibilities of the committee and the purpose and responsibilities of the board (P. Schwartz, 1991). Both entities are designed to advance this vision and the chair of board development understands this requirement.

The chair has a strong belief system regarding the work of the agency and is able to use the board's beliefs, values, and ethical commitments in framing the responsibilities of board development. The chair understands that board development is a long-run venture for the board, sometimes taking up to two years before tangible outcomes are realized. And the chair values progressive learning and the role of the board development committee in developing the knowledge base of the board as a system. By selecting a chair who is strong in several or all of these properties the board is increasing the probability that the board development committee is itself a high-performance system.

The appointment of the board development chair is a critical decision on part of the board as a whole. The board understands that the chair is not a newly recruited person but someone who has some continuity with the board, and perhaps has held other highly responsible positions within the board. The chair is selected because of his or her knowledge and understanding of the board and the agency and the continuity he or she brings. From a systems perspective, the chair may be an institutional leader who understands the values the agency stands for, the role of the agency in the community as an institution, and the need to protect and advance the character of the agency (Bennis, 1993b).

The chair may be an ancestral leader who was involved in the founding of the agency. Or the chair may be a generative leader who is very concerned with the stewardship of the future of the community service agency. What is for sure, however, is that the chair is a leader. By virtue of this, the chair is deeply concerned about the well-being of the agency. And the chair is concerned about the well-being of the people who are served by the agency, the impact of the agency on the community problem or need that gives purpose to the organization, and the agency's achievement of its vision.

These qualities are likely most important to the achievement of strong leadership at the head of the committee. Certainly, there are other qualities that can be sought in a chair: someone who is probably well positioned in the agency's community. The person is networked, has a community presence, and can reach a diversity of people who can serve on the board or who can suggest other people who can serve. Yet these are not essential prerequisites for leadership of the board development committee. It is probably more important for the members of the board development committee to be the ones who are positioned, to be the ones who are networked, and to be the ones who can reach out to others. The board chair will be concerned about the operation and performance of the actual committee, and therefore its composition becomes very important to effective performance.

Having other committee members who can reach out to others, to identify new candidates, and to conduct discrete aspects of board development business will be important complements to strong, visionary leadership. Committee members who "think" development will not be put off by the practical tasks involved in strengthening board performance through recruitment, self-evaluation, curriculum development and training, leadership development, and planning.

The board's vision of the agency will serve as a good reference point for identifying and selecting committee members. Having a strong consumer focus within the vision may suggest consumer board members who can serve on this committee. A strong vision of helping youths to appreciate and become involved in the arts may mean that artists—both young and old—join this committee. The membership of the board development committee is where vision, networking, and planning come together to be translated into basic outcomes of having the right people with the right commitments and the right knowledge and understanding join the board of the community service agency (Kouzes & Posner, 1987).

Relationship of the Board Development Committee to Board Structure

Relationship to the Executive Committee

The board development committee is central to the work of the community service board. But it is one of perhaps several committees and task forces sponsored by the board. In this sense, the board development committee is part of the board's internal structure and network of committees, task forces, and advisory groups.

The board development committee exists as an entity within the context of the by-laws of the board. The executive committee sanctions existence of the committee through these by-laws and gives the committee its charter, its purpose, and its mission. It is critical to recognize that ultimately the board development committee is responsible to the executive committee for achieving its purpose. This observation has importance primarily because the basic conception of "board development" within the board will initially lie in the executive committee. It is this committee that will have expectations about board development; will conceive of board development as an essential function, structure, process, and product of the board; and will define the parameters of board development for the committee.

It is therefore important for the board development committee to understand its charge and its charter from the perspective of the executive committee. Over time, the committee will become increasingly important in educating the executive committee of the board about board development. And as the board development committee becomes more sophisticated, and more skilled in bringing development about, the committee will become increasingly active in helping the executive committee and the board itself to shape their own expectations about board development.

Thus, in terms of its educational role, it is important for the board development committee to actively define for board members what development is, its purpose, and how it can be undertaken within the committee and within the board. Alternatively, it is essential for the executive committee to think through its initial expectations of board development, to prioritize these, and to translate these into a charge that is relevant to the board development committee.

Relationship to Standing Committees

The board development committee must have strong links to other standing committees of the board. Weak links will mean that the board development committee and its members simply lack relationships with other board members and structures that are important to the execution of board development work. Alternatively, it is important for the board development committee to create with some forethought those relationships with other committees that will enable the board to develop as a whole system.

To create these linkages, the board development committee will want to link to the chairs of standing committees within the process of board development needs identification, board development planning, and the establishment of board development outcomes that are enthusiastically endorsed by the chairs of other standing committees. Here are some essential tasks:

- Identify the membership needs of standing committees on a routine basis and identify these needs and responses to them in the board development plan.
- Create a membership data bank that identifies candidates and makes essential information about them available to standing committees.
- Sponsor informal gatherings that bring committee members and chairs together to interact solely for the purpose of helping people to get to know one another.
- Identify and build an understanding of the knowledge and skill needs among the members of specific committees and work with the board in making training opportunities available to address these needs.
- Facilitate leadership development in the anticipation of succession of the chairs of committees, and help the board to have leaders ready to assume these assignments.

Other tasks can be undertaken with specific committees to advance the substantive work of the board. For example, development of the knowledge base of the board through continuing board education can anticipate the strategic formulation work of the planning committee. An understanding of the agency's resource development plan by the board development committee can foster the identification of people whose affiliations, networks, and community positions can in turn facilitate the achievement of resource development outcomes.

These tasks mean that the members of the board development committee are continuously interacting with the members of the various standing committees to obtain an understanding of the development needs of these committees. The board development committee, as a consequence, becomes an important partner in supporting the committee structure of the board.

Relationship to Task Forces and Advisory Groups

A board committed to a broad scope of participation and involvement of community members, staff, and users of agency services will most likely sponsor a number of task forces and advisory groups as key tactics in increasing input of information into board dialogue, debate, and decision making. These kinds of structures will require board members to chair them, staff members to assist with administration, and community members who are involved in them. The board development committee can be pivotal in helping the board to organize and launch these task forces and advisory groups. Certainly this kind of participation and involvement can be facilitated through the committee's board candidate database.

Members of the board development committee can work closely with the board chairs of these structures and staff who are assigned to them in identifying candidates who will make promising participants. These structures also offer the board development committee an opportunity to move candidates into involvement and participation within the board as a way of screening these people for subsequent board membership. The board development committee may also work closely with board chairs of these structures and assigned staff in the orientation and education of task force or advisory group members.

Relationship to the Board Chair

Many board chairs come into the office with strong conceptions of how they want to develop their boards and the specific changes they want to make to strengthen board performance. Board development chairs most likely will want to interact with the chairs of their boards in the identification of what these leaders consider to be essential changes to how the board functions, membership development, and the development of the structure of the board.

The board development committee can assist in the identification of these needs, aims, and outcomes and bring these into board development plans so they can be addressed. Indeed, at the beginning of any board development cycle, the committee should meet with the board chair or president to interview this person about his or her conception of board development and essential or needed changes. This meeting may actually involve the executive committee, but, ultimately, the board chair or president should be viewed as the chief architect of board development. The perspectives of the board chair may actually initiate the board development process. The board chair may identify these perspectives when the board initiates long-range, strategic, financial, or capital planning. These perspectives may be communicated during a "state of the agency" address when the board president outlines the challenges the agency faces and the initiatives the agency will undertake to meet these challenges.

It is likely when a new chair is appointed or elected to lead the board, that board development will be on the minds of those affiliated with the board. A new leader indicates a time of change and transition for a board. It represents a time when the vision of the agency will be reexamined, major policies appraised, and work of the board reviewed. Thus, board development naturally emerges at a time when an agency may examine and establish new directions and new processes of undertaking its work. The board development committee can meet with the newly entering chair and the departing chair to review what has been achieved in board development over the previous term and what could constitute a board development direction for the upcoming term.

From my experience, I have found these conferences to be very productive. They help not only to evaluate the status of board development and the priority that will be given to it, but also offer an opportunity to create a framework or specific theme guiding the development of the board. This theme may emphasize knowledge development, structural organization of the board, membership or leadership development, the expansion of the size of the board, or a combination of these themes. An incoming board chair may find such a conference useful in establishing a meaningful board development agenda.

Conclusion

This chapter offers an overview of the board development committee and its scope of work and responsibilities. This scope broadly construed moves the committee away from a sole focus on the nominations process and expands the focus to a consideration of several ways a board can go about its own development. There are five responsibilities:

1. perpetuating the board through membership development,
2. self-evaluation of board performance,
3. building the knowledge base of the board,
4. leadership development, and
5. the formulation of the board development plan that offers the board development committee a framework within which it can operate to advance or otherwise strengthen the board.

The successful execution of these responsibilities cannot be realized without a board chair and a membership committed to high expectations of performance. The board development chair, in particular, holds a pivotal role in leading the execution of these responsibilities and perhaps without this leadership the board development process will simply falter. A board development committee willing to undertake these responsibilities offers a community service board a specific structure in which to install the mission of development.

We cannot overlook the important role undertaken by the board development committee and how it implements this role through relationships with other structures of the community service board. The board development committee does not execute its responsibilities in isolation from these other structures but rather purposefully links to the executive committee, standing committees, task forces and advisory groups, and the board chair to form an overarching agenda of board development.

Subsequent chapters build on the work of the board development committee by expanding substantive discussion of board membership, development of individual board members, leadership development, board self-evaluation, and the board development plan. This discussion will help further frame how board development unfolds within the context of the boards of community service agencies.

Questions for Board Discussion

1. Does your board need a board development committee? If so, what is the charter of this committee?

2. Should this charter incorporate the five core responsibilities identified in this chapter? Refine the charter of the board development committee on the basis of its scope—that is, the extent to which it incorporates these five responsibilities.

3. How do you define the qualities of a "good" board development committee? What are its expectations within the context of your board?

4. What are the qualities of the chair of the board development committee you propose for your board? Is there a "good" candidate from within your board?

5. Who should become members of the board development committee? Are these members currently available within your board?

6. How will the board development committee relate to the executive committee? What is its calendar of activities? How does this calendar fit with the major annual responsibilities of the board as a whole?

7. How will the board development committee mesh with other standing committees? What is the role and responsibilities of the board development committee in the support of the missions of these standing committees?

8. How will the board development committee mesh with task forces and advisory groups? What is the role and responsibilities of the board development committee in the support of the missions of board-sanctioned task forces and advisory groups?

9. How will the board development committee take direction from the board chair?

10. What developmental needs does this chapter illuminate for the board? How will the board act on these needs?

▪11▪

Leadership of Board Members

The Newcomer Board Chair Testifies at a Policy Forum Sponsored by a Public Substance Abuse Agency

Please excuse me today. I do not come here as an expert on the problem of recovery. I own a business and as someone in recovery I have made it a policy of my work to employ as many people who are in recovery as possible. Today 30% of my workforce are people in recovery. I joined the Newcomer board three years ago at the invitation of Jerry Pearson who at the time was the chair of the board's personnel committee. Mr. Pearson learned of me through a newspaper article and after reading it followed up with a telephone call to let me know of the work of Newcomer. Since joining the board of this agency I have learned much about recovery as a process of personal growth and change. I am here today to share this knowledge with you. I have a simple message and it is this. It is a mistake for this public agency to ignore the vocational rehabilitation needs of people who are in the process of recovery. Let me offer my perspective. It is a product of my own experience with recovery, my experience as an employer of people in recovery, and my service on the Newcomer board of directors.

Differential Perspective on Board Leadership

Leadership does not happen automatically within the boards of community service agencies. Leadership has to be purposively developed with an eye toward what is needed by the agency to bring about its vision and to make this vision happen in the context of the community served by the agency. Informal surveys among board presidents and agency CEOs convince me of the importance of board leadership and the essential role leadership plays in advancing the work of the community service agency. When asked about what is essential to the good if not exemplary performance of their boards, presidents of these structures will invariably state that it is the leadership of board members that makes the critical difference (Jacques & Clement, 1991). When I pose this question to executive leaders of agencies, they too assert the importance of board leadership. Indeed, one agency executive said to me that her board is composed of "heavy hitters" from the community. She however quickly asserted that she wished that her board was made up of leaders rather than the individuals she described using baseball metaphors. When I expressed some surprise about this she noted that her board really did need people who could think about the agency in a visionary manner and who were willing to do the work to move the agency toward this vision (Kouzes & Posner, 1987).

What is leadership within a community service board? This question is not easily answered. Let's take a moment to reflect on it. Leadership does indeed involve visionary thinking and visionary acting (Koestenbaum, 1991). Of course, some board members think in broad terms while others think in more focused narrow ways. One chief executive officer describes his board as a balanced one in relationship to vision: "My board is composed of people who envision the grand forest. Other members of the board have visions of specific trees. They are all welcome to contribute; they all contribute something that I don't or cannot. But more important, they complement one another. It takes the entire board to envision the big picture and the small picture." This CEO is describing a board that is developing its leadership. The board and CEO recognize that visions come in different packages, have different scope—but they all share the same substance and content from the perspectives of values, desires, and outcomes (Koestenbaum, 1991).

So, leadership is about vision. It is about being able to bring a desired and exciting end state into the mind of the board. But board leadership also is about acting. It is not confined solely to thinking about what can or should be. The community service board undertaking its quest of development must also think about leadership as acting—acting on behalf of the agency to fulfill this vision (Jacques & Clement, 1991). Acting can come in many forms for the community service agency. It involves making critical decisions that shape the substance of the agency. While writing this chapter, I was interrupted by a telephone call from one particular community service agency the board of which is crafting a policy statement on business diversification. The board wanted my help in framing a policy statement. A board task force of visionaries had been assembled, a wonderful and impressive group of people deeply committed to the child welfare mission of the agency. They were acting on the vision by making this critical decision. They were leading.

Another form of action finds itself in advocacy. The board and its members advocate for the advancement of the agency. The board is mindful of the well-being of the agency, but the direction and substance of its advocacy is more driven by the vision. The leadership action here focuses on the achievement of the agency's vision. Board members act externally to garner the dollars, tools, equipment, and legitimacy—that is, the resources—that are relevant to the agency's vision (Nanus,

1992). The board member who testifies at a hearing and who acts to frame the funder's understanding of how the agency will make use of requested resources is acting as a leader. Leaders shape how we perceive the world and interpret organizational life (Schein, 1992). In a political context, leaders engage in co-optation by shaping the values of external stakeholders (Selznick, 1957).

An additional form of acting in a manner that is mindful of leadership is found in a board member's execution of specific tasks relevant to advancing the work of the board. The member may bring information to the board, educate other board members about environmental issues or challenges, or foster the development of those committees the work of which is essential to the performance of the board. One board member confided in me her conception of herself as a "foot soldier" of her board. "I do the mundane things but in retrospect they add up, and the board is better off because of this pedestrian work." She shared this self-appraisal with me when she was awarded a community service award by a state program recognizing contributions to the nonprofit sector. Her fellow board members nominated her to this prestigious award, and they authored a memorable letter of recognition. It began this way: "For your leadership . . ." This board member understands something that can be easily overlooked. Board leadership rests in the details, in the specifics. It is not merely the vision that is important.

Let me include one other form of leadership-inspired action undertaken by board members (Jacques & Clement, 1991). Some leaders come to the fore during periods of crisis. The agency may find itself in compromising situations—politically, legally, financially, or ethically. A board member arises to the moment and acts to inspire confidence and to support problem solving or situational management. A friend of mine—an attorney—is the quintessential crisis manager. In fact, I think she lives in crisis and thrives on crisis. She once told the board president of an agency that if he really wanted her service, he would respect her desire to be only called on during crisis. "You can expect me to be a good citizen of the board between crises. But when you need me, call me!" It seems like all of her energy and focus were brought to bear on the crisis, and she could muster her extraordinary intelligence, motivation, and clarity of thought to work with the agency in finding solutions that were consistent with its vision. The message of this board member needs to be understood. She is telling this agency to use her assets, and it is within the situation that these assets will emerge and her leadership will shine (Bennis, 1989).

Variation in Board Leadership

This brief perspective on board leadership suggests four important types. Each type of leadership possesses a specific purpose within the board, and the types taken collectively illustrate the diversity of board leadership as well as its potential complexity (Bennis, 1989). A board that is engaging in board development may want to reflect on whether each type of leadership is available to it, and what forms of leadership are especially needed given the distinctive purpose and character of the community service agency and its stage of development (Bass, 1981):

1. *Transformational Leaders:* Moving the agency from vision to action is the principal focus of transformational leadership. The transformational leader is concerned with surfacing and framing an overarching vision of agency performance and in framing and inspiring action (Yukl, 1989). These kinds of board leaders are concerned with the "big picture" regarding agency existence, identity, and success. As leaders, they are concerned with the identification and use of values in response to the achievement of specific organizational outcomes. Mission performance and mission integrity will be of great importance to these board leaders (Bennis, 1993a).

2. *Transactional Leaders:* Board members who subscribe to this form of leadership are interested in relationships and the formation of relationships with stakeholders who are essential to the success of the agency. These leaders are willing to accept the vision of the agency and will subscribe to it with energy and commitment (Bennis, 1993a). They likely are disinterested in its formation, but recognize the importance of being informed and influenced by the overall direction of the agency. Transactional leaders within the board enjoy representing the board at important policy, funding, and community forums. They are interested in influencing the behavior of those organizations, entities, bodies, and individuals who have a significant if not substantial impact on the community service agency (Yukl, 1989). Transactional leaders want to know about "who we need to get to" and "who we need to influence." Although the transformational leader may be idealistic and even romantic about agency purpose, the transactional leader is more political in orientation and action (Pfeffer, 1992).

3. *Task-Oriented Leaders:* These board members focus on the agenda of tasks that are involved in the board's conduct of business. They are interested in "what needs to be done" and evaluate their board leadership in terms of what gets done in relationship to board business. These board members are most likely the heart of any community service board. They chair special events, organize fund raising, participate in committee work, and lead task forces. Without this kind of board leadership, the board will likely become inert and momentum will appear to be sluggish. From my own experience serving on boards and working with them, task-oriented leadership is seen by agency personnel as that form of leadership most indicative of the sincerity and commitment of

the board as a whole. Thus, when a board is seen by agency personnel in negative light, it is usually because these personnel begin to see the board, as one staff member shared with me, "contributing little, and doing nothing." A board with a record of productivity often earns the approval of staff who perceives the board as a whole as deeply concerned and committed. Task leadership and its contribution to board organization, productivity, and organizational legitimization cannot be easily discounted (Misumi, 1985). It may be one of the most important forms of board leadership.

4. *Situational Leaders:* These leaders form the crisis response capacity of the board and perhaps the agency. Situational leadership is not routine leadership, and those board members who feel comfortable with rising to the occasion and addressing agency disruption may not be visible until they are called on. These board members may constantly occupy the background, but the board and the agency soon senses their importance when they do rise to the occasion and begin to exercise their leadership in visible and explicit ways. Leaders who are oriented to situations track the board and the agency actively although quietly. They keep their eye on what is going on, looking for opportunities to step in when they are needed. These "situations" may arise out of a range of events or circumstances. Nonetheless, situational leaders are focused on issue management and they are often willing to bring their expertise to bear in the successful resolution of these issues (Coates, 1986).

Some situational leaders may have specific expertise, such as the malpractice attorney who is available to an agency to negotiate or otherwise address a specific legal concern. Other situational leaders may have expertise relevant to the agency during periods of crisis, such as the financial expert who was able to assist a small community service agency successfully handle an audit conducted after the misuse of funds by an agency administrator. I have found that situational leaders enjoy the heat of the moment. They are often in professions and in jobs that demand crisis responses and they feel more able to offer the agency leadership and assistance within a specific situation, rather than on an ongoing basis. Independent of expertise, these leaders contribute energy to the board during what can be overwhelming or trying times. They mobilize, organize, and focus the board during troubling situations.

Balancing Leadership within the Board

The leadership of board members can influence the character of the board. How this leadership is integrated to create a working culture and system also is critical to the formation of board character. Unfortunately, community service boards may not consciously think of the necessity of this balance and, as a result, find themselves with a composition biased by one particular form of leadership. Think of the board that is composed solely of situational type leaders. Little routine or ongoing work will be completed by this kind of board. Think of the board made up of task-oriented leaders. Much may get done but the board risks that this production may be unrelated to vision. Think of the board whose members are transformational leaders. The board has a strong focus on vision and a clear sense of where it wants to go but little capacity within the board to achieve the necessary and required movement. And think of the transactional board. Board members are eager to form relationships with stakeholders but do so without any sensitivity to vision, mission, and subsequent task.

These biases can distort the board and its internal operations. They underscore the importance of thinking about leadership within the board comprehensively and differentially. By *comprehensive*, I mean that the board—particularly through the work of the board development committee—thinks purposively about the scope of leadership needed within the board. *Scope* in this context refers to the availability of board members who represent the various forms of leadership: transformational, transactional, task, and situational. Simultaneously, the board development committee is able to think about the leadership needs of the board differentially by appraising what kind of leadership is needed at a particular time or moment in the lifespan of the board. For example, a community service agency that is experiencing considerable change in its environment may need to augment its transformational leadership to maintain a viable and relevant vision. A community service agency that is experiencing revitalization may require more situational leadership to negotiate the environmental and policy issues emerging immediately in the life of the agency (Gilmore, 1988).

Differential thinking about leadership within the board development committee, however, does not mean that the leadership within the board should be homogeneous, that is, of one type. Balance does require a representation of all types of leaders, whereas differential thinking requires the board development committee to reflect on what form of leadership may be specifically needed at any given time.

Leadership and Board Development

Like in any other area of board development, the development of board leadership requires sensitivity to the role of the board in the community service agency. Hard and fast rules cannot and should not be applied here. Board development is a creative process that gets into the nuances of where the community service agency is going, what it wants to achieve, and how it wants to get to its preferred destination. The fostering of leadership within the board becomes informed by data and by need. Thus, some general parameters can be defined for the board development process:

I. The board can undertake a periodic audit of its leadership assets. Each board member is understood in terms of a preferred leadership approach, the mix of leadership approaches the board member uses in board work, and how the work of a board member fits into the leadership fund of the board as a whole.

II. The gaps in leadership at the board level can be identified in this audit. And a set of leadership needs is identified, ones that are relevant to subsequent or future recruitment drives. Leadership gaps can express themselves in

A. the absence of an encompassing vision and the inspiration needed to get to this vision, which is suggestive of a gap in transformational leadership;

B. missed opportunities to form critical or strategic linkages with other organizations, with funders, with the media, or with key community groups that indicate the need for transactional leadership within the board;

C. low productivity within board committees or even nonexistent or nonoperational committees indicative of the need for task oriented leadership within the board; and

D. a lack of board responsiveness to impending or current crisis situations that are not addressed within the board. Inertia characterizes the board at the very moment that urgency, energy, and motivation are required by board members so that they can take needed action. This gap signals the need for situational leadership.

III. The audit of leadership gaps and strengths within the board can be used within the context of the board development plan. The board's leadership needs are identified, and these needs can be used to guide the process of searching for and screening candidates.

IV. The socialization of leaders into the board can become an intentional focus of board development training and education. Board members can become conscious of their leadership preferences and approaches, and the board as a whole can become more conscious of their leadership assets and gaps.

V. An informal understanding of leadership roles can emerge within the board and every board member can begin to frame their work from a leadership perspective, understanding their value and importance to the advancement of the board through the exercise of their leadership gifts.

These overall parameters do not dictate prescriptive requirements for board leadership and its development. However, these parameters underscore the importance of each community service board becoming more conscious of itself as a (if not the) principal leadership structure within the agency. And these parameters suggest that each board can influence its own fund of leadership by becoming conscious of its strengths and assets in this area, and in acting to develop those leadership assets it needs through a balanced and differential recruitment and training process.

Conclusion: Leadership in the Support of Board Development

Although it is important to reflect on the role of board development in the fostering of leadership, it is also important to reflect on how leadership supports board development. This presentation of leadership reflects a systems view of leadership in which the major dimensions of performance are incorporated into the leadership structure and process of the board itself. In this manner, the comprehensiveness and balance of leadership within the board supports its own effectiveness in the execution of the commerce and work of the agency as a whole. Board development requires the integration of vision, relationships, task, and situation. The various forms of leadership address these four imperatives discussed in the chapter. They also relate to the development of the board as a multidimensional system outlined in section 2. Transformational leadership is relevant to the institutional and functional development of the agency and board in which the articulation of purpose, meaning, and aims become paramount within the policy and local environments in which community service is undertaken. Task-oriented leadership relates to the performance dimension of the board as a system within which the actual work of board governance and stewardship is executed through group, committee, task force, and individual action. Situational leadership can cut across institutional, functional, and performance dimensions offering the board and the agency a resource to maintain these dimensions and to achieve continuity and coherence during periods of demand and stress. And finally, the lifespan dimension favors a differential perspective on leadership in which board leadership needs and requirements are carefully balanced and matched to the stage of organizational development of the community service agency.

In this way, leadership supports the development of the community service board as a system. Also, leadership shapes the character of the agency (Bridges, 1992). This system is dependent on its leadership so that ends are articulated, functions are executed, performance is achieved, and key relationships are maintained (J. Gardner, 1990). The leadership system of the board can achieve the stability and continuity the board needs to govern and steward while it fosters a capacity to be responsive to environmental turbulence that any community service agency is bound to experience given the dynamics of contemporary societies and communities.

"Leadership in the support of board development" means that the board must look to its leader to strengthen the board. Leadership and board development intersect in a reciprocal fashion. Balanced and diverse leadership is required to further the development of the board as a system. And purposeful and intentional board development is required to foster the diversification of leadership.

Questions for Board Discussion

1. How do you conceive of leadership within your board? Given your board development mission, and your vision of board performance, what leadership needs does your board face right now?
2. Who are the transformational leaders within the board? What is their distinctive contribution to how your board operates and performs?
3. Who are the transactional leaders within the board? What is their distinctive contribution to the performance of the board?
4. Who are the task-oriented leaders within the board? What do they do on behalf of the board? How do they improve the performance of the board?
5. Who are the situational leaders within the board? What assets do they offer to the board and to its performance? What value do they add?
6. How does your board balance leadership? Or does it fail to balance leadership? What are the consequences—either positive or negative—of the board's leadership pool at this time?
7. How does your board develop leadership and focus existing leadership on the tasks of board development?
8. What developmental needs does this chapter illuminate for the board? How will the board act on these needs?

■ 12 ■

Board–Agency Interface

Two Agency Staff Members Discuss the Board

Jan: I made a presentation to the board the other night.

Kim: Why?

Jan: The board wanted to know how my program achieves the purpose and vision of the agency. The members wanted to hear from a program administrator and not the executive director.

Kim: I didn't think the board really cared about what we did.

Jan: Wrong. They were very interested and asked insightful questions. In fact, I think I cleared up some of their misconceptions about serving people who cope with HIV.

Kim: I didn't think we have much to offer the board. The members seem so remote.

Jan: This wasn't my impression. They are sincere about their interest in our work. In fact, I was asked to meet with the board development committee to plan a task force on serving new groups coping with HIV and AIDS.

The interface between the board and the community service agency is a critical one, deserving considerable attention on the part of the board. This development can be undertaken to better integrate the board and the agency, and to make governance a more effective and proactive process. The community service board is dependent on both the executive and the staff of the agency. Purposeful alignment of these two entities can make the organization more effective in its community service work and foster a stronger sense of collaboration among all levels of the agency.

Development of this interface can be achieved in several different ways. The board can foster the integration and coherence of the organization through the creation of an agency identity that connects the members of the agency through vision, beliefs, and empathy. The agency identity can strengthen the sense of enterprise among organizational members and foster a sense of common purpose among board members and agency staff.

The interface between board and agency can also be fostered through the integration of major systems that enable the board and the agency to undertake its work in key areas in a complementary manner. The integration of major systems can involve the sharing of information, the integration of training and education, complementary planning, and the integration of administrative and organizational tasks.

The interface between the board and the agency can also be found in the involvement of agency staff in the board system. In this area, the board creates specific staff roles to foster interaction, to ensure that the board remains relevant to the community service agency, and to increase the actual productivity of the board.

And, finally, the interface between board and agency can be found in the relationships that are established and perpetuated in the collaboration between the board and the agency executive. The success of the overall interface between the board and the agency often is determined by the attitude of the chief executive officer toward this integration. An executive who is threatened by board members being too close to agency staff may prevent a strong interface from developing. Alternatively, an executive who sees the board and the agency forming the same system will be devoted to ensuring that this interface is strong and that it is a productive one for the agency as a whole.

The purpose of this chapter is to explore some aspects of the interface between the community service board and the agency it stewards. The assumption is that a strong, deliberate interface will foster agency performance and create a more coherent organization.

Fostering and Integrating Institutional Identity

A strong sense of institutional identity was underscored as critical to both board and agency in chapter 3. The development of this identity solely within the board creates the risk that it will be isolated here and that there will be no diffusion of the identity to the agency as a whole. Thus, the board may emerge as having a stronger identity than the other parts of the agency, and board members may find themselves frustrated when other agency members do not share the same sense of purpose, vision, or beliefs. Alternatively, if the board fails to develop an institutional identity while the agency develops a strong sense of purpose, then agency members may discount the importance of the board, and the commitment of its members (Pascarella & Frohman, 1989).

Board development and agency development can join at the interface created by the need to foster a common organizational identity. These two entities can be integrated through the crafting of a common narrative or story that connects people and explains what the agency stands for, what the agency is trying to achieve, and what makes the agency distinctive (H. Gardner, 1993). This grand narrative is essential to the success of any human system and requires board and agency members to work together in its creation and diffusion (H. Gardner, 1995).

The institutional dimension of the board system underscores the importance of creating this grand narrative that explains why the agency was founded, the spirit of community service that animates the work of the agency, and the critical values that form the substance of the agency's work (Bennis, 1989). Defining and articulating purpose and basic expectations are the purview of the community service board. And formulating vision also is a key responsibility of the board. In other words, the board is responsible for the management of agency identity by articulating "who we are" (chapter 7) and "where we are going" (chapter 8).

But this responsibility is not confined merely to the board ensuring that purpose, expectations, and vision are committed to writing or that these statements of identity are incorporated into agency policies and used as reference points to make critical agency decisions. People who compose the agency whether as service staff, administrators, or board members must share this narrative and the purpose, vision, and expectations that flow from it. It is the board's responsibility to ensure that the grand narrative or story of the agency truly binds people together into a common enterprise (H. Gardner, 1995).

The board must see to it that the ownership of the narrative is shared between the board and the agency. Certainly the role of the chief executive officer is critical here because it is this person who will most likely serve as the principal agent responsible for the internal dissemination of the story (McCall, Lombardo, & Morrison, 1988; Wareham, 1991). The board can make this an important responsibility of the executive and judge its own leadership and the leadership of the executive on the basis of how well this narrative is disseminated within the agency.

The board and executive work to make the narrative a living document within the agency. Board-sponsored events in which the narrative is made explicit lend themselves to the formulation of an agency vision jointly developed by board members, staff, and even the people and community members who are served by the agency. The board sponsors these events with the purpose of creating a sense of common enterprise, by building understanding of the narrative and the vision that results from it, and by creating a shared understanding of the distinctiveness of the agency and the enterprise it seeks to undertake.

These events can come in the form of retreats, annual planning sessions, or grand meetings of the agency as a whole. The form of the event is not important. But three things are important:

1. The event is sponsored by the board and is the responsibility of the board;
2. The event is inclusive of many different stakeholders who care about the success of the agency; and
3. There is an opportunity for the members of these various stakeholder groups to work together in creating a common narrative, a common set of expectations, a common vision, and a shared sense of distinctiveness.

This kind of board work is truly governance in action because it requires the board to reach out to the members of the agency to include them in fashioning the basic policy structure of the agency expressed in its sense of identity.

Without the interface formed by this identity work a community service agency may experience a cleavage that separates the policy makers of the agency, that is, board members, from the policy implementers. This cleavage can result in great social distance, poor collaboration, and a basic fragmentation of effort, when "ends" are not linked to "means."

The creation of a strong interface characterized by shared understanding and the formation of good working relationships between board members and staff can lead to other important developments. One of these is the development of shared empathy between the board and the agency. To be frank, it is easy for board members and agency staff to become alienated from one another, and as a result negative stereotypes emerge that are usually both inaccurate and counterproductive. Working together to establish, renew, and disseminate grand narrative, vision, and expectations can also create mutual understanding of the critical role board members and agency staff play in the success of the community service enterprise. Board members, staff, and consumers come in contact with one another to discuss and formulate agency identity. As a result, members of each group can earn a strong sense of empathy for the nature and challenges of board work and for the challenges they must meet in working toward the vision of the agency. Also, board members and staff alike can learn the issues service users face in using the services and opportunities offered by the organization.

Mutual empathy for the challenges faced by the various members of the community service organization forms the interface between board and agency. This interface is really psychological in quality. This mutual empathy in turn offers members an opportunity to create a shared set of outcomes. These outcomes in turn can facilitate the integration of the performance of board and agency.

Staff Roles in the Board System

Staff can play an integral role in the work of the board and in the fostering of board development. In agency cultures that create considerable social distance between the board and agency staff, staff involvement in the board actually may be frowned on.

Alternatively, those agencies that seek to build bridges between the board and the agency, staff are seen as a significant resource to fostering board performance. I have seen staff serve in numerous roles in the boards of community service organizations.

Staff as Board Meeting Participants

Certainly the most basic of these is the staff member as a participant. In one agency, staff members look forward to the monthly board meeting, and a staff representative is always available to listen in on board deliberations. This is not done to become privy to agency politics or to monitor the board. Staff participation is a desired and constructive element of these meetings. A knowledgeable staff person is available to respond to board issues when invited. The executive director has come to expect a staff person to be available so that board members receive a better understanding of the experiences of the workers of the agency when this cannot be offered by the executive directly. Indeed, in another agency, the presence of several staff members from line positions at board meetings is a symbolic demonstration on part of the organization's commitment to building bridges between policy implementers and policy makers.

Staff Members as Board Liaisons

Another role of the staff member is that of liaison to board committees, task forces, advisory groups, or other board-sponsored structures. Typically, I have found liaisons in large community service organizations to be senior administrators but this is not necessarily an imperative. In other agencies, I have seen line staff assume a great deal of responsibility in facilitating the work of a board-sponsored task force. Indeed, it appears from much of my consultation work that the most appropriate staff appointment as liaison to a board group has more to do with the interest, motivation, and substantive expertise of a staff member than it does with his or her position in the hierarchy of the agency (Larson & LaFasto, 1989).

This conclusion is based on the demanding role of the liaison. This position incorporates numerous responsibilities. These include convening meetings, helping the chair to formulate the working agenda, sometimes facilitating the work of the committee, taking minutes of high quality and publishing and disseminating these, producing the final product of the group, and facilitating input into the group by various constituencies. Agencies may find that it is problematic to appoint service personnel to board committee assignments in lieu of an administrator who has more flexibility and time. Yet such appointments, if supported by some relief time from direct service responsibilities, may offer a staff member an exciting reward or professional development opportunity, particularly relevant to his or her preparation for a future leadership position within the agency.

Staff as Members of Committees or Task Forces

Agency staff also can serve as members of board-sponsored committees or task forces. They may serve on search committees for a new executive director, or on a task force authorized to investigate services to a new geographic location or population. Staff may serve on standing committees like human resources to help the board understand the implications of the policies it establishes in this critical area of organizational performance. Membership of agency staff on committees may indicate an area of potential conflict between the agency and its staff as when unions win the right to appoint members to key committees.

However, from my own experience, staff membership in board committees usually indicates the existence of a strong partnership among the board, the chief executive officer, agency staff members, and perhaps consumers whose input is seen as essential to the formation of good decisions and the establishment of relevant direction by the agency as a whole. Agency staff as members of certain board-sponsored structures can offer many assets to governance. Particularly relevant is technical expertise, practical experience, and perspective that board members recruited from outside of the agency may not be able to offer.

Roles as Board Educators and Trainers

Staff members can also serve in education and training roles for the board. A community agency, a literacy council, located in a rural area depends on its staff members to organize and implement an annual program of board training. Like many of their colleagues in other community service agencies, these staff members possess advanced degrees in human services and education. They faithfully attend state and national conferences on literacy. Several of these staff members serve as officers of state professional associations and two of them teach at local colleges and regularly serve as workshop faculty at conferences. Staff members help the board to understand the problem of illiteracy, the state of the art in literacy education, and the theory and practice incorporated into the programs offered by the agency. This best practice itself shows how board development can become a joint enterprise of board and staff members.

An inventory of the knowledge, skills, credentials, and professional development activities of community service staff will reveal the extent to which they can serve in educational and training roles for the board. Staff members who fulfill these roles do not muddle the lines of authority between the board and the agency executive. Staff members often know a great deal. Numerous staff members are devoted to their professional work and see as a basic professional responsibility the advancement of their knowledge base. As staff members return from conferences, as they gain knowledge and skill through higher education, and as they execute ancillary roles in the community as faculty and educators of professionals, why should a board squander or ignore such a readily available resource (Kaufman, 1990)?

Roles as Colleagues of Board Members

Those boards seeking to strengthen the interface between themselves and the agencies they steward may also consider the important contributions staff can make to governance as colleagues of board members. Often community service boards sponsor planning events or processes in which they feel it is necessary and productive to involve staff as contributors and participants. Staff colleagues can serve important roles in strategic planning processes in which boards may establish committees or task forces to examine specific aspects of the agency's purpose, performance, and strengths and needs as well as to analyze environmental forces. Rather than staff being confined to liaison roles, these agency members are directly involved in the work of the committees and task forces, having equal standing with board members in undertaking planning tasks and activities. The collegial relationships do not obscure who is a board member and who is a staff member but, rather, lower or reduce hierarchy and the rigidity in service to the formulation of a plan that captures multiple sources of input and involvement. The adoption of this kind of "planning culture" may actually produce more creative strategic thinking as well as a plan that has more validity than one the development of which is confined to the board, and staff are relegated to marginal duties and roles in the planning process (Schein, 1992).

Board and staff members also can interact as colleagues in the preparation for accreditation, particularly in the phase typically referred to as the self-study. During this phase, the agency has to undertake a comprehensive self-assessment. The first time through accreditation can be the most trying and challenging period experienced by a grassroots organization. The first accreditation often demarcates the transition of the agency in its own lifespan from the founding stage to growth and maturation.

Collegial relationships that are in place at all levels of the agency give an organic and fluid character to interactions across and among people from different parts of the organization, which can serve as an asset to the self-study process. The process will require the formation of committees, task forces, and problem-solving groups and if the coordination is centralized at the board or executive level, people whose perspective and input are critically needed may be simply omitted. The agency that has groomed collegial relationships at all levels of the agency, and particularly between board and staff members, will be in a better position to undertake complex developmental tasks such as those that need to be successfully executed during accreditation. The agency that has established these kind of relationships will be likely seen by members of an external accreditation team as an organization that is strong in communication, interaction, performance, and coherence. These qualities are often a product of the development of a strong interface between board and agency.

Supporting the Board–Agency Interface for Staff Members

There are a number of tactics an agency can undertake to strengthen the board–agency interface. On the staff side, the agency can integrate board responsibilities into staff job descriptions, committing a small portion of weekly responsibilities to staff involvement in the board. The more demanding these responsibilities become, the more relief time staff members should receive, particularly from direct service responsibilities. Staff members with interest and relevant talents can take special assignments to work on projects having significance and importance to the board system. For example, rather than bringing in an external consultant to complete an environmental audit for the board's strategic plan, staff members were solicited for their interest. Three staff members agreed to undertake this work and were offered by the agency director an administrative attachment to their salaries to compensate them for the extra time they invested above and beyond their normal responsibilities.

For an effective interface to be realized between the board and agency, the membership and work of the board really cannot be a mystery to the members of the agency. Those staff members who are to become constructively and productively involved in the board need insight into how the board operates.

One community arts agency has initiated staff training to better prepare agency staff for involvement in the work of the board. This training incorporates (1) staff orientation to the board and to the members of the board; and (2) staff training and education for board involvement that includes content on how to serve effectively in roles as meeting participants, liaisons, educators, and training, and colleagues. The executive and associate directors share responsibilities for this training to demonstrate how important productive involvement is to agency performance and to offer the principal executive leaders of the agency opportunities to establish the expectations and standards for board involvement.

But an agency and board have to go beyond knowledge acquisition on part of agency staff to make this interface real and productive. The formation of productive and effective relationships between board members and agency staff members is probably the most important ingredient to the achievement of an interface that works for a community service agency. The formation of relationships requires board and staff to get to know one another as people, to interact in positive contexts, and to establish an understanding and empathy for each other's work (Bolman & Deal, 2007).

Board–staff celebrations are a basic tactic that can be undertaken by an agency to foster a positive interface between board and staff. Of the past 10 board retreats I have conducted, only one community service agency regularly hosts board and staff celebrations or social events to mark accomplishments, to celebrate holidays, and to recognize the contributions of staff members. This agency goes to great lengths to organize and execute three celebrations a year that are sponsored by the board:

1. An annual board–staff breakfast in which the board prepares a meal for staff members
2. An annual agency retreat in which the agency's institutional identity is reexamined and either changed, or reasserted
3. An annual winter festival in which the spiritual, ethnic, and racial diversity of the agency is celebrated through exhibits, educational events, and performances

A task force on board–agency relations is responsible for planning and offering these events.

Readers may find this set of celebrations to be too elaborate for a board of a community service agency to sponsor. These events may very well be demanding, but they enable this particular board of this particular agency to build a strong and viable interface between two groups—board and staff—that can drift apart, or fail to even establish basic working relationships. This particular agency is very interested in creating community within the agency that supports high performance (Weisbord, 1987).

Board–Executive Relationships

An effective interface between the board and agency often lies in the hands of the executive director. Board development seriously undertaken by a community service agency will create significant if not substantial responsibilities for the chief executive officer. Indeed, if I have heard a consistent comment from agency executives when a board invests in board development, it is that board development itself redefines the role of the executive director, and makes the executive much more sensitive to the needs of the board.

An effective interface requires an executive director who is open to people interacting, to becoming familiar with one another, and to working collaboratively (Wareham, 1991). The model of the agency as hierarchy in which only the executive director interacts with the board, and staff members confine their attention to direct service work, now may be arcane. There is the perception in community services that resources are tighter, community expectations are higher, and performance demands by purchasers are higher than ever before in the brief history of many community service agencies. Internal collaboration may be more important than ever.

The executive director that seeks collaboration, and the melding of people together into temporary, ad hoc, yet highly productive groups in service to the achievement of highly valued agency outcomes, may not think twice about the politics of crossing the board–agency divide (Waterman, 1990). This executive is interested in fostering the horizontal development of the community service agency, rather than the organization's vertical dimension. Horizontal development means that the agency must learn how to become outcome driven and solution focused through the work of people who come together from very different perspectives and backgrounds but who are nonetheless bound by a common purpose, vision, and grand narrative (Weisbord, 1987; Vaill, 1991).

Yes, this executive recognizes that staff members have their own responsibilities, as does the board. But for this executive, these different responsibilities and accountabilities can intersect through collaboration between board and staff the purpose of which is to advance the institutional identity and performance of the agency.

Whether the interface is strengthened or even established will be most likely a decision of the board chair and the executive. Indeed, the chair–executive relationship is probably the most fundamental ingredient in establishing and fostering board development to begin with. The partnership between the board chair and the executive will be expressed through the adoption of a common agenda of board development—one framed to advance the vision of the community service agency. The vision frames the board development agenda. And it is this agenda that will define whether a viable interface between the board and the agency is even an aim of board development.

Conclusion

Some readers may say that such an interface is a luxury and really does not serve a purpose beyond perhaps creating more familiarity between the agency and the board. I disagree. There are some fundamental outcomes that this form of board development can yield to the agency as a whole.

Reflect for a moment on when agency staff and board members are likely to interact. Times of crisis are probably the most reasonable response. Board officers may meet with staff when there are substantial changes in the agency environment that demand retrenchment, for example. The development of a strong interface does not guarantee that retrenchment will never occur. It does mean that the board and the chief executive officer have established relationships with agency staff. These relationships can contribute to the formulation of planning and problem-solving mechanisms to better negotiate retrenchment and, as a consequence, can create a more valid retrenchment plan than if the board is isolated from the agency and left to its own devices to plan for cutbacks.

A board may interact with staff when an executive director leaves. Again, like in the situation with retrenchment, the board without a strong agency interface may need to spend an inordinate amount of time interacting with staff to organize a search process. Or the board may even disregard staff involvement and input into selection and simply conduct the search on its own, bringing in staff at the last moment to review several candidates.

Issue management is another case in point. A serious issue emerging in the environment of the agency can have serious repercussions for agency performance and effectiveness. The board may need to collaborate with staff to address the issue in a holistic manner. The executive may need both board and staff involvement to organize a response to the issue and to influence its outcome.

One community service agency experienced considerable vandalism by local neighborhood children. The anger many local children felt toward the agency because they could not use its recreational and athletic facilities that were reserved for the children with developmental disabilities the agency was serving during the day was understood by the community service agency as a loss of community support. The incidents gained notoriety in the press, and the agency was labeled as insensitive to the needs of the local community. The timing of this issue was inconvenient if not poor. It came when this nonprofit, grassroots, educational facility was negotiating with the school system and the city to upgrade its facilities to expand early intervention programs. The board was shocked by the press coverage, as were members of the staff. The executive director was able to rely on the work he devoted to build a strong interface between staff and board. The board and the staff all met, some 50 people, to examine why the agency had neglected to consider the needs of the neighborhood in which its school was based. There was a feeling that they had missed the obvious, that a dimension of their vision needed to incorporate the needs of local neighborhoods. The board sponsored a joint board–staff task force to meet with neighborhood leaders to identify the needs of local youths. The resolution was an expanded vision of the role of the facility in the local community, one that redefined how this agency conceived of itself as an organizational citizen. Successful issue management was really a function of the strength of this agency to join the leadership of the board, the executive director, and the staff in resolving this critical issue.

These are some of the crises that can challenge the interface and that can call for a strong bridge between board and staff. The creation of the interface without reference to any specific crisis can offer the community service agency the opportunity to be proactive and anticipatory. The creation of the interface will take energy and forethought. But likely it is energy well invested.

Questions for Board Development

1. What are the principal strategies used by your board to link its work with the work of the community service agency? Have these strategies helped the board to create a stronger integration or bond with the agency?
2. How do the board and the agency integrate its systems, particularly ones pertaining to data management, information, and evaluation?
3. How do board members maintain an awareness of the needs and issues faced by the agency and by its personnel?
4. How does the board establish an integrated identity within the agency? How is this identity shared between board and agency?
5. What special events or celebrations does the board sponsor to make visible its support of the agency and its personnel?
6. How does the board establish productive staff roles within the board system? How are staff members encouraged to become involved as participants, liaisons, task force or committee members, educators and trainers, and as colleagues?
7. How do staff members become aware of the functions and work of the board? How do staff members keep their understanding of the board up to date?
8. How do the board and the executive director collaborate on an integrated agenda of board and agency development?
9. What developmental needs does this chapter illuminate for the board? How will the board address these needs?

■ SECTION FIVE ■
DEVELOPING BOARD MEMBERS

Like the chapters composing the previous section, the three chapters of section 5 further address the pragmatics or particulars of board development. The theme of this section is the development of individual board members.

Chapter 13 discusses the recruitment of board members and the anticipation of the membership and leadership needs of the board through a consideration of the kind of members who should be identified and recruited to board service. The chapter outlines the audit of board membership needs. Discussed in this chapter are membership characteristics and demographics required by the vision of board and agency performance, specific membership assets required by the board, membership contributions to the properties of the board as a whole, and contributions of membership to system development. This chapter then moves on to consider tactics for the identification and screening of potential board members and procedures useful to actual recruitment.

Chapter 14 focuses specifically on the development of the individual board member within the context of the board system. Preservice and ongoing orientation is identified as essential to preparing board members and to maintaining their currency with the issues and challenges faced by the community service agency. The education of board members is then discussed with an eye to the core curriculum of the board and the dissemination of knowledge that is the foundation of good board performance. Content pertaining to the mentoring of board members for subsequent leadership within the board system is examined with a priority placed on the nurturing and support of (1) inexperienced members, (2) nontraditional members, and (3) the future leadership of the board.

These two chapters lay the foundation for a consideration of succession—its anticipation and planning. Emphasized within chapter 15 is the requirement to prepare the board for subsequent turnover among its leadership. Succession planning and preparation are presented as a logical outcome of a systematic approach to board development undertaken by leadership that is charged with the responsibility to perpetuate and develop the board as a system.

Succession as thoughtful and deliberate is underscored, and the avoidance of urgency and crisis is highlighted within this chapter. This particular chapter identifies the aims of succession planning and the need to build succession on the assets of previous board development work.

■ 13 ■

Anticipating Board Membership

Two Business People Discuss Their Service on Community Boards

Pete: My board needs members badly. My job is to come up with a slate of potential members. The slate needs to be ready for the next board meeting in June. Don't you chair the board development committee of the Haworth board?

Karen: Sure I do.

Pete: How about some recommendations.

Karen: We work on our nomination platform all year long. In fact, our database of potential members is now up to 60 people.

Pete: Will you share about four names with me?

Karen: Not on your life!

Development of the actual membership of the board may be one of the most important strategies for strengthening the board as a system. Previous chapters have pointed out that boards can follow the same developmental phases as the agencies they sponsor and, therefore, boards must be cognizant of their membership needs over time. And boards require a number of properties that are fundamental to the board's performance as a governance body. The right members bring these properties to board service and when they combine with the ones brought by other members, they define the distinctiveness of a particular agency's board.

Unfortunately, many boards may not invest the forethought that is needed to anticipate what kind of members they require. The nomination process may be haphazard and may fail to follow a definitive plan of action. Candidates for board membership may be nominated to the board because they are known to other board memberships as friends or colleagues.

This chapter asserts the necessity of approaching the recruitment of board membership in a more strategic manner. The identification, nomination, and selection of board members can be undertaken in a manner that attempts to match the needs of the agency and the board with the qualities, characteristics, and assets of candidates. Ultimately, anticipating board membership is driven more by the board's need to fulfill organizational or agency vision than by whether some "good" candidates are available through the networks of existing board members.

Anticipating the membership of the board may be the most traditional approach to board development but nonetheless it can be the most critical. What is a board without excellent members? What is a board without committed and energetic people? Ultimately, the quality of a community service board comes down to its membership and then to how it is organized and how it undertakes its work. The anticipation of its membership, however, requires a board to reflect on what it needs and how the fulfillment of these needs will strengthen its culture and the manner in which the board functions (Bolman & Deal, 1997).

Auditing the Membership Needs of the Board

The anticipation of the board's membership needs requires the board to audit its membership, its vision, and what it wants to achieve. Thoughtful planning of board recruitment and nominations is driven by these considerations. This anticipation, operationalized in board procedures through the membership audit, can focus on four principal areas:

1. membership demographics and characteristics,
2. specific membership assets the board requires,
3. membership contributions to the properties of the board as a whole, and
4. contributions of membership to system development.

Auditing Membership Demographics and Characteristics

The principal question guiding the audit of the membership needs of the agency board lies in whether it has the diversity to support the achievement of the agency's vision and principal platforms (Helgesen, 1995). The developing board will be very concerned about the demographics and characteristics brought to board service by its members and potential members (Shaw, 1996). People in leadership roles in community service must recognize more than ever that the citizens served by their respective agencies do not necessarily come from all walks of life. Many community service agencies respond to the needs and challenges experienced by the members of minority populations who often compose groups that inordinately experience oppression, disenfranchisement, discrimination, and stigma (Fetterman, 1996).

Questions pertaining to whether the board is composed of members who have these firsthand perspectives of the needs and problems addressed by the agency become important in auditing board composition. The board may need to examine how social factors like gender, race, ethnicity, sexual orientation, and socioeconomic status influence the business of the agency and its vision and identify board membership needs based on these factors. A vision of diversity and flexible access to service may dictate the need for a board that mirrors what is sought in staff and user characteristics. Indeed, the board may be so concerned about its own development in this area that it requires the membership to mirror the diverse demographic characteristics and qualities sought in service staff and in the people served (Fox & Miller, 1995).

The achievement of diversity in board demographics and characteristics may be essential to the development of empathy among board members for the people who offer services and for the people and community receiving services. Empathy among board members and strong aspirations for the agency may be more easily achieved among people who identify with professional staff and people who receive services. Shared demographics and qualities may reduce social distance between board members, professional staff, and people who are served. Anticipating these kinds of qualities in board members may serve as a strong communication to the community, to funders, and to the agency that the board is very serious about reaching those people in whose lives the agency seeks to make a positive difference.

Concern about the demographic composition of the board also may stimulate an understanding among board members that the board and the agency must strive to create new networks linking the agency to the community and subgroups within the community (Hegelson, 1995). Too often, membership relies on the elite networks of the members of the board. Board members well connected to corporations, businesses, government, and social clubs may draw their nominations from these groups. They can overlook other critical (and perhaps more important) community networks that will bring the board into contact with members of minority populations, diverse groups, and groups that may have difficulty in gaining access to the leadership structures of community agencies. Board connections to these community networks may not only facilitate the recruitment of board members, but also better position the agency as a whole to recruit staff members and to conduct outreach to service populations.

Auditing the board composition in terms of membership demographics and characteristics and using the agency's vision statement to conduct this kind of audit can enlighten the board to what it needs in terms of diversity. The tone and content of the vision may remind board members that they are in the business of serving people who experience serious social problems and related deprivations. Such an audit may also alert the board to the necessity to capture this voice within the board through the recruitment of people who experience the problem or need first hand.

In other words, a basic board development question here is, to what extent does the board incorporate representatives of those people the agency serves?

This overview of the board membership audit is based on a critical assumption not every board member, aspiring board member, or community service administrator will agree with. I am not advocating an elite board membership whose principal service to the agency is to link with elite structures within the community. Alternatively, I am highlighting the need for a community service board (as opposed to a board of a private sector organization) to get as close as possible to the community it serves and to the people it seeks to help through community service. Indeed, this kind of board development work may be very distinctive of those grassroots boards that seek to enhance the well-being of people by developing a strong empathy and understanding of their situations and a strong commitment to acting in ways that will produce substantive benefits for the people the agency serves.

Auditing Membership Assets

Another aspect of the membership audit may involve the examination of the extent to which the board has those assets that will support the achievement of the agency's vision. These assets come in different forms and they have importance at different periods of the lifespan development of the agency and the board. Often times, a community service board may prioritize the recruitment of members who have specific managerial technical skills in areas such as accounting and budgeting, human resources and personnel, finance, information technology, marketing, and risk management. It is not unusual for agencies in the founding phase to have a board composed of advocates who may lack substantive managerial skills often found among board members who come from the private sector. Alternatively, other technical skills more indicative of social and human services may be critical, such as knowledge and experience with housing systems, income maintenance, health and medical care, education, and the arts, depending on the purpose and substantive focus of the agency.

The risk in recruiting members on the basis of their technical assets is that the board does not fulfill its ultimate purpose as a visionary and policy-making structure, but merely becomes a repository for surrogate staff members who are only called on to deliver technical assistance to the agency. Balance is needed here. Anticipation of board membership needs to take into consideration the kinds of technical skills board members require and the extent to which these need to be represented among the board leadership. Balancing these assets against other needed assets and against the demographic needs of the board reflects the complexity of board membership development.

A board of an agency responding to the housing needs of people with HIV and AIDS went overboard in the recruitment of board members with substantive knowledge in the acquisition and management of housing. Most board members had knowledge of housing financing, mortgage banking, development, and real estate. The board had the skills to help people obtain housing but it had little know-how about how to help people sustain their housing. The board did not anticipate the social service needs of the people it served, particularly in the areas of independent living, transportation, chore services, case management, mental health care, and substance abuse treatment. Consequently, the board was ill prepared for addressing from a policy perspective its vision of helping people to not only get housing, but also to hold on to it successfully.

Another asset of board membership lies in the networks brought to board service by individual board members. These networks can be to the populations needing service, substantive technical resources, to resources and dollars, to the media, or to critical industries that are vital to the success of the agency. Board members not only represent their own individual skills, qualities, and abilities, but also represent a social network. What kinds of networks are needed by the board and by the agency?

These networks do not only mean connections to other people and resources, but also to knowledge networks. For example, the neurologist on the board of an agency serving people with epilepsy not only brings her connection with health care systems, but also may have critical connections with research universities that make her very knowledgeable about those best practices relevant to advancing the agency's vision. Her own research and the networks created to sustain this research may be quite instrumental in advancing the community well-being of people coping with epilepsy. The audit of the networks of board members can further enlighten the board as a whole to the kinds of knowledge, linkages, and organizations represented or not represented among board members. This kind of audit can also alert the board to what kinds of assets it wants to acquire through future membership development.

Another asset that can be considered in the anticipation of board membership lies in knowledge of the problem or need addressed by the agency, understanding of the situation experienced by people served, and advocacy perspectives relevant to the people served by the agency. These assets mean that relevant members have a good understanding of what is happening in the need or problem domain addressed by the agency. Members have an understanding of what problems or issues people face, the state of the art that is emerging in the service domain of the agency, and the policy and program systems established to respond to the need.

These assets return us to the necessity of a board possessing a good sense of the social problem or issue it seeks to address and doing so with some clarity and understanding (Shaw, 1996). Board members who bring these kind of assets tend to be technical experts in their chosen fields of service or they can be consumer advocates who understand need from the perspective of the people who are served.

These assets can be quite central to the formation and achievement of agency vision. The individuals who bring these kinds of assets may be important to the board and agency staying on track in their work.

Finally, there are those board members who bring symbolism as an asset to the board (Fox & Miller, 1995). These may be individuals who are very visible within the community and recognized for their outstanding work on behalf of the community. They may receive media attention for their commitment and work. Their affiliation with the agency strengthens the standing of the agency. Their involvement in the board stands for something to the community and to potential donors.

These individuals are not to be confused with wealthy or affluent community members who lend their name to the agency. They are not elite members whose names on a letterhead constitute their principal involvement with the board. Rather, these individuals have developed a substantive track record in the problem area addressed by the agency and have been recognized for their wisdom, commitment, and substantive skill as problem solvers. Symbolically, if they affiliate with a particular agency, then other people in the community may interpret the agency as sharing a boldness of vision and commitment with these community leaders (Bolman & Deal, 1997).

One board of an agency devoted to the employment of people with disabilities was able to recruit the president of the state association of parents of children with developmental disabilities. The president was recognized throughout the state for her sincere and untiring commitment to the advancement of the well-being of children and their families. She was not merely an advocate, but was a symbol of a social movement. She was recognized for her work promoting inclusion in the arts, community development, educational access, and family support. She kept her membership on other boards to a minimum and her consent to join this particular board was an endorsement more powerful than the best accreditation. Symbolic assets are not to be discounted in board development (Douglas, 1998).

Auditing the Properties of the Board as a Whole

An audit of board membership and the anticipation of board membership needs take into consideration the properties of the board as a whole. Here, the board is seeking to address those properties that are basic to the achievement of high performance. Included within the mix of anticipated needs is not only membership demographics and specific assets, but also those qualities that will make the board more effective as a whole. Several important questions here involve how much energy does the board possess? Is there inspiration and motivation for the work undertaken by the community service agency? And is there a moral commitment to the advancement of the social cause undertaken by the agency?

How much energy does the board possess? In situations in which the board's energy is low, or is on the wane, board development should take into consideration the recruitment of members who will bring more energy to board service. It is not unusual that a board loses energy during periods of transition, and that this loss of energy is an indicator that board development through membership recruitment is critical to the viability of the board and of the agency. Board members with high energy may translate this energy into challenging aspirations for the agency, for the well-being of people served, and for the people who are offering service. It can also be translated into higher expectations for the board as a whole. Recruitment of several members who possess high energy may establish a needed enthusiasm within the board and create, in general, an invigorating effect on overall board performance and effort (Maslow, 1998).

Do we have a vision that inspires and motivates? The visionary competence and performance of the board as a whole have been discussed in previous chapters. Board development uses the vision as an advanced organizer—that is, board development is actually framed by the vision because, after all, this is what the agency ultimately stands for and what it wants to ultimately achieve. A vision is a living concept. It lives in the minds of board members, in the board as a system, in the leadership of the agency, and in the minds and performance of service staff. Identification and recruitment of board members who are committed to the vision, who will help bring it about, and who will contribute to its change cannot be overemphasized.

The board's vision can be precarious (Selznick, 1957, 1992). Boards may become preoccupied with technical aspects of running the agency, they may become preoccupied solely with resource development, or they may merely exhaust its previous vision (Kotter, 1998). Thus, the board members who bring symbolic assets, as well as those assets relating to an understanding of social problem or community need and advocacy, may be vital actors in the development, preservation, advancement, and rejuvenation of vision. Nonetheless, a fundamental consideration guiding board recruitment is whether a particular candidate can advance the agency's vision and how the candidate can substantively do this through contributions that make use of the perspective, motivation, and assets he or she brings to board service (J. C. Collins & Porras, 1998).

Do we have a moral–ethical commitment to the advancement of the people and community we serve? No matter what assets people bring to board service, the creation of a board with a strong moral–ethical commitment to service can differentiate an excellent board from a mediocre one. A moral–ethical commitment is another way of inquiring into what motivates the membership of a particular board candidate. Certainly, motivators will vary among candidates. Some people want recognition whereas other people want to fulfill an expectation of their employer.

Other people may want to "give back" whereas other people are deeply committed to the idea of community service and to the idea of helping other people make substantive progress in their lives (Coles, 1993). Who is the better board candidate? This is hard to say because as any board understands, good people with specific talents can be lost to a board by making too many judgments about their motivation to join. Yet there is a greater willingness to take responsibility, to achieve results, and to perform among people who possess deep purpose than those people whose commitment is more instrumental in nature. Board development benefits from the recruitment of people who are not only talented, but also deeply committed to the cause reflected by the service vision of the agency (Coles, 1993).

Do we have commitment to continuous improvement? Board candidates can come to board service with a positive attitude toward continuous improvement. There is no perfect board, but there are boards that are moving toward an ideal end state and they are working to become conscious of this end state. They are also working to improve those processes that will help them to achieve this end state (Hamel & Prahalad, 1994).

Using this question to anticipate board membership requires the identification of people who have energy, who will commit to a vision, and who are motivated by ethical commitments (Kline & Saunders, 1993). Improvement encapsulates those other qualities but it also requires a board member to take practical steps to change processes, procedures, and policies that guide the work of the board (Kotter, 1998).

I know of one community service board that each year holds a board retreat that brings together board members with the executive leadership of the agency. At this retreat, the board examines its vision for the people served, for the people offering service, and for the board as an independent entity. It asks basic questions about what has been achieved vis-à-vis the vision, and it asks even more basic questions about how the board can improve. Four basic aims are established as a product of this work:

1. aims pertaining to the improvement of the work of the board as a whole,
2. aims pertaining to the improvement of the work of board structures and members,
3. aims pertaining to how the board and agency works together, and
4. aims pertaining to how the board can bring about substantive outcomes relevant to its vision.

This is a community service board that over the past several years has purposefully recruited people who are talented and committed and who bring tangible assets to board service. Yet one of the most important screening criteria it has used is the willingness of a board candidate to assume responsibility for the improvement of the board (J. C. Collins & Porras, 1998). It is no surprise that the attendance at the annual board retreat among board members is some 97 percent.

Do we have a commitment to progressive learning? A developing board is clear about its learning requirements and learning norms. This means clear identification of preservice orientation designed to help members understand the board before service begins, continuous orientation requiring board members to keep on top of changes in the board and the agency, and substantive training designed to help board members master their roles. The basic question here is whether potential board members are committed to the fulfillment of learning expectations.

Potential board members may be somewhat ambivalent about making a commitment to progressive learning. Any success with continuous improvement will only be possible with a learning system developed within the board. This learning system is a fundamental asset of board member development (as discussed in chapter 14) and therefore serves as a good way of screening potential board members. As discussed in previous chapters, a "good" board knows the agency in some depth and with some sensitivity. It knows about the issues the agency faces, the outcomes the agency seeks to create, how it seeks to create these outcomes, and the resources needed to support good agency performance.

Some of this knowledge comes naturally through board work both at general meetings and within board committees, task forces, and other board structures. Yet progressive learning also requires an intentional agenda of knowledge development that helps all members to master the knowledge base of the agency. In the anticipation of board member recruitment, a basic question may involve the willingness of board members to acquire this knowledge. Will candidates make a commitment to participating in a progressive agenda of board learning and education?

Auditing Development of the Board as a System

A good community service board comes down to people, an observation made at the beginning of this chapter. Yet it is not people per se that fully makes a board effective. The organization of people into a system is ultimately what the community service agency is trying to achieve. It is through this system that integrates well-selected people into useful leadership roles and that binds them together into a unity driven by purpose and meaning that really forms the substance of the effective community service board (Zander, 1993).

In section 2 of this volume, the four dimensions of the board as a system were introduced and each dimension was discussed in terms of its contribution to board development. The board will want to appraise board system development when the recruitment of new membership is anticipated. The identification of membership needs in terms of membership demographics, substantive assets, and contributions of board candidates to the properties of high performance can be used to appraise whether a particular slate of members will enhance the development of the board as a system:

■ Will board candidates contribute to the development of the board as an institution by helping to clarify values and beliefs, forge a stronger more relevant vision, and help the agency to achieve a better position in the community as a permanent, viable community institution? In general, how will each board candidate contribute to the institutional development of the board?

■ Will board candidates strengthen specific functional roles within the board and balance these roles so that no one perspective entirely engulfs or dominates the board? Are there board members who will help the agency to stay conscious of its founding values? Are there board members who will help the agency to achieve a strategic position? Are there board members who will help the agency to prepare for its future? Are there board members who can help to expand the scope of citizen involvement in the agency? Are there board members who can help the agency to adapt to external expectations? What functional roles does the board need to develop? Or what kind of functional balance needs to be achieved within the board? In general, how will each candidate contribute to the functioning of the board?

■ Will candidates strengthen the performance of the board? Will these candidates improve board leadership, particularly within specific committees or task forces? Will they strengthen the network of the board? Will they increase productivity and the achievement of critical tasks? In general, how will each board candidate contribute to the performance of the board?

■ How will board candidates contribute to the board given the phase of board lifespan? Is this candidate needed during the founding phase? Is the candidate a good fit with growth and maturation? Can the candidate make substantive contributions to the stabilization of the board and agency? Can the candidate help the board to renew and rejuvenate?

Examining how proposed board candidates will contribute to the four dimensions of system development will remind decision makers that the purpose of board development is not merely to recruit new board members, but to strengthen the board as a system within which high performance is valued and achieved. Exemplary community service requires such system development.

Identification and Screening of Potential Board Members

Identification

There are a number of tactics that can be useful to the identification of potential candidates for board membership. Certainly, one of the most powerful of these is the manner in which the board uses the membership of board task forces and committees. Expanding the scope of involvement in various board structures through the inclusion of people who are not formally board members offers the board an opportunity to observe these participants. The board can then evaluate the contributions these people make to the work of the board task force or committee and the qualities they demonstrate through their service. Thus, this involvement offers a natural opportunity to screen a candidate.

And this involvement offers the board to an opportunity to socialize the candidate into board service. Prior to their formal entry into the board, candidates can obtain an understanding of the institutional framework of the board and agency and their functional role on the board. They can learn how they can contribute to the performance of the board and how they can address the needs of the board given the phase of the organizational lifespan the board is negotiating. Through my own consulting experience, I have observed three boards streamline dramatically their membership recruitment by working to expand and manage the scope of involvement in board structures, rather than focusing their energy on the annual recruitment of board members who are not known to the board as a whole.

There are other tactics that can prove useful to the identification of board members. Certainly, the most traditional tactic is the use of the personal networks of board members. Board members, however, may have substantial biases in their networks and such a tactic may be ill suited to a policy aim of diversifying the membership of a board. Yet it stands as one means supporting the recruitment of members.

Staff certainly can be another source of membership recruitment. Staff come into contact with consumers, consumer advocates, other community service professionals, educators, researchers, and professionals from business and government. A board conducting recruitment may want to consider the development of a nominating questionnaire (see Table 13-1) that obtains input from the staff of an agency.

To be sure, the board will want to be sure that staff members understand the needs of the board and how these needs interface with the agency as a whole and the lifespan of the organization. Staff members may also be apprised of the demographics, characteristics, assets, and contributions sought by board members. An added asset of staff involvement in the board recruitment process is that it can strengthen the staff's understanding of how the board functions and what the board wants to achieve on behalf of the agency.

Those agencies that adopt a social marketing approach within their communities may also find it easy to employ a community scanning approach to the membership recruitment drive. The marketing leadership of the agency may scan key informants in the community identifying potential board members and use local newspapers and professional journals to search for candidates that meet the needs and requirements of the board (Grace, 1997b). Ongoing identification of potential

TABLE 13-1: Questionnaire for the Nomination of Board Candidates

Purpose of the Questionnaire

This questionnaire is directed to the staff members of the agency who often come into contact with individuals who may be effective and well qualified members of the board. You are free to nominate people from all walks of life who you feel can make a valuable contribution to the development of the agency and to the achievement of the agency's mission. The nomination form requires you to provide information about the nominee's strengths, why you have nominated the person, and how the nominee can be informed of his or her nomination.

1. In what situations have you worked with the nominee? _____

   _____

2. What are the strengths of this nominee and why do you feel these strengths will serve the agency well?_____

   _____

3. How will the nominee benefit from his or her participation on the board? _____

   _____

4. How can the nominee advance the mission and aims of the agency?_____

   _____

5. What perspective can the nominee bring to the board and to the agency?
   _____The perspective of a recipient or person the agency serves.
   _____An advocate for the people the agency serves.
   _____A business perspective.
   _____An industry perspective.
   _____A community service perspective.
   _____The perspective of government, either state or local.

6. What is significant about the nominee's background that helped him or her to form his or her perspective? _____

   _____

7. Please prepare a brief citation that summarizes why the nominee will make an effective board member:_____

   _____

   _____

8. Please supply information for how the agency can follow up with the nominee:

   _____

   _____

   _____

candidates can be banked in a database that if maintained and updated can offer the board a current list of potential candidates.

Screening

Screening candidates for board membership can be intensive requiring board members to meet with candidates and to appraise them in relationship to board recruitment needs. This process will be facilitated if the board has these things:

- Updated background information on a candidate, including resume or curriculum vitae
- An understanding of the board's principal development needs, typically encapsulated in the board development plan (see chapter 18)
- A list of screening questions that can guide the initial interview (see Table 13-2)
- A questionnaire that can be completed by the candidate (see Table 13-3)

Those community service boards that have created a recruitment system typically follow four steps:

1. Initial contact is made between the candidate and two board representatives. The initial contact is guided by the screening questions. The two board members can reach an understanding initially about whether the candidate does or does not meet the needs of the board.
2. The candidate completes the questionnaire and this offers the board development committee or recruitment officer of the board an understanding of whether a screened candidate is appropriate for further consideration.
3. A more in-depth face-to-face interview and information session is conducted with the candidate to orient the person to the board and agency, and to performance expectations. The candidate is interviewed about the contributions he or she can make to the board. The candidate is asked whether he or she is interested in being recommended to the board.
4. The board development committee or recruitment officer summarizes the recommendation if positive and the rationale for board membership. This rationale identifies the match between the board and the candidate. A recommendation of the candidate is made to the board. The board then invites the candidate to become a member and establishes initial service contributions the candidate can make.

Conclusion

This chapter highlights the anticipation of board membership as a systematic process. Anticipation of board membership seeks to establish a linkage between the

TABLE 13-2: Screening Questions for the Initial Interview of a Board Candidate

1. What do you know about the agency and what do you know about its purpose and mission?

2. What is your experience with board service? What has gone well with your previous service, and what has not gone well?

3. How do you think and/or feel about serving the agency as a board member? What are your expectations of yourself as a board member? What are your expectations of other board members? What are your expectations of the board as a whole?

4. How do you describe your motivation to serve as a board member? Where did this motivation come from?

5. What does your employer think about your involvement as a board member? Is your board service meaningful or important to your employer?

6. What does your family think about your service to this board? Is your board service meaningful or important to your family?

7. Are there personal experiences that you feel make you well suited to work with the agency? What are these experiences and how do they influence your feelings about board service?

8. Do you have direct or personal experience with the social issue the agency addresses? How do you feel this direct experience will influence your board service?

9. What previous volunteer work have you undertaken? What did you like or dislike about this work?

10. What substantive skills or knowledge do you possess that you feel can make a contribution to the work of the board? What professional credentials do you possess that you feel are relevant to board service?

11. How much time and effort do you want to commit to board service? What kind and/or scope of responsibilities do you want to undertake?

12. What can compete with your board service? How will you balance board service with your other responsibilities?

13. How do you characterize your leadership style or approach? Do you want to get involved in the board as a leader or eventually as an officer?

14. Are there limits you want to place on your involvement in the board? These limits may relate to frequency of meetings, availability of time, or scope of responsibility.

15. Are there other things you want the board to know about you and your background that you feel are important to your candidacy as a board member?

16. How important is board service to you at this time in your career?

TABLE 13-3: Board Service Questionnaire for Candidates

Is board service important to you at this time in your career?

____Yes

____No

Do you have adequate time to address the matters or business of a board each month?

____Yes

____No

In addition to board meetings, are you willing to work on task forces or committees?

____Yes

____No

Does the agency represent a social issue or need with which you are proud to affiliate?

____Yes

____No

Is the work of the agency meaningful to you professionally?

____Yes

____No

Is the work of the agency meaningful to you personally?

____Yes

____No

Please indicate the skills or knowledge you want to gain through your service to the board and agency?

_____

_____

_____

Please indicate the contributions you seek to make to the board?

_____

_____

_____

How will the board and agency benefit from your involvement?

_____

_____

_____

_____

developmental needs of the board and the recruitment of specific board members. The anticipation of board membership actually involves the explicit identification of board development needs and board recruitment of promising candidates is undertaken by making a match between the candidates and the board.

Board development needs come in many different forms but can be structured through a consideration of membership demographics and characteristics, specific substantive assets needed by the board, contributions of the candidate to the properties of the board, and contributions of the candidate to the board's development as a system.

Recruitment of specific members unfolds through a networking and marketing approach that can be orchestrated through the scope of involvement of potential candidates in board structures and through the networks of board members and agency staff.

The recruitment process, however, is only designed to bring new members into board service. It is really not designed to prepare board members thoroughly for board service.

This preparation requires a board to be conscious of the purposeful development of each board member. The next chapter examines how orientation, continuing board education, and mentoring are useful in the development of board members.

Questions for Board Discussion

1. What are the principal membership needs of the board? Do a quick audit of the board and identify what these needs are currently? How will these needs change in the near future? What does the board's vision, performance expectations, and board development mission suggest about these needs?

2. Do the demographic characteristics of current board members take into consideration the diversity needs of the board? Of the agency? Do the characteristics of current members link the agency to important social movements in the area of community service in which the agency works?

3. What are the principal membership assets within the board? Are the assets essential to the achievement of the agency vision available within the board? To what extent do board members have the social, knowledge, networking, technical, and emotional assets to lead the agency?

4. What does the audit reveal about the properties of the board as a whole involving its energy, motivation, and commitment?

5. To what extent is the board developing as a coherent system, including its institutional, functional, and performance features and within the context of the organizational lifespan?

6. Does the board possess policies and procedures that enable it to identify and screen potential board members so that it develops a slate of candidates that will contribute to the mission of the board and the vision of the agency?
7. What developmental needs does this chapter illuminate for the board? How will the board act on these needs?

▪14▪

Socializing and Educating Board Members

A Board Member Presents Her Perspective on the Direction
the Agency Can Take in the Next Year

We all seem anxious about what direction we will go in the next year. I must say that I could not really speak to this issue when I first joined the board but now I have some confidence in my perspective. The agency is committed to offering normalizing service alternatives to people with developmental disabilities. But, based on what we have learned through our board training program, the field is moving beyond normalization. I am captivated by the idea of inclusion. Perhaps we should establish new corporate aims—ones designed to help young adults to participate fully in mainstream institutions without reference to their disabilities. Of course, from my perspective, employment, housing, and recreation are the important sectors of our community that should serve as our focus. The board training we have received indicates that best practices like personal futures planning, circles of support, and supportive community living need to become routine ones within the agency. Obviously, I am not an expert in these areas, but the training has really illuminated my understanding of what this agency can do in this community.

Why should the board of the community service agency invest in the development of its own board members? Certainly, board members come to agency service well prepared. Often they are professionals accomplished in their own fields. Attorneys, physicians, educators, and business people are just some of the individuals who come to board service with a great deal of technical expertise to offer the board and the agency. Many of these board members have been recruited on the basis of their fine reputations within the community and their dedication to social causes. Other board members, consumer advocates, for example, may come to agency service with a special kind of energy and devotion to a cause. They can have firsthand experience of the problem or need the agency seeks to address, and they may have high aspirations for how the agency can make a positive impact on this problem or need.

But talent and motivation are necessary but perhaps not sufficient to exemplary board performance. Board members, like other people involved with the community service agency, need to ground their knowledge in the work of the agency. And, as a result, board members can develop a keen awareness for the distinctive features of the agency, how the agency frames its work, the needs and issues faced by the people served, how the agency undertakes its work, and for the substantive outcomes it seeks to produce.

Development of this grounded knowledge within the board is an outcome of a commitment to the development of the individual board member (Knowles, 1990). This development is accomplished through three principal tactics. One tactic involves the approach the board and agency takes to the orientation of its new members and to the continuous orientation of its existing members. Orientation offers the board and the agency a means to help new members develop a basic understanding of the board and the agency. It also offers a means to keep members current.

A second tactic involves continuous education of board members. Compared with orientation, continuous education of board members offers opportunities to add depth of understanding (Knowles, 1990). It offers to board members opportunities to grapple with the nature of the needs of people served by the agency, technical dimensions of the agency's work, and policy forces operating in the agency's environment. Continuous education well done means that board members are intellectually prepared to undertake critical decisions often required of the board in enlightened and insightful ways.

A third tactic involves the mentoring of individual board members. Mentoring is certainly popular in corporate circles and is recognized as a tactic for linking experienced with less experienced organizational members. The more experienced mentor is able to teach the less experienced person about the nuances in organizational culture and instruct this person in how to complete tasks, interact with superiors, and navigate the demands of everyday work life (Guarasci & Cornwell, 1997). In the context of this chapter, mentoring is framed as a tactic used by the board to nurture newcomers. These newcomers may be those individuals who are new to the board. Newcomers may be individuals who are new to board work and, as a consequence, have little experience in undertaking board level responsibilities. Newcomers may also be individuals who are new to specific roles within the board, particularly those individuals who are undertaking officer or key leadership positions within the board.

Knowledge acquisition aside, these three tactics for the development of individual board members have an important aim in common. They all enable the board to socialize its members into the institution and structure of the board as well as into the performance system of the board. Successful socialization into the board requires each board member to become knowledgeable of values, beliefs, roles, and norms within the board and to internalize these in relationship to board performance (Vella, 1994). Thus, "socialized" board members understand how they fit into the board as a system or as a group, and how to behave and to perform in the pursuit of board sanctioned and endorsed outcomes. Each of the tactics enumerated above contributes to the socialization of board members. Orientation offers board members the opportunity to understand the board as a whole and how it fits with the history, culture, technology, and environment of the agency. Continuous education offers board members opportunities to develop their knowledge base with knowledge here broadly construed to incorporate values and beliefs, philosophy, theories, and explanations about why and how the agency works (Knowles, 1990). Mentoring offers an individual board member opportunities to learn about a specific role and to acquire the knowledge, attitudes, and skills needed to execute this role successfully.

Orientation

Most community service boards I have encountered have been very concerned with the orientation of their new members. Indeed, if there are two tasks that are traditional board development ones, they are the nomination of new board members and the basic orientation of those members to the board and the agency. Orientation is often conceived as a one shot event, however. A new group of board members is identified and if this cohort is considered large, a board feels that it has to undertake a training event dedicated to board orientation. However, in these situations, I have often observed that existing board members want to participate in this orientation, and even some senior level staff members will express a desire to become involved. The orientation event offers a time when all board members evaluate the currency of their knowledge base and understanding of the board and agency. They can use this event as an opportunity to become current.

The orientation event, I have found, is a stimulus for other board training activity. For example, in preparation for the orientation, senior staff may review the currency and adequacy of agency policy material. Marketing and promotional material may be reviewed and updated. More important, in the context of board development, the board manual and board policies and procedures may be reviewed and updated. The entire board manual may be restructured in preparation for the board orientation. Thus, the orientation often becomes much more than a training and information session designed to bring new members into the board. It often becomes a board event that is undertaken annually to help all board members to become oriented not merely to the basic foundations of board work but to how the practices of the agency and board have changed over time. Thus, orientation can address these three things:

1. how the agency has changed and developed over a period of time,
2. how the work of the board and the manner in which this work is undertaken by the board has changed, and
3. what board members—both new and existing—need to know and understand, and perhaps how they should think about, their roles on the board to undertake their work effectively.

Whether the community service board pulls apart the aims of orienting new members to the work of the board and to orient existing board members to organizational changes in the board and the agency, the board must address the orientation needs of both of these groups. Thus, it is wise to consider orientation to possess a preservice function and a continuous function.

Preservice Board Orientation

Ask any existing board member, one experienced with the culture of a particular community service board. Board work is complex. It takes time to learn about this work and this learning is a function of involvement and participation. The creation of an experienced board member probably takes years and not merely months. Indeed, the loss of an active and engaged board member is literally a loss to the board as a whole—to the knowledge and practice base of the board as a collective organizational entity within the community service agency. I point this out to consider the magnitude of service a board asks of a new board member. There is much to learn, to know, and most of all, to understand. Board recruitment has most likely identified and selected highly motivated board members, but they are newcomers in a very ambiguous situation.

Preservice board orientation must be designed to reduce this ambiguity, to equip the new board member with enough knowledge to begin service, and to help him or her join the group as an active board member who is known to other members as a person, professional, and contributor. These are the aims of preservice board orientation. Let me state them in more official language:

■ Help new board members understand how the board enables the agency to achieve its purpose. This requires new board members to obtain a basic introduction to the agency and its work.
■ Help new board members to understand how the board operates and their initial roles within the board as contributing members. This requires board members to become familiar with the expectations of board membership

and how the board functions during the course of the year, during a meeting, and within committees and other structures.

■ Help new board members establish relationships with other board members by helping board members to get to know one another. This requires the board to personalize its members and to establish a common bridge of human understanding and familiarity among its members.

Community service boards approach these aims in different ways. As noted previously, some boards sponsor a new board orientation to which new members, current members, senior leadership, and agency partners (for example, funders) attend perhaps for the entire session or a segment of it. It is likely that these orientations take a full day and a board covers a range of content. A portion of the day is devoted to essential background on the agency, on the nature of its work, and on how it sustains itself. Another portion of the day may be devoted to an orientation of new board members to the programmatic structure of the community service agency in which overviews of specific programs are offered by staff and consumers. A third portion of the day may be devoted to the by-laws and governance role of the board, the structure of the board, to how it conducts business, and how the work of the board relates to the work of the agency. Following this portion may be an orientation to the role of the board member.

Throughout the day, this orientation integrates opportunities for board members to get to know one another. Formal introductions of new and existing board members may be followed by structured breaks during which small groups of board members undertake informal introductions and discussions, meals during which board members interact, and structured group exercises designed to help people to get to know one another.

This kind of orientation format that devotes an entire day to the orientation of new board members often is favored by those community service agencies that undertake a seasonal routine of board recruitment and selection so that a critical number of new board members enter service at the same time. Thus, for example, if four new board members enter board service in the spring or entry is staggered so that six new members enter service during winter and spring, it may be useful for the agency to sponsor its new board member orientation in late spring. A relatively large cohort of entering members may justify the commitment of a full day that a formal orientation may require.

Other boards may have different routines. Their approach to addressing the orientation aims identified above may come through the preservice orientation of members using an individual format. An agency serving the community through cultural development undertakes the orientation of new board member on an ongoing basis because it is quick to fill vacancies and its board nominations process works continuously to ensure that needed board members are identified and screened.

The board appoints an existing board member to serve as an "orientation coach" who guides the board member through a series of orientation experiences that are stipulated by a board orientation checklist (see Table 14-1). These experiences involve an overview of the agency conducted by the executive director and key staff. Board members can then observe key agency programs, participate in an arts outreach activity, and become involved in a guided discussion with agency staff about the work of the organization. Other orientation events can include an orientation to the board conducted by the board president, an orientation to the role of the board member conducted by the board vice president, and the dedication of a segment of a board meeting to the introduction of new members. The board favors this kind of preservice orientation because it enables it to be flexible, to tailor the orientation to new members, and to incorporate more experiential material than a one day orientation format allows. The orientation is completed when the checklist is exhausted, which is usually accomplished within six weeks and is the board's self-stipulated quality standard assigned to orientation.

Orientation aims may be achieved in one more way. A board of one community service agency devotes an extra hour to each monthly board meeting in the fall of the year, a part of its seasonal calendar in which new board members join the agency. New board members and interested existing board members stay for this hour and a formal orientation program is offered that covers agency purpose, program structure, role of the board, and role of the board member. The entire new member orientation is covered in three one-hour sessions. The orientation is consolidated because the board and agency sponsors a continuous process of board education that is open to board members, staff, and consumers of the agency. Thus, all board members receive continuous education about the board and agency and, as a consequence, the board has discovered that new member orientations do not have to be comprehensive events.

Continuous Board Orientation

A board's commitment to the development of its members can also come in the form of continuous board orientation. This kind of orientation is most important and productive during certain periods of the lifespan of the community service agency and its board. The agency that is in the founding phase of its development may find that it requires considerable exposure of its board to new knowledge so that it is competent in formulating vision, mission, organizational identity, and critical values. The founding board may need to spend a considerable amount of time contemplating the purpose and commitments of the agency. It may need to consider such aspects of the agency as what is meant by community service,

TABLE 14-1: Orientation Checklist for the Myers Arts Outreach

Board Member: _____. Orientation Coach: _____.

Initiation Date: _____/_____/_____.   Completion Date: _____/_____/_____.

Orientation to the Board
Responsibility for Coordination: Board Chair or Designee

1. Completion of the board member contract.	Yes	No
2. Overview of the organizational vision.	Yes	No
3. Overview of the agency mission and principal plans.	Yes	No
4. Orientation to the board calendar.	Yes	No
5. Overview of board culture and practices.	Yes	No
6. Introduction to board members.	Yes	No
7. Q & A session with board member.	Yes	No
8. Orientation to board policies.	Yes	No

Orientation to the Agency
Responsibility for Coordination: Executive Director

9. Orientation to agency policies and procedures.	Yes	No
10. Overview of all agency programs.	Yes	No
11. Overview of financial system and structure of the budget.	Yes	No
12. Overview of licensure, certification, and regulatory requirements.	Yes	No
13. Overview of community and service recipient needs.	Yes	No

Programmatic Orientation
Responsibility for Coordination: Senior Staff Member

14. Observation of a service program.	Yes	No
15. Introduction to and interaction with staff members.	Yes	No
16. Participation in arts outreach activity.	Yes	No
17. Lunch with staff members of a program.	Yes	No
18. Interaction with service recipients.	Yes	No

Debriefing
Responsibility for Coordination: Executive Director

19. Lunch with several board members to answer questions.	Yes	No
20. Review of the board member contract and its clarification.	Yes	No

who are to be the principal recipients, and what the agency should accomplish on behalf of the community. This work requires a continuous orientation to what is occurring within the agency and within the context of its policy and organizational environment.

Agencies experiencing growth and maturation may find that much about their agency and its environment is changing and that critical decisions are needed to navigate these changes successfully (Stacey, 1996). The agency may be involved in negotiating contracts, applying for grants and preparing grant proposals, obtaining gifts, and establishing and formalizing policies in anticipation of accreditation. The board has to be aware if not knowledgeable about these developments. More important, it needs to work with the agency executive in the anticipation of these activities and the demands they place on board policy making.

An agency negotiating renewal may also place new knowledge and information demands on a board. A strategic plan the aim of which is to renew the relevance and vitality of an agency may require new kinds of initiatives, new investments, and new resources (Stonich, 1982). Board members need to be aware of these and must be oriented to what is occurring within the context of an agency policy of renewal.

Continuous orientation of all board members means that no one board member is operating in a vacuum characterized by blind spots, misunderstandings, and lack of relevant information. Continuous orientation is not designed around any one impending decision. This kind of work gets into the actual policy process within the board. Rather, continuous orientation is enlightenment oriented. It is designed to open the eyes of each board member and to increase his or her fund of knowledge about emerging developments or actual change that is occurring within the agency and its environment. Continuous orientation during periods of change means that each board member will be oriented to these changes and to what is occurring in anticipation that future decisions, policies, or actions are needed from the board.

This kind of orientation is not a burden for a community service board to undertake. However, I have found that continuous orientation is the first to be eliminated from a demanding schedule of board activity. This means that continuous orientation has to become a ritual of board work. This in turn requires the board as a whole (and each board member) to develop a belief and expectation that their continuous orientation to what is happening within the community service agency and its environment is a top priority of board work. Without this ritual, often achieved by making continuous orientation a fundamental aspect of a board meeting, such orientation—and the information and knowledge it communicates—will not be realized within the board. Board development will most likely suffer—in other words, board members will not be prepared to execute their roles as stewards or trustees of the agency with foresight and preparation.

Continuous orientation can be nested in the roles of specific board members and participants as well as the products of the board. Using the first 10 minutes of any board meeting, the board chairperson can highlight issues, developments, and change that have substantive importance to the board and the agency. Typically, board chairs introduce meetings and this introduction can be literally highlighted within the board meeting agenda as an "orientation to new developments" or an "orientation to agency changes." The agency executive director can follow this up through a more focused description or analysis of these changes in the executive report to the board. This, too, does not have to demand a considerable investment of time but, rather, can involve a brief accent on substantive changes. Complementing this verbal presentation can be a restructuring of materials that are disseminated to board members in advance of a meeting. An "orientation report" can offer a listing of changes and developments in a brief format. Those agencies using the World Wide Web or Internet can post orientation reports on their Web or home pages.

Continuous orientation has one principal outcome. Board members should feel current with the agency and not "in the dark." Board members should feel like they have requisite information about what is occurring within the agency and within the environment of the agency. This connection to the agency is achieved by a commitment of the board to the individual orientation of each of its members and of the board as a whole. Preservice orientation offers members a framework for how the agency and the board works, and, of equal importance, it helps each board member to join the board as a group. Continuous orientation recognizes that each board member needs to be mindful of agency changes and developments and that this information may not be disseminated through other channels like board committees, newsletters, and informal contact. A commitment to continuous orientation is really a commitment to the continuous development of the knowledge base of each board member.

Core Curriculum

Orientation—whether in the form of preservice or continuous education—is not sufficient to build the depth of knowledge needed by each board member. Reflect on the substantive nature of the decisions made by board members. When you examine them, their importance to what the agency does and how it does its work cannot be minimized or dismissed. Indeed, a distinguishing attribute of a high-performing board is that its decisions steward the development of an effective agency. Good decisions require information and, more important, require on the part of board members knowledge that is relevant to the development of the agency it stewards. Recently, I observed the board of a community service agency negotiating the organizational phase of growth and development. On the agenda of the board was a decision about whether accreditation should be pursued by the agency and what specific accreditation addresses the substantive needs of the agency.

The board conceived of this decision as relevant to its role within the agency. But it was obvious from its deliberations that it was not prepared to make this decision. An overwhelming number of board members understood the external pressure to obtain accreditation, but they did not understand the variety of accreditation types and sources, the demands of preparation placed on the agency and the board, and how accreditation could be achieved in an efficient manner. From my perspective, this was a board that did not anticipate how changes in its environment created a need for new knowledge among board members and the board as a whole.

Continuing education is vital to the development of individual board members. Board members need to know a lot, not merely about their fiduciary or trustee responsibilities, but also about their role in the development of the community service agency. Knowledge requirements vary by board. They depend on the nature of the community service agency and the kind of work it is involved in. More important, however, knowledge requirements vary by vision, expectations, and aspirations. A course of knowledge building within the board that is vigorous, current, and substantive will be a product of several sources of expectations (Carlson, 1996). It will be a product of those boards with high expectations for themselves. Those boards with a vision of exemplary performance on their part will endorse this kind of knowledge building. And those boards with an expectation that community service will be exemplary will commit themselves to this course of action.

There is one principal aim of continuous board education: to help develop among board members a depth of understanding that results in informed and insightful decisions about the direction, vitality, and viability of the community service agency. Orientation really is designed for awareness and initial understanding. Continuous board education challenges board members to acquire depth of understanding. This depth of understanding is achieved through the formation and implementation of a board core curriculum designed to offer each board member opportunities to gain the knowledge and understanding needed to steward the agency.

The core curriculum within the board can serve as the focus for board development. It can emanate out of the board's development as a system with institutional, functional, performance, and lifespan dimensions and informed by vision, energy and aspirations, ethical commitment, and commitment to continuous improvement. It is one of the basic tactics undertaken to make the board a viable and vital entity of community service. Why take the time to create a core curriculum? Why take the time to make continuous education a focal point of board development? The key foundation of board development work is the development of knowledge about the agency on part of the full board.

Continuous education, directed by a relevant core curriculum, does not have to be onerous for the agency or for the board. Continuous board education needs to respect some realities about board work. Education is not an end in itself and it should enable board members to understand the substantive challenges facing the community service agency. Also, board education must link with and inform other board responsibilities to make it synergistic and productive for the board member. Through their participation, board members should obtain a good understanding of how to perform. The curriculum needs to be renewed periodically and incorporate changes that are occurring within the environment of the agency. And time is limited so every educational activity no matter how brief must contribute value to the functioning of the board.

The board does not formulate a core curriculum because education of members is valued as an end in itself. Board members have other personal avenues to pursue for their own edification. The purpose of board education is to improve insight and understanding. Thus, the core curriculum is crafted around the substantive challenges facing an agency and the knowledge that is incorporated into the curriculum possesses strategic significance to the agency.

This imperative is best demonstrated through example. An agency negotiating the growth and maturation phase is addressing multiple issues and challenges emanating out of its desire to improve the well-being of the youths of its community. The agency is a voluntary one. No one from government or business directed this agency to be formed. Indeed, business leaders, educators, youth advocates, and government officials joined together as individuals to found the agency and to establish its identity in relationship to advancing the well-being of youths in their particular community. The problem was apparent in their daily lives. Numerous youths were not doing well whether in their families, in schools, in employment, and in preparation for adulthood. Alarming indicators having to do with drug use, teen pregnancy, and status offenses illustrated the problems dramatically.

The agency negotiated the founding stage. The original board fully understood the challenges facing the agency. It was prepared to steward the agency during its early stages. As these founding members retired or left the community, new members came on board. These members were not as informed or knowledgeable about the original need for this agency. Changes to the need itself and its manifestation within the community called for a fresh look and perspective within the board.

The board president, an alumnus of the original founding board, in partnership with the executive committee and the chief executive officer, first identified the need for a core curriculum. They knew that the curriculum had to focus on basic parameters of the agency's business. Board education needed to build the depth of knowledge of board members on a continuous basis and it needed to be implemented in an economical manner. Finally, it needed to be renewed annually to reflect substantive changes in the challenges facing the agency.

These performance parameters were achieved through the creation of a five-part continuing board education series sponsored by the board for board members, staff members, and other interested parties (like task force and advisory group participants). The five-part series focused on youths in the community and addressed these topics:

1. The changing needs of youths in the agency's community
2. Policy changes in the state and local communities that created opportunities to better support youths or that hindered the support of youths
3. New practice models and approaches found effective in increasing the success of youths in their communities
4. Standards of quality in youth services
5. How the agency measures up to new practice models and standards of quality

The core curriculum was implemented in three ways. First, several sessions were offered at regular board meetings and limited to 30 minutes. Resource materials were disseminated to board members to support their understanding through updated board education manuals that contained a section on the core curriculum. Staff from the agency served as faculty of these sessions. These educational sessions were followed by a morning board-staff training event held on a Saturday to facilitate participation. The theme of this educational event was "Standards of Quality in Youth Services: The Status of Arbor Agency." This educational event anticipated the annual internal audit of the agency that was linked to the renewal of the agency's strategic plan and that in turn contributed to the agency's self-study in preparation for reaccreditation. This educational event was then followed up with a final session within the annual board retreat that educated the board about the challenges the agency faced in meeting exemplary standards of service. During the course of board self-evaluation, it was revealed by a majority of the board members that the educational series offered them a much better understanding of the challenges the agency faced and a better understanding of the role of the board in addressing these challenges. One board member's comments are instructive:

> Of all the boards I have served on, the board education series has helped me to become more aware of how important my decisions are to the well-being of the agency, and to the youth it serves. The knowledge I obtained helps me to be more respectful of this agency and the work of the staff. I'm more understanding than ever before of the challenges we must all meet in preparing this agency to make a positive impact on the lives of youth. If we can make this kind of education permanent, I feel that we have a major board asset.

This board achieved the four criteria needed to make board education a developmental tool. Board education was not treated as an end in itself. Rather, it was designed to support the knowledge development of board members in relationship to their responsibility of stewarding the agency toward higher levels of performance. Indeed, the content of their training reflected the board's commitment to exemplary service development within the community and in linking service development to the substantive needs of youths. Board education was connected to other board and agency responsibilities and products, specifically the renewal of the agency's strategic plan, and the preparation of the agency for its reaccreditation. The development of the board and its individual members through education was naturally linked to its governance and the tasks that needed to be completed to govern the agency effectively. Board education and performance can go hand in hand. And finally, the board education series recognized that time is precious and a premium in the lives of board members. Through the integration of board education into standing meetings and board events like retreats, time commitments were minimized.

The downside of board education is that it does not become relevant, continuous, and economical. Board members are bogged down with too much extraneous information, and the knowledge acquired does not have direct applicability to their membership roles. The board member quoted above implied that there is a challenge to make this education a routine and permanent feature of the board and how it undertakes its role within the community service agency. Without a means of renewal, of changing board education as the situation of the agency and the youths and community it serves changes, then board education as a tactic of board development will likely stall.

Preservice orientation, continuous orientation, and continuous board education form a developmental agenda for the community service board. This agenda will be visible within the discrete agendas of specific board meetings in which time is allocated to substantive orientation and education of board members. The expectations of board member orientation and education will be encoded into the board's mission statement and into the core policies used by the board to undertake its own development and work. The deliberations of the board's executive committee will also reflect the orientation and educational needs of board members. Thus, board development is linked to the ongoing work of the board and is recognized as an essential feature of board work by the membership. In other words, board work and board development really cannot be separated in practice.

Mentoring of Board Members

New members of the board represent the future of the community service agency. As noted above, many come to board service with varying degrees of experience with community service boards. The development of new members and the preparation of members for new roles within the board suggest that the development of individual board members can be undertaken through a system of mentoring.

Not all board members require mentoring. Some will bring into service a deep understanding and sophistication about their roles within community service. Some board members will have experience with several different types of boards while others will bring experience as officers of community service boards. Some board members will benefit from productive preservice orientations and continuous orientation of high quality. And their participation in regular board meetings will be sufficient to build their knowledge and skills as board members.

Mentoring can be used in a targeted manner by those community service boards interested in fostering the knowledge, skills, and leadership of specific board members. Mentoring and mentoring assignments should be well thought through and executed by a board and reserved for special circumstances. Those situations in which mentoring is particularly warranted involve (1) the selection of a board member who is relatively inexperienced, (2) the selection of consumer members who may not be readily integrated into the board, and (3) the preparation of board members for new or existing leadership positions.

Mentoring of Inexperienced Members

Community service boards are always in search of talented members who bring energy, aspirations, and commitment to their positions as board members. It is not unusual for members who are relatively inexperienced in the operation of community service boards to join after being identified by existing board members. These inexperienced members may be identified in the community and may be seen as relevant candidates. They may be identified within board-sponsored task forces or they may have served as community representatives within board advisory groups or committees.

Despite a strong professional background, good intentions, and strong motivation, these inexperienced board members may require some extra attention and development by the board. Their motivation makes them good candidates for mentoring relationships in which an experienced board member pairs with them to teach them substantive content about board operations or the nuances of board culture. Or the experienced board member may simply reach out to an inexperienced member to offer support during an initial period in which board participation may be found to be ambiguous and somewhat confusing.

A mentoring relationship is not structured or even formal. Informality may be the most appropriate attribute to attach to this kind of relationship (Vella, 1994). Nonetheless, mentoring relationships can become powerful tactics in the socialization of new members in the anticipation that these members can emerge within the community service boards as strong leaders.

A mentor is basically responsible for forming and sustaining a supportive relationship with the new board member. The mentor may reach out to this member.

He or she can schedule informal gatherings the subject of which is the operation of the board and how the new member can get involved and make a contribution. Luncheons, early morning breakfasts, dinner before an evening board meeting, and periodic telephone contacts may be the vehicles of mentoring. During these informal contacts, the mentor and new member can flag issues and discuss them. Most important, the new member has someone to touch base with and to clarify board expectations concerning new member performance, identify the assets the new member can share with the board and the agency, and formulate a plan for getting involved within the board.

New board members can gain a great deal from a good mentor. They can gain more clarity of purpose and increase their confidence. They can clarify the contributions they can make and formulate a realistic set of expectations of what to contribute to and get from board involvement. Mentors themselves can gain from this kind of relationship. Some board mentors have expressed to me that mentoring offers them a concrete way of engaging in board development and of strengthening the board through development of an individual member. Mentors have commented that they feel more connected to the board and more "generative" in the sense that they are helping to prepare the agency for its future.

Other mentors have emphasized the benefit of preparing people specifically for the roles they will eventually vacate. For example, one board member strong in financial accounting was instrumental in bringing into board membership a junior associate from a large managerial consulting firm. The board member knew he was retiring and understood the valuable contribution he made to the financial development of the agency. However, he knew that his relocation to another community would make his continued service impossible. He saw mentoring the new member as an opportunity to achieve continuity in the substantive area of his expertise. Luncheons with the new board member helped the retiring member to share his six years of knowledge about the agency and its financial practices with the new member. Subsequently, the new board member was amply prepared to take over the leadership role the retiring member relinquished.

Mentoring of Nontraditional Members

Some community service boards have been quite proactive in the recruitment to board membership of people who represent the users or consumers of agency services as well as those individuals who are direct recipients of these services. These so-called "consumer members" may be people who bring an identity as a consumer to the board, and their perspectives may be critically needed to more effectively inform board decision making. Some consumer board members may also represent minority perspectives or those of underserved populations who are not normally included in the service population of the agency. Their perspectives also can add consumer sensitivity and responsiveness to the board. Other consumer members may be family members of people who are served or they may be consumer advocates whose direct knowledge of the need or problem addressed by the agency can strengthen the board's performance.

For some boards, this kind of membership recruitment may contrast sharply with past practices. In the past, "consumers," whether they came in the form of direct recipients of services, advocates, or family members, may have been seen as unsuitable board members. They were too biased in their perspectives, too conflictual in their interactional styles, or merely not connected enough within the community to foster the success of the agency. Increasingly, however, consumers—or people with first-person experience with the problems or needs the agency is established to address—are the most relevant board members. They have an understanding and knowledge base that other board members may simply lack. And they may have a strong empathic feeling for what the agency is trying to do.

The introduction of board members who are considered to be consumers may be a significant challenge to a board. Thus, it is important for a board to develop bridges between traditional and nontraditional members. In their lives outside of the board, members may operate in very different social spheres. Consumers may experience misunderstanding, negative stereotypes, patronizing attitudes, and outright social rejection. A board that has made considerable progress in the development of its own diversity may not experience these kinds of challenges. Community service boards composed of traditional members from industry, the professions, and government may find it difficult to reduce social distance.

The risk here is that nontraditional members may be isolated within the board. They may not be accepted as serious members who have substantial knowledge and skill to share with the board and the agency. This isolation may communicate to the agency that consumers, family members, and members of minority populations are not to be taken seriously. It may communicate to the community that an elite board structure has little consideration for the people whose needs form the reason the agency exists.

Mentoring established to bring nontraditional members into the board membership may be a tactic that is essential to a policy of diversity within the board. Mentoring of nontraditional members can be undertaken in the same manner that it is undertaken with inexperienced members. Established board members can reach out to incoming nontraditional members, and through informal contacts such as the telephone, e-mail, luncheons, dinners, and conversation the new member can be involved in the board as a contributing member.

The demeanor and commitment of board mentors are critical to success. It is likely that the social characteristics and demographics of the experienced member are different from the nontraditional member who is new to the board. Differences in race, ethnicity, language, sexual orientation, gender, and socioeconomic status may create some awkward interactions at first. They may amplify conflict that is communicated verbally and nonverbally. These are potential barriers to the success of the mentoring relationship. They can offset the successful integration of non-traditional members into the board. Yet resolving these barriers successfully can establish strong relationships between the established board members and non-traditional newcomers. Successful resolution of the barriers can establish models for the board as a whole. Mentoring relationships become symbols supporting the attainment of diversity within the board.

A mentor as a symbol of welcome can serve as an important ritual of board functioning and development. One community service board new to a membership policy of diversity conducted an assertive outreach program to identify and select nontraditional members. Several members were selected for board membership on the basis of their firsthand experience with recovery from the use of substances. Up to this time, the board had been composed of business owners, treatment profes-sionals from the substance abuse service system, and community and professional leaders. The addition of these new members signaled a new direction for the board. The board organized a welcoming at the orientation meeting. The hopes and aspi-rations for the contributions these new members could make to the strengthening of the board and to the creation of an agency more responsive to recovery were discussed with a great deal of excitement. Opportunities for "mutual mentoring" were identified. Existing board members were assigned as mentors to help the new members coming into the board. New members were seen as mentors who could help the board as a whole better understand recovery, outreach, and the challenges inherent in making the agency more responsive to the people it serves. This board has been so successful in its policy of diversity that the distinction between nontra-ditional and traditional members has since fallen to the wayside. In other words, consumerism is well situated and established within this board.

I have seen other boards that have not been so successful. Few supports offered to nontraditional board members by established members have created consider-able social distance. In one instance, factions developed within the board that has set those who are "consumer advocates" against those who are seen as only com-mitted to traditional service. The resulting conflict has fragmented the board and has reduced its productivity. Working out a policy of diversity among board mem-bers and the development of a support system that would help these new members to become central to the operation of the board may have reduced or even elimi-nated this conflict. Mentoring can serve as one tactic to form relationships among people who would otherwise not interact. Forming mutuality of purpose between people who have very different characteristics may be an aim of mentoring within this context.

Mentoring for Leadership

A program of board mentoring seeks the preparation of board members for new or existing leadership positions. An effective board has numerous leadership positions that require knowledgeable members to fill them (Bolman & Deal, 1997). Some community service boards may become comfortable with a limited number of members who fill leadership roles over long periods. When there is a transition in leadership, the board finds that no one is prepared for a given role (Kets de Vries, 1989). A community service board with a commitment to agency development will find that its own leadership development is essential to the realization of agency success.

There are numerous leadership roles even within a relatively small community service board. Officers, committee chairs, advisory group and task force chairs, and substantive leaders who focus on board education and planning are the types of roles leadership development needs to consider. Yet these are formal leadership roles. Informal leadership should not be neglected, and any planning for leadership development should also address the development of roles that are relevant to task completion, group facilitation, emotional inspiration, and vision. Leadership development is an essential feature of any developing board.

Perhaps all community service boards should consider the membership of current leaders to be impermanent and transitory. After all, a change in job, health, or family situation can quickly remove a leader from service to a community service board. One day a board leader may announce to the board that a change in life circumstances means that the person will have to step down from either a leadership position or even the board.

An awareness of these possible contingencies means that the board can begin to anticipate some possibilities and prepare for these through leadership development. Mentoring as a leadership development tactic within the board may prove indispensable. Key leaders within the board may have informal or formal expectations that an incumbent for their role be identified and that this person be groomed for the existing position. Perhaps the person is identified as an associate chair of a committee or as a coleader of a task force. The president-elect or executive vice president of the board may be two formal positions that actually represent roles and people who are being mentored for leadership within the board.

Some boards may not designate formal leadership development positions. A community service board develops a cadre of four to five members who are mentored in overall board operations. As leadership positions within the board become open, one of these members is transitioned into the role and offered specific technical assistance or mentoring by senior board members so that he or she is able to handle the expectations of the position. The board development committee holds the responsibility for identifying candidates for leadership positions and for the four to five leadership development roles. The board development committee also is responsible for ensuring that these four to five individuals receive mentoring from key board leaders. Annually, the board development committee works to anticipate leadership vacancies, the movement of new leaders into these vacant roles, and the identification of individuals who will receive leadership development. The committee ensures an ongoing process of leadership development within the board itself.

Mentoring for leadership may be somewhat different than the other forms of mentorship identified above. It is likely that candidates for leadership will be exposed to many different roles within the board and perhaps will receive short-term assignments to help them to understand these different roles. These candidates may get special attention from the leadership of the board and the board development committee may actually identify the content of the mentoring relationship and process for these candidates. But mentoring is neither prescriptive nor highly structured. Candidates for leadership positions need the attention of the people filling the roles they will eventually assume. They need to obtain a basic understanding of how these roles are executed in practice. Thus, mentoring that focuses on how board practice is implemented within a given leadership role is beneficial to the preparation of the future leaders of the board.

Conclusion

The development of individual board members is a conscious process within the board that unfolds through preservice orientation, continuous orientation, continuous education, and mentoring of specific board members. The responsibility for the development of individual board members lies in the board development committee the mission of which involves the perpetuation of the board. The fostering of knowledgeable board members who have a good understanding of the work of the board and the purpose and aims of the agency are fundamental to the perpetuation of the board.

The purpose of all of these tactics is to reduce the ambiguity felt or perceived by new board members or by board members who are assuming or will assume new roles within the community service board. As ambiguity is reduced, knowledge and understanding of role and performance begins to emerge. Achievement of a good understanding of role and performance is probably the outcome that is sought through the individual development of board members. It is this outcome that will not only strengthen people as individual board members, but also advance the board as a collective system responsible for the success of the community service agency.

Knowledge and understanding are not only individual achievements, but also collective ones. Thus, development of individual board members also results in the collective development of the board system. Board knowledge and understanding means that the board as a collective understands itself as a system and how this system connects to the agency as a whole. Board knowledge and understanding mean that the board as a collective is better able to meet the five challenges discussed previously in this volume. Board members know (1) who they are on the basis of agency purpose, expectations, and distinctiveness; (2) the vision of the agency; (3) how the agency will get to its desired destination; (4) what inspires the work of the agency; and (5) how performance will be judged. This knowledge is essential to an empowered board. An empowered board can mean empowered community service.

Questions for Board Discussion

1. Does the board possess an organized approach to the initial and ongoing orientation of board members? Does the orientation help board members to become knowledgeable of the values, beliefs, and norms within the board and their specific roles? Does the orientation help board members to understand the agency fully and what it is seeking to do through community service?

2. Does continuous board orientation help board members to stay abreast of internal agency changes and changes in the external environment of the organization? Does continuous board orientation help board members to maintain an understanding of changes in the state of agency practice?

3. Does the board support the development and implementation of a core curriculum? To what extent does the core curriculum help board members to remain current in their understanding of the technology of the field and of best practices?

4. Can the board support an active mentoring program for new board members? To what extent can the board ensure the mentoring of board members who will subsequently assume vital leadership roles within the board?

5. What is the logic by which the board socializes its members into the culture of the board and into the institutional framework of the agency?

6. What developmental needs does this chapter illuminate for the board? How will the board act on these needs?

■ 15 ■

Anticipating and Planning Succession

The Members of the Board Development Committee Hold a Conference Call

Sally: It may be premature to start thinking about nominations for board leadership positions, but I think the committee should have some ideas about candidates for Robert's vice president position. We all know that Robert is ill and that he will not continue on with the board for much longer.

Ryan: John has been with us for a year and he is showing considerable interest in the agency and the board. He handles both his work and board responsibilities with a great deal of responsibility and he is always available for special projects.

Tom: John has previous board experience and we need to hold on to him. I think he will make a very good board president three years from now. He has expertise in financial planning and marketing. These are the skills we need right now and in the near future.

Sally: I propose that one of us talk with John and get his commitment to advancing within the board. We should then put together an informal mentoring plan that prepares him for an officer's position within the board. He may or may not move in to the vice president's position since that is dependent on Robert's situation. But after the mentoring plan John will be prepared for a leadership position, whatever it is.

Succession Planning as a Challenge to Board Development

The ease of succession planning and succession itself indicates the extent to which a community service board is developing the leadership it requires for effective performance (Kets de Vries, 1989). Certainly, succession planning is a challenge to board development. It requires the board to anticipate its leadership needs far in advance of people leaving key positions, and most of all it requires a board to anticipate its leadership needs in terms of institutional advancement. I have found that some boards discount succession and fail to look forward in the grooming of the future leaders of the board who will serve in critical positions to advance community service. At the time when there is a vacancy, these boards often scramble around to find the best candidate to fill the needed role.

Most likely, however, the board finds the most willing person. Other boards may simply treat succession as a pro forma activity dictated by the by-laws. These boards ensure that people are aligned perhaps as president elect or in other roles to assume officer positions in the future. Sometimes these boards are more anxious to have people designated in the line of succession and may fail to identify people who really can fulfill the future needs of the board and of the community service agency.

The importance of succession cannot be discounted. And the challenge it poses to leadership cannot be discounted. Succession is the gradual, orderly, and sequential process of change in the membership of a community service board (Hult & Walcott, 1990). It does indeed reflect the transition in governance of the board as one leader leaves a position and another assumes office. We witness this kind of orderly succession in our own government at local, state, and federal levels as executives and legislatures, council people, and mayors leave office and new ones come into these positions (Hult & Walcott, 1990).

Succession is thoughtful and deliberative in practice. The board invests considerable thought into the succession process to ensure that it is orderly and sequential. Members of the community service board have an opportunity to deliberate the kind of leadership that is needed given the direction and stage of development that characterize the board and the agency it governs. Succession is predictable; it should not catch the board by surprise. It is not crisis-oriented because even though there may be unexpected vacancies owing to a death, job change, or family situation of an incumbent, the board has prepared board members to step into critical roles and to execute them with some familiarity and confidence. And it is not haphazard. The community service board commits to a seasonal process that involves a process of identifying potential candidates from within the board, develops these candidates, and integrates them into the nomination process so they can subsequently become part of the senior leadership of the board.

Aims of Succession Planning

What is sought through succession planning and its execution? First, the community service board has available a pool of leadership from within the board to fill critical roles, which at a minimum are dictated by the board's own by-laws. I stress here that this pool is from within the board because it may weaken the board and the agency considerably if the board attempts to recruit new members who are inexperienced in the nuances, traditions, and dynamics of the board. Board development in this manner is consistent with the continuous demand placed on the board to groom its own leadership as discussed in chapter 11. Second, succession planning gives some rhythm and order to the annual work of the board. Indeed, I have found several community service boards that coordinate succession with transitions in board planning, review of by-laws, and self-evaluation so that the new leaders of the board come into office or into their terms with their own agenda for which they are responsible. Third, succession planning aims to produce for the board as a human system both continuity and change. The grooming of new leadership and its subsequent movement into key positions within the board continues and perpetuates the board as an entity. The possibility that the transition of these new leaders parallel processes of self-evaluation, planning, and legal self-appraisal creates opportunities for institutional change and development (Fombrun, 1994). Thus, board perpetuation, continuity, and change are fundamental aims of succession planning within the community service board.

Building Succession on Board Development Assets

Succession planning and the successful execution of succession amplify the role board development plays in the perpetuation and continuity of the community service board. A board that invests energy in the anticipation of board membership and the systematic and deliberate development of individual board members will reap rewards through the realization of a succession planning process that is most likely uneventful and fluid. The board development committee will have ensured that leaders are identified and prepared through continuous orientation, training and education, and most of all through mentoring in key secondary leadership roles.

A board that pays attention to its own institutional development establishes a strong identity within the board and the community service agency. A strong institutional framework to the board system means that any new leader will operate within a set of expectations for perpetuating this identity (Houle, 1997). Appraisal of the challenges faced by both board and agency will suggest the kind of functional leader needed by the board within the context of its own lifespan and the developmental tasks dictated by a particular stage of the organizational lifespan.

The board will be in a better position to identify the types of members needed in the next generation of board leadership. Indeed, one community service board, cognizant of its needs to "get back to its founding values," deliberately selected a seasoned ancestral leader to serve as president-elect. This selection was based on the idea that the agency as a whole was going to work in the next three years to solidify these values and to integrate them into the operation and performance of the agency. Purposefully matching institutional needs with succession may be one of the most powerful means for changing both the board and the community service agency.

Effective succession requires that basic board development assets be in place. The selection of new leaders does not occur in a vacuum but is informed and steered by the board's own insight into its stage of development, purpose, direction, strategies, and desired outcomes. These expectations equip the board with a set of tools to appraise its leadership needs. These expectations as a framework steering selection of these leaders, however, only will be as good as the members who are prepared to assume leadership. A principal, if not primary, asset of succession is board members who are equipped with the understanding and sensitivity to undertake the leadership roles they will move into. Succession and the development of individual board members go hand in hand.

Preparing for Succession

Development of succession planning as a process within the board can produce significant value found in the achievement of order and continuity. There are four elements critical to succession planning within the community service board.

Element 1

The development of an awareness within the board of the potential or expected turnover in the incumbents of key leadership roles. This awareness, and the anticipation it can produce among members, requires the board to prepare for these vacancies created through natural movement out of roles by members who have fulfilled their terms. It requires the board to anticipate vacancies created by those members who wish to step down from formal leadership roles, or by members who leave the board unexpectedly. The board requires time to contemplate annually the task of preparing for succession by considering the vacancies that can emerge in leadership roles, the leadership needs that the board and the agency must or wants to fulfill, and the availability of candidates who are prepared to assume leadership. The awareness of succession among the board comes early enough in the annual cycle of board work to anticipate subsequent nominations and installation of new leaders.

Element 2

Involved here is an institutional appraisal of what is needed in key leadership spots using as a reference the board's understanding of its vision for the agency, of the distinctiveness of the agency, and the platform of development the agency is negotiating. Annual appraisal of leadership needs, the identification of members who can fulfill these needs, and the matching of these members to specific vacancies form the actual content of succession planning undertaken by the community service board.

Within this element lies the scope of leadership the board requires. The board should reflect on how broad or narrow this scope is. A broad scope will require the community service board to address leadership needs created by succession of the principal board leader, that is, the president, or chairperson, executive officers of the board, and the leaders of key committees. A narrow scope of succession planning focuses only on filling those officer positions in which there will be expected vacancies. The choice about the scope of succession planning lies in the hands of board members.

A broad scope can be quite demanding and places considerable pressure on the board to generate a range of candidates for key positions. However, without this attention to filling all formal leadership vacancies that emerge within the board, the board risks injury to its own system of performance. Given the importance of committees to board performance, not deciding to bring committee leadership appointments within the scope of succession planning may reduce the continuity and momentum of board work. Some committees, I have found, may falter because they lack needed and thoughtful leadership appointments by the board as a whole.

Element 3

Another key element of succession planning involves the internal structuring of the board itself in terms of the creation of positions that are built into the structure to support the fluidity of succession. Certainly, many by-laws of community service boards call for a president-elect, which is a position that anticipates succession. The designation of this role recognizes the critical position of chair or president and the complexity inherent in preparing a new incumbent for this role. The president-elect benefits from the exposure to the board work "as if" he or she is the president without having the formal responsibilities of this role.

Community service boards can also engage in succession planning by identifying other "elect" or "quasi-elect" positions. One large community service board, for example, has created several vice president positions that anticipate succession. These positions are aligned in an orderly process with the senior vice president groomed to fill the president-elect position and the next vice president groomed to step into the role of senior vice president. This succession planning reduces much of the controversy surrounding who will move into senior leadership positions within this board. But it can produce a significant drawback. It may produce a board that is too bounded by tradition with major decisions becoming executed in predictable and routine ways. This particular board is dominated by "group think" and has not created through its own succession planning process a means of rejuvenating or renewing itself. Although its succession process has created considerable continuity in board direction and performance, this board is not able easily to chart and execute new directions for institutional development.

The creation of "coleadership" or "associate leadership" positions within board committees is another variant on the theme of the board member–in-waiting. Succession within committees can be managed by asking each committee to groom another member to take over the chair of the committee in the event a vacancy is created. The associate leader or cochair can share responsibilities for leading the committee and running actual meetings. The benefit here is that the committee will not likely experience an impasse in its work and require an immediate candidate to fill this vacancy. The cochair or associate leader has moved through a development process informally and likely has been mentored by the actual chair. The cochair is experienced in the operations, work, and dynamics of the committee, and is prepared to carry on with its work.

Element 4

The fourth element of succession planning involves the nominations process of the board. This process can be disjointed and crisis-oriented if the board has not invested energy in creating and executing a systematic process of succession planning. However, as noted previously, planning for succession as an annual process can result in a fluid and perhaps routine nomination process. The board early in its annual cycle has become aware of its succession needs and has appraised its leadership assets and requirements. It has matched these assets to its succession needs within a defined scope that may be either broad or narrow. The board also anticipates succession to a certain extent through the structuring of auxiliary leadership roles that lie in succession to principal positions within the board.

The nomination process is part of succession within the board. It defines what positions are open to succession. Thus, a board with a broad scope of succession will need to constitute a nominations slate that reflects this scope. It is likely that such a board will identify positions that move well beyond the president and key officers to flag the nominations of committee chairs, cochairs, and perhaps even the formal task leaders of the board.

Some nuances in the nomination process involve the reduction of controversy in the selection of board leaders. In a predictable succession process, members understand the board's leadership needs and the rationale for the nomination and selection of candidates. Also, in a routine succession process, members understand that a rhythm is needed in the deliberations of the board and in the work of the board committee responsible for succession. Thus, planning and preparing for succession are not one-shot processes but form a continuous responsibility of the board. What entity should handle the succession process? It is lodged logically in the board development committee. Succession planning and preparation offers a clear agenda to the work of this committee outlined in chapter 10:

- perpetuating the board through membership development,
- improving the productivity and performance of the board,
- building the knowledge base of the board and fostering leadership within the board, and
- tracking and evaluating board performance.

Succession planning is a logical outcome of a systematic approach to board development undertaken by a committee charged with perpetuating and developing the board as a system.

Conclusion

Succession can be framed as the "cycle of succession" within the board. This cycle is initiated through awareness building on part of the board as a whole in which formal leadership needs are identified and appraised. It proceeds to an institutional appraisal in which leadership needs are matched with the assets of board members. The cycle then proceeds to structuring the board for succession, the creation of a nomination slate that captures the consensus and understanding of the board, and results in the installation of new leaders in an orderly and predictable manner. The perpetuation, vitality, and viability of the community service agency lie to a great extent in the manner in which the board undertakes the planning and execution of succession.

Succession is a time of transition. It opens up opportunities to develop the agency and the board as an institution with continuity and presence in the community. It opens up opportunities for renewal and reinvention. And it opens up opportunities for the agency and its principal leadership structure, the board, to reassert organizational identity, and to push the agency ahead to new avenues of change and development.

The planning and preparation of succession should not be ignored. It is a set of elements and related activities that can be easily ignored in the process of board work. Ignoring it, however, can create peril for a board. Paying attention to it and grooming it purposefully can result in substantial developmental gains for a board.

Questions for Board Discussion

1. To what extent does the board need to address the succession of its leadership? Is the board anticipating this succession and the leadership needs it will create in the present, the near future, and the distant future?

2. In what areas will the board experience succession? What specific needs are created within the board by virtue of specific people leaving specific roles?

3. Does the board possess a succession plan that incorporates specific aims and strategies for the achievement of these aims?

4. Is the board tracking turnover within the board and reviewing this turnover on a periodic basis?

5. Is the board tracking changes in its environment and the implications of these changes for the future leadership requirements of the board and agency?

6. Does the board have procedures for preparing members for a fluid succession through the creation of associate or elect positions?

7. Has the board established a nominations process that allows it to be disciplined, consistent, and anticipatory in the identification of candidates, the preparation of slates of nominees, and the deliberation of candidates for key leadership positions?

8. What developmental needs does this chapter illuminate for the board? How will the board act on these needs?

SECTION SIX
Moving through the Cycle of Board Development

In this section, the pragmatics and particulars of board development are captured through the metaphor of a cycle with its own rhythm and tempo established by the unique character and substance of the community service board. Chapter 16 identifies the pivotal role of self-evaluation within the board development cycle and lays out the purpose and relevance of this form of evaluation to the developing board as well as the definition, aims, and process of self-evaluation.

This chapter complements the content offered in chapter 17 that addresses the board retreat. The retreat is viewed as an extension of self-evaluation and offers the board an opportunity to further reflect on the appraisal of its strengths, needs, and opportunities. The organization of a retreat is highlighted and is framed as part of a seasonal cycle of renewal undertaken by a community service board.

Chapter 18 is the capstone of the board development cycle. It examines the board development plan that can be thought of as the product of self-evaluation, the board retreat, and the formulation of the board development mission. The plan seeks to "concretize" board development into a substantive working document that identifies (1) the strengths and limitations of the board, (2) the need for board development, (3) the incorporation of the board development mission, and (4) objectives and work plans that follow from the need and mission. The plan is a reminder to the agency board that although its ultimate purpose is to govern and oversee the organization, it must reflect and act on its own development to advance community service.

■16■

Self-Evaluation of Board Development Needs

The Board Chair Discusses the Annual Report on Board Development Needs

I am excited about this year's report. The board development committee performed an important service for the board. The report identifies the many advances we have made in the area of board development. For example, we attracted five new members all of whom contribute critically needed substantive skills to the board. In addition, the board has increased the productivity of its committees. In particular, the committee on long-range planning has completed an integrated strategy on financial, facility, and technology change. And the human resources committee has brought the agency into the modern age on personnel.

As with any success, new challenges arise. Certainly the annual report on board development needs identifies some new aims the board must strive toward. The board's vision statement indicates that this agency will become known for its exemplary work in bringing the arts to people with disabilities. The agency needs new, unrestricted resources to achieve this and it is the responsibility of the board and the CEO to put this resource development in motion. The board development plan identifies this as the principal theme of the coming year. We need to build the expertise, motivation, and foresight of the board in this area. In other words, we are strong enough to become an exemplary resource development board, an achievement that will mobilize the entire agency.

Evaluation is an important activity of many boards of community service organizations. These boards devote themselves to the evaluation of agency performance in terms of the agency's financial status, the establishment and use of various policies, and the work and outcomes of the chief executive officer. Perhaps a substantial amount of time is devoted to evaluation broadly defined as judging the merit of the agency's context, inputs, products, and key organizational processes (Gray et al.,

235

1998). However, many boards may fail to include within the scope of their evaluative activities self-appraisal of their own performance.

Purpose of Self-Evaluation

Self-evaluation may be one of the most critical aspects of board development. Through self-evaluation the board initiates the process of board development. Whether undertaken in an informal or formal manner, it is through self-evaluation that the board identifies its own strengths and needs, translates these strengths and needs into strategies that contribute to board development, and formulates a mission and plan to guide the actual work of board development. Evaluation within this process of board development can be viewed as an initial part of a cycle through which a board moves to appraise its development, to formulate a direction and to plan its own development so that changes in the board are anticipated and executed with foresight and purpose.

The principal reference points for this cycle is the board-defined vision of the agency and the aspirations the board holds for the agency and for the community service in which the agency engages. This vision and the aspirations it represents are important elements of the agency's own institutional framework that offer self-evaluation a reference point for the consideration by the board of its most salient development needs. Thus, ultimately, self-evaluation enables a board to identify, analyze, and frame its most important areas of board development.

Self-evaluation offers a board of a community service agency an opportunity to reflect on its own development in relationship to the vision, aspirations, and the challenges faced by the agency in becoming a significant force in the improvement of the quality of life of people and their communities. As with any improvement process, evaluation is critical to development because it is difficult for a human system to undertake self-directed change without insight into its own needs (Stringer, 1996). Self-evaluation offers the board an opportunity to identify and contemplate its own board development mission and, therefore, precedes the formalization of the substance and content of this mission. Thus, one principal product of self-evaluation is the creation of a board development mission (see chapter 9) based on the development theme most important to board members in a given period.

Definition of Self-Evaluation

Self-evaluation of board development is defined as the board's own appraisal of its functioning and performance in relationship to where the board desires the agency to move in the execution of its vision of the people served or the principal community need addressed by the agency. The board seeks to judge the merit of its own performance as the principal governance structure of the agency and to reflect on and identify those changes needed to the board to strengthen the board as a system.

Thus, self-evaluation enables a board of a community service agency to do these things:

- Identify those needs for development that are informed by the vision of the agency and the aspirations the board holds for the agency and the people it serves.
- Actively consider the challenges the board faces and how the board needs to change to meet these challenges.
- Contemplate and reflect on the board development mission.
- Translate the identification and appraisal of board development needs into a plan that enables the board to achieve its mission.

Timing of Self-Evaluation

The timing of self-evaluation is an important consideration by any community service board. As the boards of community service agencies become more formal, typically an outcome of moving from the founding stage of organizational development to the growth and maturation or stabilization stages, they often consider their own development in relationship to the agencies they sponsor. These boards will likely consider the movement through some kind of seasonal cycle in which critical board tasks are allocated to certain periods of the year in the anticipation of producing for the agency important products such as the budget, a strategic plan, or policy review and development.

The formation of a seasonal cycle within which board and agency development tasks and activities are undertaken are characteristic of a board that is becoming increasingly thoughtful and purposeful in its role vis-à-vis the community service agency it governs. Nested within this seasonal cycle may be critical board development tasks such as board nominations, orientation, and perhaps some kind of training event. It is not surprising to learn that these tasks are not systematically identified, and organized in relationship to agency vision, aspirations, and challenges (Argyris, 1990).

A seasonal cycle of board development reinforces the ongoing work facing the board in perpetuating itself and in strengthening its performance so that it can support the agency fully in meeting successfully the challenges it faces. This seasonal cycle of board development may coincide with budget formation and with strategic planning. The cycle brings board development into the rhythm of agency development.

Board self-evaluation may be scheduled biannually or annually. Less frequent evaluations may jeopardize board performance and relevance. Those boards that wait for self-appraisal to be stimulated by an external event such as changes in the agency's policy environment, new certification or licensure requirements, or the demands of accreditation may open themselves to the loss of legitimacy and relevance. It is important to be purposeful about self-evaluation to undertake pro-active measures that are self-directed and that prepare the board and the agency to anticipate and act on changes (Argyris, 1990).

Most of the community service agencies I have worked with favor an annual self-evaluation that occupies a critical period of the board's seasonal work. For example, one nonprofit rehabilitation agency undertakes its self-evaluation in August of each year. The board has accumulated four major points of self-evaluation and now has assembled an impressive agenda of changes and a record of proactive and self-initiated board development accomplishments influenced by its own evaluation activities. The end of August has been chosen by this agency because it fits the timing of the board's institutional work. The tactical choice of August is both symbolic and substantive.

It is symbolic because this period is one of "going back to work" after the summer months. For this agency, board meetings purposefully trail off during the summer months, although board committees and task forces continue to meet. Family vacations, sporting events, avocations, and the lure of recreation may all compete during these months with formal board service. The coming of the fall season signals to the agency that work must begin again in earnest, and that attention must be paid to the vigorous and vital work of the coming months initiated by a new fiscal year. Although much administrative work has been accomplished during the summer months on such products as the new budget, human resource policies, and resource development, the fall season symbolizes the harvest of these products and the need to put them to work in the formalization of agency performance.

Symbolically, there is no better time to perform self-evaluation of board development than after a summer of productive agency and committee work. The board can use its self-evaluation to consider or reconsider the vision and direction of the agency. And it can use self-evaluation to consider its direction, and the challenges it faces by identifying and considering the improvements needed by the board to support the performance of agency in the upcoming year. This symbolism communicates to the agency that the board is cognizant of these challenges and is willing to continue its own development in service to agency development, performance, and ultimately effectiveness.

Substantively, this agency is concerned with identifying those areas of board improvement that are going to make a real impact on the performance of the community service agency it governs. For this agency, the coordination of budget, strategy, and board development makes good institutional sense because it enables the board to reflect on substantive challenges and to make the appropriate changes or improvements to the board that will empower the agency. In one year, for example, this board totally realigned its committee structure on the basis of a new agency strategy of strengthening resource development. The new committee structure reflected the corporate aim of diversifying resources through (1) business development, (2) new forms of contracts available through managed care, and (3) new campaigns to increase community giving. The new board structure was a product of self-evaluation, which in turn stimulated a search for new members, an augmentation of technical skills within the board, and the orientation and training of existing members in substantive areas of resource development.

This agency also has been successful in coordinating board self-evaluation with the evaluation of its chief executive officer. The two events occur close together based on a board premise that agency performance is a function of strong coordination of board and executive around a set of relevant agency outcomes. The board has found that when these two evaluations are undertaken close in time, the board has a better understanding of its role in the development of the chief executive officer. And the chief executive officer has a better understanding of his or her role in the advancement and strengthening of the board. The board and executive have been successful in using the period of late August to coordinate the substantive outcomes of agency strategic planning. This planning is driven by the agency vision and incorporates the improvements required of the board and the executive that are needed to advance this vision (Hinings & Greenwood, 1988).

This is a good example of how board development can be linked to agency development. They do indeed coincide and should coincide. The example illustrates that the board's self-evaluation is not undertaken within a vacuum. The theme of coordination is important. Coordination of self-evaluation with the cycle or rhythm of the year, the coordination of self-evaluation with major tasks like strategic or vision planning, and the coordination of self-evaluation with executive evaluation help the agency and board to integrate these various organizational activities. They all complement a common institutional purpose—namely, to get each major aspect of agency performance integrated so that the organization is more effective in advancing its ultimate vision of community service (Jacobs, 1994).

There is no normative framework for the timing of self-evaluation that fits all community service agencies. But all agencies need to consider the rhythm of their own annual development that typically incorporates a greater institutional cycle or framework of planning for ends, budgeting and garnering resources, monitoring performance, and evaluating both means and ends. For some, this rhythm is determined by a fiscal year; for some, this rhythm is established by the calendar year; and for others, it may be suggested by an overarching agenda of routine projects and milestone products.

Agencies will vary in their work and in their routines established to accomplish this work. Bringing self-evaluation into this rhythm and into a seasonal routine of work can serve as a resource for board and agency effectiveness. Self-evaluation as a regular event in the seasonal life of the board adds a discipline that focuses the attention of board members on how the board needs to develop in relationship to the positive difference an agency is trying to achieve in the lives of people and communities it serves.

Process of Self-Evaluation

The process of self-evaluation is initiated by the recognition of the board that it is indeed an important undertaking. This endorsement of self-evaluation reflects the board's overall commitment to board development and to the role development is assigned within the context of agency governance. Strong commitment to board development will most likely produce strong commitment to self-evaluation. Weak commitment to board development will most likely produce a correspondingly weak commitment to self-evaluation.

Boards committed to self-evaluation try it out and then, from my experience as a consultant, institutionalize self-evaluation within the context of board development. This institutionalization often is achieved through the formulation of a board policy on self-evaluation that underscores its importance to board development, the process of self-evaluation, and its use in service to board development. As the board policy on self-evaluation of a community arts program reflects, this policy makes this form of evaluation a regular feature of board work:

> It is the policy of the board of the Center City Arts Consortium to conduct an annual evaluation of its performance for the purpose of identifying essential areas of board development that are important to facilitating the agency's achievement of its vision and defining purpose in the arts. Self-evaluation will coincide with the processes of budgeting, strategic planning, and evaluation of the executive director. It will culminate in a written plan incorporating the board development mission and it will summarize substantive areas of board development.

It is noteworthy to identify and discuss each of the principal steps needed to complete the process of self-evaluation. Four steps are most salient: (1) identification of key areas of self-evaluation, (2) formulation of an approach to data collection, (3) compilation of the results, and (4) use of relevant data and information.

Key Areas of Self-Evaluation

The self-evaluation sequence can follow the content outlined in previous chapters. Self-evaluation can begin by examining and appraising the systemic framework of the board. An examination of institutional identity focuses on the clarity of purpose, overarching narrative or story, and the sense of enterprise that exists within the board. This aspect of self-evaluation offers the board an opportunity to reflect on whether the board as a whole has an overarching understanding of the agency and its role in community service. Critical here is whether the board has a foundation that will serve the board's formation of vision and direction, and whether board members have a "consensual" sense of direction. Indeed, as emphasized in previous chapters (for example, chapters 7 and 8), the formation of this agreed-on direction, based on how the board interprets or explains agency purpose, may be the most fundamental outcome of board development. Self-evaluation can reveal the extent to which the board possesses this consensual understanding.

Self-evaluation of the board's functioning may focus on the extent to which the board as a whole has incorporated those perspectives needed to foster the comprehensive development of the community service agency. Here, self-evaluation examines and appraises the extent to which the board exercises its adaptive, strategic, civil, generative, and ancestral functions. Self-evaluation can offer board members an opportunity to appraise the current status of the board in these areas, and to anticipate using agency vision, direction, and challenges as reference points for what is needed in these diverse but important functional areas.

The performance dimension of the board system can also be examined and appraised through self-evaluation. It is here that the board will evaluate the more operational aspects of its work, particularly the adequacy and effectiveness of board organization (Zander, 1993). Self-evaluation of the adequacy and effectiveness of board membership, group life, structure, network, task performance, and products can lead to critical appraisals and decisions concerning the current status of board organization and modifications that are demanded by other dimensions, the agency's environment, and the agency's vision.

It is within the performance dimension that the board may examine the contributions of individual board members versus its collective performance. There is an important subtlety here that is worth mentioning. I have found that several boards define self-evaluation as a time to focus almost exclusively on individual performance. These boards actually undertake the evaluation of each board member, and make decisions about continuing service on the board as an outcome of these evaluations. Board development here is construed as an individual issue resolved by getting more committed and devoted board members.

My work with boards emphasizes the collective product of the board as a whole (Zander, 1993). Certainly, evaluative issues pertaining to the contributions of individual board members arise, and to whether each member is "right" for the board. However, I view the evaluation of individual board members to be within the domain of developing board members, and a focus on individual evaluation at the time of self-evaluation may drain attention and energy from understanding the collective strengths and needs of the board as a whole. Thus, in this context, "self-evaluation" really pertains to the evaluation of the board as a collective entity responsible for agency governance.

The evaluation of the board as a system should also take into consideration the organizational lifespan of the agency and the board. This is a somewhat complex situation but important to considering where the "board is at" in relationship to agency direction and stage of development. Some boards discover through self-evaluation that they are truly out of sync with the agency. Often, this means that the board's development and role are well behind the development of the agency as a whole. Other times, it means that the board is out of sync with the environmental challenges and developmental challenges the agency faces (Shanklin & Ryans, 1985). A community service agency facing accreditation in the growth and maturation phase may require a board that is active in advancing the human resource policy system of the agency. If ill equipped to perform in this area, the board's leadership may prove inadequate. Most likely, this scenario is not unusual. Such situations may come to the surface when a community service agency is becoming more formal to achieve legitimacy in its policy, task, or community environments.

Self-evaluation can amplify areas that demand board attention and that are ultimately tied to the development of the board as an essential system of the community service agency. Certainly, as the board examines its own development as a system, it will likely become aware of the "development work" it needs to undertake to better define "who we are," "where we are going," "what will inspire us," and "how to judge our performance." These are substantive challenges to overall board development and emanate out of the institutional and functional dimensions of the board as a system. Opportunities for proactive development will be lost if the board does not approach these challenges through self-evaluation and self-reflection. Self-evaluation therefore needs to address the substantive areas outlined in section 3.

The self-evaluation of the board as a system and of the "challenges of board development" can lead to a consideration of those changes needed by the board to support board development as well as the development of individual board members. In terms of "supporting board development," self-evaluation can consider the strengthening of existing board leadership and the interface between the board and the agency. "Developing the individual board member" can identify the specific types of board members that are needed, the fostering of effective succession, and the ongoing mentoring, orientation, and training of key board members.

Thus, a comprehensive evaluation of board development will take into consideration strengths and needs in four key areas: (1) developing the board as a system, (2) meeting the challenges of board development, (3) supporting board development, and (4) developing individual board members.

Capturing Relevant Data and Compiling Results

I have found boards of community service agencies to differ in their preferences on how to capture data. Some boards prefer a highly structured approach to self-evaluation in which a structured and formatted questionnaire is designed and disseminated to various respondents. In other cases, boards prefer a less structured, more exploratory approach to data collection. However, in both cases it is important for a board to consider the advantages of involving a third party in the data collection process or having this third party work in a manner that is consistent with the data collection preferences of the board.

However the board undertakes self-evaluation, the reference point is the purpose and vision of the agency. Board members use this reference point to frame their immediate task, which is to evaluate those areas of development the board requires. Self-evaluation of board development can follow a traditional survey approach, but this may not get to the richness and nuances the board desires.

Although a structured survey offers an agency more economy and efficiency of data collection, a more open-ended and probing interview approach can actually turn out to be more productive. This approach requires a third party, typically a trusted agency staff member, or an external consultant or volunteer to interview each board member. These interviews can be undertaken on a face-to-face basis, by telephone, or through interactive computer technology. The aim is to identify board development challenges from the perspectives of board members, to identify their rationale for identifying these challenges, and to frame board strengths and needs from the perspective of board members. Interviewing a board of approximately 15 members can be quite challenging, but it can offer a set of very valid perspectives grounded in the experiences of a specific board.

These kinds of data—whether captured through questionnaire or interview—should lend themselves to the formulation of a tentative set of "board development needs" related to agency vision, direction, and challenges. The analysis of these data should not establish specific priorities but rather illuminate the range and variation of issues perceived and interpreted by board members, and any consistencies that cut across board members.

The compilation of results need not involve analytic rigor. The person responsible for compiling the data should be able to bring together a good listing of issues in memorandum format. Sometimes analysis is called for, such as when there is some controversy among board members about board development. In one agency, "consumer perspectives" represented on a board were perceived to be in conflict with "establishment or professional perspectives." However, when the data were analyzed using these various perspectives, the board learned that there was not much conflict in substantive issues pertaining to board development. Indeed, the majority of members were fairly consistent in identifying what they referred to as the four major overarching issues facing board development. These were (1) strengthening the performance of the board's committees, (2) creating a committee structure that was more relevant to the agency's program development challenges, (3) strengthening the information exchanged between board and agency, and (4) ensuring that all board members were oriented and trained in real time.

Compilation of results should go beyond merely an inventory of the issues faced by the board. It should also illuminate the strengths of the board. It should help the board to see itself in a balanced light, one characterized by strengths that can serve as board development assets, and needs that must be addressed to further strengthen the board. Compilation of results can serve as an information asset in that it can foster awareness of board members of the work at hand, and what must be preserved in light of further board development.

Also, compilation of results should allow a primary theme about development to emerge. It is likely that the board as a whole has discussed board development needs and issues, but perhaps not in a systematic or organized manner. The consistency of needs and issues will likely converge on a principal theme that can serve as the substantive focus and content of a board development mission. This theme converted into a board development mission can subsequently focus the attention of the board as a whole on what it is trying to achieve on behalf of the agency. "Making the agency financially viable." "Getting the word out about our effectiveness as an alternative health care provider." "Stewarding the future of the agency." "Advancing our professional standing in a changing health care environment." Various boards found these themes useful as products of their own self-evaluation and to guide subsequent board development.

Given the busy personal and professional lives of board members, it is critical that the report consolidating the data about the board's status is focused. The memorandum format is a useful one. This format can briefly communicate strengths, needs, issues, and next steps to board members and can prepare them for further deliberation of these data in a forum designed to translate these data into substantive board development aims and objectives.

Using the Data

The data are collected for one purpose—that is, to help the board to organize its thinking about its own development. The principal memorandum that serves as one important product of the self-evaluation of board development summarizes the findings. It is designed to communicate the strengths, needs, and issues framed by board members; to foster reflection on these strengths, needs, and issues; and to promote deliberation among board members about the most important objectives to establish in the area of board development. Thus, the use of these data is found in individual and group cognition concerning board development. The self-evaluation stimulates the awareness, reflection, and deliberation among board members regarding board development. The data are most relevant and effective when the board as a group can make up its mind about the possible priorities and potential objectives undergirding board development.

The self-evaluation report is disseminated to board members, committee members, task force members, and relevant staff members in the spirit of learning and in the spirit of change. The report is not and should not be a "doomsday" document designed to incite the board to action in a context of anxiety. It is part of the history and governance of the agency. It is a report to foster and facilitate decision making in a specific and discrete area: board development.

Conclusion

Table 16-1 offers an example of a board development memorandum that reports on self-evaluation data. It is designed to build board members' understanding or awareness of strengths, needs, and issues. And it is designed to foster consideration of possible substantive directions for the board. It is designed to move board members on to the next step in the process of board development. This next step is the board retreat. The self-evaluation report will assist the board to prepare for the retreat. It will help members to contemplate priorities and directions for board development. And it will help members to frame what they consider to be a limited set of the most important priorities the achievement of which will move the board ahead in its own development.

Questions for Board Discussion

1. Does the board engage in a systematic process of self-evaluation, including its need for development, its performance, and its outcomes?
2. Does the timing of the self-evaluation process coincide with other major institutional activities like long-range planning, strategic planning, budgeting, and executive appraisal?
3. Is the self-evaluation used in board decision making worded so that areas of concern or improvement within the board can be identified in relationship to the advancement of the institution?
4. Is the scope of the board self-evaluation broad enough to consider all major dimensions of the board (institutional identity, functioning, performance, system development)?

TABLE 16-1: Example of a Self-Evaluation Report to the Board of the Johnston Center

TO: All Members of the Johnston Center Board

FROM: Charles Andrews, Chairman of the Board

I want to thank all of you for your participation in our annual self-evaluation that involved an in-depth interview of each board member to identify the board's development objectives for the coming year. This document summarizes the results of these interviews and was prepared by the center's external consultant. As you know, the annual self-evaluation coincides with the evaluation of the center's president and the updating of the corporate annual plan. Each board member will receive summaries of these activities in a separate electronic transmission.

Reaffirmation of the Center's Institutional Direction

Board members share a deep commitment to the success and effectiveness of providing community health and social support services to people coping with long-term illness. Members of the board concur on the continuing relevance of the center's vision, to help each person coping with long-term illness to achieve a personally satisfying quality of life in a community of his or her own choosing. The principal aspirations of the board focus on helping recipients to define their own quality of life aims and to fashion for themselves a range of effective support services to assist them to achieve safety, satisfaction, and health in supportive community living. Board members want the center to be known as an institution that offers compassionate support to people who seek its services.

Evaluation of the Functions of the Board

In the past two years, members of the board feel that they have concentrated on securing the financial stability of the agency during a rapid and tumultuous period of change in health care practices and reimbursement systems. Over two-thirds of the board members, however, feel that this adaptive and strategic work has reduced the board's focus on its civil, generative, and ancestral functions. These board members feel that the board should encourage more community and recipient participation in the deliberations of agency policy and in the formation of its advocacy agenda. And these board members feel that the board should now focus on planning for the long-term future of the agency. This "capacity building", from the perspective of the majority of board members, should focus on the development of resources to help the agency to build and sustain critical organizational assets like recipient transportation alternatives, the acquisition and ongoing expansion of information technology, and the creation of a benefit structure to maintain an effective complement of staff members. Board members are very concerned that the agency will relax its founding values in order to adapt to the new health care environment. Thus, some board members suggest that the educational program of the board revisit these values and reinforce them.

Evaluation of the Performance of the Board

Board members perceive themselves, in the words of one member, as "a hard working bunch of dedicated leaders." Over the past two years, the board has successfully fostered a strong policy focus that has resulted in the president's completion of an excellent and relevant strategic plan. This plan has enabled the agency to position itself as a principal provider of community-based, recipient-centered, and integrated support services for people coping with long-term illness. Yet the board has not attracted new members who bring the perspectives of recipients into the governance of the agency. Also, the energy of health care advocates is missing from the board even though over the past year the board expanded its size by 25%. This expansion has added "new hands" but few board members really know one another. Consequently, an informal, friendly and warm atmosphere is missing from the board, according to the majority of members. There is a strong interest among board members in the achievement of group cohesion within the board. And current members want to lay the foundation for a long-term plan guiding the development of the agency in partnership with the people the agency serves.

Organizational Lifespan and Its Implications for the Board in the Coming Year

Board members consider the agency to be in the stabilization phase in which major threats in the current health care environment have been successfully addressed by the board and administration. A majority of board members are worried that the board and the agency will become complacent. These members want to make sure that the agency does not ignore its founding values, its aspirations for the people it serves, and the humanistic values it brings to the the provision of community health. The future is difficult to anticipate, according to these members but the leadership of the organization must use its vision to bring about a future of success and effectiveness. Modifications to the board membership to meet this challenge include (1) bringing into the board members who represent the "voice" of emerging needs in the community; (2) inducting new members who represent or who are themselves recipients; and (3) bringing into board service members who understand innovation in community health care provision and long-term community care. Many board members want to escalate "institutional aspirations" for service and product innovation.

The Theme and Objectives of Board Development

Board members endorse a theme for the upcoming year that focuses the attention of the board on leading the agency into a future of innovation in the support of people coping with long-term illness. Five objectives can guide the development of the board in the next year.

1. The board will strengthen its generative, civil, and ancestral functions by revisiting and reaffirming the founding values of the agency, involving recipients in governance, and by undertaking long-range institutional planning to keep Johnston true to its vision and purpose over the next decade.

2. The board will sponsor several informal dinners so that board members can visit, socialize, and get to know one another better.

3. The board will replace out-going members with people who are either service recipients, advocates for people with long-term illness, or knowledgeable of innovation in community health.

4. The board will revise its corporate aspirations to heighten a commitment to innovation.

5. The board will redesign its education program to incorporate and reinforce the founding values of the agency.

5. Does the board actually produce a written board development plan that identifies areas of improvement, specific aims or goals, and strategies for achieving these aims?

6. Is the board development plan monitored during the course of the year to ensure that the board makes progress? Are reports issued at relevant milestones during the course of the year to identify progress and barriers? Does the board as a whole take action to overcome barriers to board development?

7. What developmental needs does this chapter illuminate for the board? How will the board act on these needs?

■ 17 ■

Board Development Retreat

The Board Chair's Announcement of the Annual Retreat
of the Community Arts Agency Board

In previous years, the agency's annual retreat was designed as an orientation event for incoming board members. The board's progress in making
orientation an ongoing event for new and current board members elim-
inates the need to devote the annual retreat to orientation. Most of the
board members I have talked with favor a retreat devoted to the theme
of board development. In particular, the self-evaluation of board development needs undertaken two months ago illuminated members on the
necessity of the board becoming strong and effective in the competence
of resource development. This year we will experiment with a new format
for the retreat. We will focus on continuing our board development work,
focusing attention on resource development. In particular, we will achieve
four outcomes in the retreat:

1. Identify the additional members we need in order to augment the
   board's expertise and experience in the area of resource development
2. Plan a schedule of continuing board education that will increase our
   expertise
3. Identify at least two resource development projects that will serve as
   pilots of our learning effort
4. Create a board task force that will offer leadership to this area over the
   next year

We understand the importance of this retreat, particularly given the potential benefits the agency can experience from this work. Resource development is our job in the next several years and this retreat will establish the
foundation for this work to begin.

Need for the Board Development Retreat

The self-evaluation of board development undertaken by the board itself can set in motion a process of reflection on how to undertake improvement and strengthening of the board. The board development retreat complements the self-evaluation process and is, most likely, an extension of it. The retreat offers the board of a community service agency an opportunity to reflect and contemplate where the board is heading as an organizational system, how it wants to improve its performance, and the specific actions the board will undertake in the upcoming year to achieve those improvements the board desires. Thus, the board development retreat is more about the board than it is about the agency itself. I have found that many boards are involved in annual planning retreats the purpose of which is to identify agency direction and to formulate working strategies for the upcoming year (Grace, 1997a).

The board development retreat presented here, however, specifically addresses the board's performance and not the agency as a whole. It is likely that a full day is devoted to the board development retreat, and it is not unusual for this retreat to follow an agencywide planning event in which vision, aims, and plans are articulated and agreed on by agency leaders. The board development retreat naturally links with organizational planning because frequently boards want to consider how they should develop in relationship to the needs of the community service agency and the issues the organization faces in its current circumstances.

As noted previously, the board development retreat is a concentrated period of reflection, contemplation, and discussion among board members who are united in the aim to improve their performance and the performance of the board. The felt need for a board development retreat typically emerges when the agency itself is under performance pressure or the board has established high performance expectations for the agency (Light, 1998). Board members may feel that the board as a whole can improve its effectiveness, and that this is essential to overall agency success. Competent boards recognize the need to have a plan in place that will steer the development of board. An annual board development retreat offers an excellent opportunity to these boards to lay out their plans on the basis of their own self-evaluation of their performance. These boards see the board structure as an integral part of the organization and want to ensure as part of their stewardship that the board as a critical organizational system models improvement for the agency and for the community.

Other boards, ones less organized, and perhaps those plagued by fundamental performance issues, may come to recognize the board development retreat as a critical opportunity to strengthen the very foundation of the board. Self-evaluation within these boards typically highlights that the board itself has organizational problems and may be seen as unproductive. These boards may not have a clear sense of vision of the agency and of themselves. The board development retreat in this sense may be less oriented to planning and more oriented to organizational development. Nonetheless, the board development retreat offers this kind of board an opportunity to examine performance, to evaluate, and to make some critical decisions pertaining to the "next steps" of board development.

Those boards that are early in their development, ones that are parts of newly forming community service agencies, may find that the board development retreat offers an opportunity to consider the formation of the basic framework of the board. Board members can consider and select some important developmental milestones that board members feel are critical to the formation of the board in the early stages of the agency lifespan. The board development retreat in this context may be evaluative but not in the sense that an older, more experienced board uses evaluation. The newly formed board in the first several years of its development may need to evaluate where it wants to go with little knowledge of history and past achievement to guide its way.

There are three markedly different board development circumstances: (1) the experienced board using the board development retreat to engage in improvement, (2) the poorly performing board using the board development retreat to strengthen itself, and (3) the new board using the board development retreat to initiate its own developmental process. They illustrate that the retreat is useful to any community service board. This assertion may seem obvious. But I have found many boards to be pressed for time and their members to be juggling multiple priorities and responsibilities. When someone says we need a retreat, expect many board members to discount this as an important effort. Yet it is. Board members must recognize that board meetings are typically business oriented, and the board as a whole will have little subsequent time during the course of a busy year to contemplate its basic developmental and improvement aims.

Purpose and Aims of the Board Development Retreat

The board retreat serves a pragmatic purpose within the context of a focused effort at board development undertaken by the boards of community service agencies. The aims of the board retreat are threefold. First, the board retreat serves to extend the process of self-evaluation into board dialogue. Members have an opportunity to reflect on and discuss the major developmental issues facing the board. The board needs the opportunity to ground the data obtained through the self-evaluation process in the life of the board and to explore what these findings mean to the board and to the agency. Second, the board uses the retreat to link its own development to the direction of the community service agency so there is an opportunity to strengthen the institutional and organizational linkage between these two entities. And third, the board retreat offers an opportunity to make explicit the agenda of board development that will be subsequently translated into a written plan for use by the board during the course of the year. These three aims taken together illustrate again that board development is much more than merely recruiting more members. Although this is an important feature of board development, the board retreat demonstrates the need for a community service agency to consider board development as a system through the improvement of its institutional, functional, performance, and lifespan dimensions.

Board Development Retreat in Action

Particulars of the Retreat

An example of a board development retreat in action can offer a perspective on the benefits of this kind of meeting. The setting is a U.S. Midwest city and the protagonist is the board of an agency devoted to early childhood education. The agency sees itself as a major innovator in the provision of early childhood services to families of limited income and means. This is the fourth year in which the board has conducted a retreat principally devoted to the consideration of its own development. For this board, the fourth board development retreat means that this board is formulating its fourth board development plan. Historically, the agency's development was well ahead of the board's development. This occurred for a number of reasons, but it meant that the board four years ago was small, unstructured, and unproductive. The new agency director and the board president felt that the weaknesses in the board reduced the community agency's ability to attract resources, achieve its vision, and gain recognition as an important community institution. It was these needs that propelled the board into its own program of board development.

The fourth board development retreat, like the previous three, is conducted in August. The selection of this month is purposeful and timely. Board members are winding down summer vacations and routine; the agency as a whole has completed its own organizational planning in preparation for the upcoming budgeting process; and the board recognizes the need to outline its board development objectives before business meetings begin in the fall. Attendance at the board development retreat is mandatory. The scope of participation is broad, including board members, community members of board task forces and committees, and agency personnel. Those people who can help the board identify and refine the substance of board development are welcomed as participants in the retreat.

A full day is devoted to the retreat. It is held at a conference center that offers food, meeting rooms, and breakout rooms for small-group work. A former board member who is a management consultant facilitates the meeting. Board or agency leaders do not facilitate because they need the opportunity to fully participate in the deliberations of the day. Twenty-five people attend the board development retreat. This is a good showing because 30 people were invited to participate. Only two people cut short their participation and leave because of family demands.

The setting is a comfortable one. During the breakfast buffet, a briefing notebook is handed out that incorporates material previously mailed to participants and additional material on the findings of the board self-evaluation. These notebooks contain the agenda for the day:

8:30 A.M.–9:00 A.M. Welcome and breakfast buffet.

9:00 A.M.–9:15 A.M. Introductions and discussion of the expectations for the retreat.

9:15 A.M.–9:30 A.M. An overview of the agency, vision, and aims.

9:30 A.M.–10:30 A.M. Review and discussion of board self-evaluation.

10:30 A.M.–11:15 A.M. Strengths and progress of the board.

11:15 A.M.–Noon Outcomes and achievements of the board in the previous year.

Noon–1:30 P.M. Lunch and small group discussions about the challenges facing the field of early childhood education.

1:30 P.M.–2:15 P.M. Challenges faced by the agency.

2:15 P.M.–3:00 P.M. Challenges faced by the board and board development needs.

3:00 P.M.–3:45 P.M. The theme of board development for the up-coming year.

3:45 P.M.–4:30 P.M. Specific board development directions for the up-coming year and next steps in the board development plan.

4:30 P.M.–5:00 P.M. Closing remarks by the president and the chair of the board development committee.

Purpose of the Retreat

The purpose of the retreat was framed at a previous board meeting. The board carefully considered this purpose because people are being asked to take a full day out of busy schedules. The board frames the purpose of the retreat as follows:

A full meeting of the KIDS board of trustees will be convened on August 22 to evaluate the development of the board over the past year and to identify the contents of a plan for the continued development. To facilitate this planning process, a summary of data from the board members' self-evaluation questionnaires will be distributed to the board prior to the meeting. The board uses this document to stimulate discussion of the strengths of the board and its principal needs for continuous development. The outcome of the retreat will be a written board development plan that will be reviewed at the first fall meeting of the board.

The purpose of the retreat focuses on the necessity of board development as a routine and core responsibility of the board as a whole. The purpose statement of the retreat notes that the self-evaluation process will continue but with an emphasis now placed on interpretation and utilization of the findings to frame and produce the annual board development plan.

Strengths and Achievements of the Board

The board invested a good portion of the morning session in the identification, elaboration, and discussion of strengths, progress, and achievements of the board. This board has previously completed three annual board development plans. Most members are sensitive to what they have accomplished and what they have not accomplished. Many board members come with prepared talking points about what has been achieved, what was not achieved because it turned out not to be important, and what was not achieved but still remains important.

Most board members focus on those strengths and accomplishments they feel are indicative of the positive functioning of the board as a whole. In general, the board feels that it is moving in a desirable direction, that it is achieving sound coordination among its members and committees, and that it has created leadership assets, particularly those pertaining to transformational and transactional leadership. It has developed a membership that is strongly committed to and knowledgeable of the service population of the agency—young children who experience poverty or limited income. These strengths and accomplishments incorporate a mix of institutional outcomes, functional outcomes, and performance outcomes. Although the board members may not have been conscious of it, they flag strengths and accomplishments indicative of the development of the board as a system.

During the previous year, the board affirms the following achievements:

- formulated a new corporate vision and set of priorities that broadens the impact of the agency on the physical health, intellectual development, family development, and community development of the young children served by the agency (the board established a framework that moves the agency from a focus on early childhood education to a focus on and commitment to early childhood development within the context of families and community);
- formulated a long-term resource development plan that calls for the creation of family development centers for young children in high-risk areas of the city;
- realized considerable progress in the board's self-organization with the establishment of successful task forces, which completed the new corporate vision and long-term plan, and the creation and implementation of a new committee structure to advance these plans;

- reinvigorated and modified the executive committee of the board, thereby making it more efficient, increasing the capacity to monitor committees, and reducing the workload of the board as a whole;
- strengthened the interpersonal relationships among board members who now know one another better, have strong working relationships, and communicate and relate to one another outside of board meetings;
- sustained the involvement of all board members and achieved an 87 percent rate of attendance at last year's board meetings;
- formulated a corporate policy statement on the outcomes that each child served by the agency should realize and the values all members of the agency (including board members) need to incorporate into their advocacy and service work on behalf of young children living in poverty;
- organized and implemented a four-part educational series for the board, available as well to staff and community members, addressing best practices in promoting the early development of young children (over 150 people attended this educational series); and
- organized an internal board development workshop and technical assistance program on resource development in anticipation of working in this area in the next several years.

Challenges Faced by the Board

These nine achievements or outcomes represent considerable work and dedication on part of board members. And they represent considerable work and dedication on the part of community members and staff members who are involved in supporting the work and development of the board. The retreat participants remain concerned about continued board development in light of the new corporate vision and the expectations created by this vision. The participants are also concerned about continued resource availability through corporate giving programs, corporate foundations, and state departments of health, mental health, developmental disabilities, and education. Changes in federal and state human service policies may change funding streams and alter current resource channels used by the agency to advance its mission and vision.

The retreat participants affirmed that the board is not in crisis but needs to be vigilant about these environmental circumstances and their implications for the board and agency. The board desires not only to strengthen itself, but also to develop in those areas that will subsequently contribute to high performance on the part of KIDS. One of these challenges is resource development. And for retreat participants, competence in resource development requires continued board recruitment and member development. The retreat participants felt that the board must strengthen its competencies and practices in the identification of relevant members on the basis of a strategy of linking the agency to community resources through board membership. A continuing challenge to board development is incorporating within the board members from key corporations concerned about young children, members who are experienced in fund development and capital campaigns, and members who are knowledgeable of best practices in early childhood intervention.

Retreat participants also identified a future threat to the viability of the board. A number of board members are reaching the limits of their tenure as specified by the by-laws of the board. Numerous people registered concern about the loss of these members. Succession planning was discussed as one way of addressing this concern, and there was considerable dialogue about how the board, relatively inexperienced in succession planning, can go about this process with an eye to grooming and fostering future leadership. In addition, retreat participants discussed the potential modification of the by-laws to eliminate terms of service and substitute an annual evaluation of performance that could determine whether or not a person continues in his or her board service.

Retreat participants also shared their concerns about the "board–agency" interface and the continued pressure placed on agency staff to respond to the information, technical, and logistical needs of a growing, more productive, and more involved board. Building an effective board–agency interface is identified as a priority. Discussed at the retreat was the timely delivery of materials, products, and assistance board members require to perform. Other issues identified as challenges include helping board members to obtain and maintain an understanding of KIDS and the environment the agency faces, deploying and advancing the vision of KIDS, and continuing to refine the roles of the executive committee and the board working committees.

Board Development Needs

The deliberation about strengths and accomplishments and the discussion of board development challenges offer retreat participants an opportunity to enumerate current board needs. The retreat participants produced nine of them:

1. strengthening the board–agency interface by getting information needed by the board to members more quickly and in a timely fashion to facilitate processing of board material prior to meetings;
2. continuing to refine norms among board members about what is considered to be "good" board performance (this involves clarifying expectations and forming a list of expectations that are endorsed by the board as a whole, and using the evaluation of the board and of board members to identify the extent to which these expectations are relevant and achieved);

3. continuing to institutionalize the board educational program so that it incorporates relevant and vigorous continuing orientation of all board members (retreat participants identified the need for an efficient continuing education program that builds the resource development competencies of board members, periodic workshops that keep board members informed about advances in early childhood intervention and development);

4. continuing to expand the information dissemination effort within the board so that all board members are aware and understand what the agency does, what its staff does, what specific programs do, and the budgeting frameworks and requirements of the agency's principal funders;

5. clarifying the board's policies and plans relating to resource development and framing the roles of board members in resource development;

6. creating an explicit plan for succession and the grooming of board leadership to fill critical roles within the board when they are open or vacated;

7. establishing a written board recruitment plan (the plan is to identify the qualities of good candidates and expand the number of active board members; it will incorporate an identification of strategic sectors of the community that need to be represented within the board and those qualities of diversity that the board seeks to incorporate);

8. continuing to refine and expand the board's information system to capture critical financial information in ways that promote decision making, facilitate the evaluation of the agency vision and mission, and understand programmatic performance and the impact of programs on the well-being of young children and their families; and

9. continuing to maintain the board as an active, viable, and exciting organizational structure that contributes "high energy" to the productive work of the agency.

Board Development Theme for the Upcoming Year

The retreat participants reflected on strengths, challenges, and needs they outlined during the previous sessions of the meeting. They were impressed by how board development is never completed and the manner in which ongoing improvement requires the board to consider continuously how it needs to function and perform in relationship to its vision of advancing the well-being of young children who live in poverty. Retreat participants also assert that the board cannot overlook the vision of KIDS, and how the board as a whole needs to be conscious of this vision, as the board executes its work and responsibilities.

The retreat participants recognized another nuance of board work. Board members must integrate the work of the board in a manner that makes an impact on the work of the agency, principally an impact on the achievement of mission and the advancement of vision. In reflecting on the theme of this year's board development work, retreat participants sought this connection: The board does not stand independent of the agency as a whole. It must be integrated.

Retreat participants felt that they needed a theme to focus the work of the board. They wanted to use the board development theme to bring them into focus and to make sense of the successes, challenges, and needs they spent a considerable portion of the day reviewing and discussing. The current momentum of the board was something they sought to preserve in the upcoming year. They also knew that the agency was advancing a new vision and a new set of outcomes and this created challenges for board development that needed to be addressed and met successfully.

What was this theme? The retreat participants decided that the board development theme for the upcoming year was "Becoming a Child-Focused Board." In previous years, the board was more focused on establishing itself as a viable structure within the agency. Now it was time, according to retreat participants, to bring young children into the center of the work and purpose of the board of this agency. This was not to say that the board was not focused on children. Indeed, many of the members come with a deep commitment to young children and to their families, and are sensitive to the ravages and injustices created by poverty. It was time to begin to unify the board around the new vision and to learn to work as a group or system fully conscious of the vision it was seeking to bring about through the agency's efforts.

This theme offers the board and its members a shorthand about what it is trying to achieve. This shorthand began to create some heated dialogue among board members attending the retreat. Members asked for the vision statement. They wanted to know something about its substance. They wanted to revisit it and to begin to make sense about how this vision will be incorporated into the work of the board. Members started to talk among themselves. A moment of doubt began to pervade the retreat. Can we really do this? Can we make this happen? How do we need to develop to make this vision of young children the center of board work?

Board development does indeed create controversy. Perhaps without this controversy and the creative energy it releases, little momentum may emerge within the board. Using the theme to frame the next steps in board development will likely create controversy because board members begin to understand that the quest for board development continues, and the board itself is embarking on a new platform of agency change.

Direction of Board Development

This is a long day. The retreat participants have been productive and have committed themselves to obtaining a sense for how board development will proceed in the next year. They have mustered a considerable amount of information concerning strengths, achievements, challenges, and needs. And they have created some controversy by setting forth a bold but brief theme that can guide the board development effort they will undertake.

The retreat now enters its closing phase. The participants are working in small groups to frame what they consider to be the direction of board development in the next year. They are formulating this direction mindful that they want to create a board that is "child focused"—one inspired by the new vision of this community service agency. The direction they frame will be a collection of aims informed by this theme. What does the board need to do to become child focused? The various small groups complete their work and they come together into the large meeting room. Each group has several minutes to outline its direction, and then the retreat participants reflect on these various directions. There is considerable overlap among these various directions and it is not difficult for the retreat participants to achieve a commitment to six board development aims:

1. Strengthen the internal deployment of the new vision within the board and ensure that board members understand the substance and rationale of the vision.
2. Support the development of board committee objectives and work plans that make an impact on the vision of the agency.
3. Strengthen and refine the board information system as it pertains to the achievement by the agency of outcomes relevant to the vision of KIDS.
4. Undertake a continuous process of board member recruitment of people who can add perspectives, skills, capacities, and contacts relevant to the advancement of the agency's vision.
5. Groom potential board leadership who can subsequently advance into important board positions and maintain continuity in the agency's vision.
6. Link the resource development competencies of the board to the advancement of the agency's vision.

Conclusion

The work of the retreat is now completed. The retreat agenda is completed and the retreat participants have framed the substance of the board development plan for the coming year. It is now time for the next step. A small time-limited task force will take the proceedings and deliberation of the retreat and shape the actual board development plan. The plan will be written and will be examined at the next scheduled board meeting in September. The board will have an opportunity to review the board development plan, correct any inconsistencies or errors, and make recommendations for its modification or improvement. After the revisions are completed and board approval is secured, the plan will become a standing document of the board.

The board development retreat can stand as a major milestone of an agency's annual work. It is such a milestone in the life of KIDS. The board development retreat stands as an annual opportunity to reflect on what the board has done, what the board is doing, and how the board can renew or revitalize in service to the agency. The board of KIDS is creating its own history within the minds of the participants who are committed to the advancement and success of the agency, and who are ultimately animated and inspired by the positive vision the agency has created to direct its work.

The pragmatic aims of the board development retreat focus on the identification and appraisal of content for the board development plan and the establishment of the direction that board development will take in the next year. The retreat contributes to other aims as well—ones that are not as formalistic as those I articulated previously, but nonetheless one should not discount them. These aims pertain to the fostering of relationships among board members and between board members and agency personnel. The board retreat itself can strengthen the interface between the board and the agency and reduce the social distance between those who occupy governance roles and those who offer services and who perform the agency's work. The board retreat can promote a general understanding of the work of the agency and, therefore, can offer informal orientation to those individuals who are not fully aware of what is happening within the agency and within its environment. In addition, the board retreat can inspire—it can remind people why they have affiliated with the agency and, as a result, renew commitment.

Finally, this case example is not atypical of community service boards. Community service agencies often pose bold visions and seek to make a positive difference in the lives of people they serve. Of course, the board work described in this chapter happened because this board is fulfilling its institutional responsibilities in relationship to the agency. It has pondered critical values and it has identified its aspirations for the young children who are the focus of agency work. They possess a vision that can become the center of board work. And they possess a vision that can influence, if not direct, board development. The board development retreat does not happen in a vacuum. It is not a one-time-only event to be undertaken in crisis or when boards flounder. The retreat truly represents a developmental process and is animated by the desire on the part of board members to improve the performance and functioning of the board in service to a larger cause.

Questions for Board Discussion

1. Is a retreat process in place so that the board can gather annually to review board development and to create the framework of the subsequent board development plan?

2. Does the retreat occur in coordination with other major planning events so that board development is well coordinated and integrated with other benchmarks of governance, such as the annual agency plan?

3. Are the purpose and aims of the board development retreat carefully considered and identified? Is a theme useful to the advancement of board development established to move the board forward in its planning?

4. Is adequate time devoted to the actual retreat? Are most members available to attend the retreat?

5. Does the retreat's agenda truly focus on board development and not on agency planning? Does the board have opportunities for identifying and discussing its strengths and achievements? Does the board have opportunities to examine next steps in board development in relationship to the vision of the agency?

6. To what extent does the board have opportunities to frame the challenges it faces on the basis of its strengths and direction? Does it have opportunities to link these challenges to the need for board development?

7. Does the board make explicit the direction it wants to take by the end of the retreat? Does it have a specific agenda of board development by the end of the retreat?

▪18▪

Board Development Plan

Executive Summary of an Agency's First Annual Board Development Plan: Purpose of the Board Development Retreat

The Board of Directors of Venture Employment Services met on Saturday, September 24, 2005, to conduct a self-evaluation of its performance, productivity, and effectiveness during 2005. The meeting offered the board an opportunity to conduct a summative appraisal of its work during the course of the year and to identify improvement issues that can be prioritized and converted into objectives. Thus, the evaluation and the identified issues enable the board to establish an agenda for board development and improvement for 2006. This retreat is timely. There will be continued expansion of services and the addition of new programmatic elements. The board appreciates that the agency has much to offer the community in the creation of vocational and employment opportunities for people with serious mental illness. The board identified its responsibility to guide the development of the agency and, therefore, prioritizes board development in 2005.

Summary of the Board Development Retreat
An important question is whether the current board size identified in the by-laws is sufficient to undertake the range of work and address the problems facing the board. Several board members feel the board should expand its size in order to compensate for attendance patterns, the introduction of a diverse pool of members and expertise, and the ability to activate all of the current committees designated by the board (Finance, Human Resources, Board Development, Facilities, and Program). The Board Development Committee has prepared a plan supporting an aim of intentional and guided board expansion. In addition, requisite policies and procedures are in place to recruit, add, and develop new members.

Implementing an active committee structure requires each committee to have a clear charge, purpose, mission, and agenda of work. Resource development, marketing, and business development are critical board responsibilities that must be addressed through the committee structure in the next year. The board underscored the necessity to expand the availability of staff members to work with committees within their respective areas of expertise so that the Chief Executive Officer is not the only agency administrator available for committee assignment.

The board chair raised an important question: "Who is responsible for preparing the agency for the future?" The absence of a timely response appears to be a significant gap in the work and structure of the board. Board members agree that this must be addressed in the coming year.

Specific Board Development Issues for 2006

1. Board Development [Structure, Composition, and Productivity]
   The board will activate all designated committees to promote the productivity of these committees, to consider and reevaluate the charges to these committees, and to consider their staffing needs.

   ■ The board will expand its size using a specific strategy to attract committed individuals who represent key sectors of the community, including media, legal services, or business.
   ■ The board will incorporate futures planning and environmental scanning, and will make these functions visible aspects of board performance. At this time the board has not decided whether it should incorporate these functions into existing or new committees.
   ■ The board will strengthen the board orientation and training process to ensure that all board members gain the requisite knowledge of Venture's business domain.
   ■ The board will clearly define member responsibilities, performance, and organizational role expectations through board job descriptions.

2. Institutional Planning
   The board will update the agency's vision that projects the organization into the future and that serves as a framework guiding program development.

   ■ The board will examine business development and the creation of a consumer-run enterprise.
   ■ The board will prepare a long-range institutional plan guiding the future of the agency.

3. Corporate Visibility and Marketing
   The board will formulate a policy relevant to promoting the dissemination of the agency's work to interested publics in the county, region,
   state, and nation.

   ■ The board will adopt a plan organizing and integrating marketing
   strategies with the aim of making Ventures more visible in communities and sectors critical to the organization's effectiveness.

The executive summary presented above offers an example of the first board
development plan undertaken by Ventures Employment Services (hereafter, "Ventures"). The board development plan is a product of the board's self-evaluation
and retreat, a process that the board has repeated now for the past four years. The
board found the preparation of the first plan to be an awkward experience primarily because board members never thought of themselves as fulfilling active and
visionary roles on behalf of the agency. This board found itself over the years drift-
ing without a strong identity and without a strong sense of its role in governing
Ventures, a small but vital resource to people struggling to find employment in a
community experiencing substantial socioeconomic change and disruption. Why
did the board commit itself to the formulation of a plan the purpose of which is to
develop and improve the board as a principal agency system? A new board chair
who was deeply committed to the advancement of the well-being of people with
serious mental illness (particularly through vocational development) pointed out
to the board and to the agency that the organization was promising more than it
was delivering. A strong partnership between the board chair and the chief executive officer set the agency on a new pathway toward revitalization and excellence.

But this is merely background. Each community service board needs to define
for itself the scope and substance of its own development. The cycle of board development outlined in this section is only a tool to serve this end. Indeed, each board
must define whether or not it will even engage in development. For Ventures, the
board realized that the aspirations and expectations of the agency were not being
met. Introspection on the part of board members revealed that they could not hold
the agency personnel accountable until they became accountable for the fulfillment
of their roles as stewards.

As the Ventures board began to look forward, it saw that the environment of
psychiatric rehabilitation was becoming increasingly complex and turbulent. The
board did not want to preside over vision failure. Neither did the board chair.
And neither did the executive director. So the board launched its own process of
development. I find it both interesting and encouraging that the board development process and the resulting board development plans undertaken by Ventures

in subsequent years have become broader in scope, bolder in content, and more demanding of high performance on the part of the board. The board of Ventures has progressed from board development plans that focus on building and strengthening the identity of the board to ones that address the strengthening of the board's infrastructure through membership development, creation of committees, and productivity enhancement.

The most recent board development plan demonstrates that this board is embarking on a new direction in its self-development and improvement. The new board development plan focuses on the manner in which the board will make substantive impact on the agency. This impact is expressed through capital improvements, acquisition of resources, and the movement to a new campus of buildings consistent with the vision of vocational development the board and agency has refined now over the past four years.

It is not my intent to belabor the experience of the Ventures board. The story merely stands as an exemplar of a board that committed itself to a developmental process not only in service to the agency, but also, more important, to people with serious mental illness who can be easily displaced by social and economic change. This example offers some ideas about the board development plan that can be generalized to the work of other community service boards. One generalization is that there are several different types of board development plans that boards can consider when thinking about the kind of plan they want to put in place. A second generalization involves the recognition that there is no correct way of formulating a plan. Boards can consider multiple elements stretching along a continuum of formality. The board development plans of some boards will be quite informal and unstructured whereas for others the plans will be quite formal and structured. There are no prescriptions here. Each board has to form a plan that fits its spirit and its culture. Each board needs to craft a plan that gives direction to its improvement. The third generalization is the most important one. It is one thing to have a board development plan. It is another thing to make use of it. Board development plans, like any plan, need to be used and this requires oversight, monitoring, and milestone evaluations. This chapter discusses each one of these generalizations.

Types of Board Development Plans

Institutional Plan

My own consultation work with community service boards suggests three types of board development plans. Please accept these as pure types that can be modified or changed on the basis of the needs and situations of particular boards. The three types offer board members models that can be considered when formulating a board development plan.

Many boards will find the institutional plan to be a relevant type, particularly those boards that are newly forming, or those boards that feel that they are adrift. The institutional plan reminds a board that one of its essential responsibilities is to strengthen the agency's identity achieved through the execution of critical decisions defining purpose, vision, beliefs, aims, and direction. The reader will see that the executive summary of the Ventures board development plan possesses an institutional flavor. The board members recognize the importance of revitalizing or even reframing the vision of the agency, and of formulating a long-range institutional plan.

The institutional plan requires the board to reflect on what the agency is about. It requires the board to examine changes and challenges, to clarify core competencies, and to tap into the hopes and aspirations of the community and of the people who experience the social problem or social needs the agency seeks to address. As emphasized previously (such as chapters 3 and 7), the board that is confused about its direction, or the board that has lost its direction, cannot offer relevant leadership either from a stewardship or trustee perspective. Boards in these kinds of situations have to lay the foundation and to create the framework that offers meaning to the agency as a whole. It is my experience that agency members, funding sources, and the people served by the agency will welcome this kind of board development. It announces to all stakeholders that the board has accepted its responsibility to steer the direction of the agency.

Also, the boards of those community service agencies that find themselves in situations characterized by environmental change and turmoil may want to consider the formulation and completion of an institutional plan (O'Toole, 1995). Substantial change in an agency's environment signals a need to at least review, reevaluate, and reconsider the institutional framework of the community service organization. Changes in environment can influence how community service is defined and undertaken within a broader context. Thus, the institutional plan is important to ensuring the relevance and coherence of the agency.

Infrastructure Plan

The Ventures board has also formulated a plan that speaks to the improvement of the board's infrastructure. Indeed, the plan summarized at the beginning of the chapter focuses more on infrastructure development than it does on institutional development. *Infrastructure* refers to the structures "lying below" or composing the board system, and supporting the work and performance of the board. The Ventures board development plan speaks to a number of board members and their substantive expertise, activation of committees, introduction of new committees, introduction of staff positions to committees, and the extent of performance that each board member undertakes.

The infrastructure plan requires the board to revisit the performance dimension of the development of the board as a system. Some of the important variables composing this dimension, as outlined in chapter 5, include membership, group life, formal structure, networking, the formalization of task, and the product of board work. These infrastructure variables support the execution of priorities and the arrangements of work and support board productivity. Those boards that are not performing or that have poor records of productivity will want to consider an infrastructure plan. This plan does assume that the board understands its direction and where it wants to take community service and the agency that engages in this service.

Many boards will find themselves formulating these kinds of plans. They will want to link vision to performance and to formulate a plan designed to achieve their priorities and guide the execution of these priorities in action. Those boards that feel a sense of stagnation will want to identify how they will organize to execute the direction they have set. They will be interested in creating an infrastructure that strengthens performance.

The content of the infrastructure plan speaks to performance directly and identifies the action steps the board needs to execute to become effective. Note in the executive summary of the Ventures board that the need for committee performance is raised several times. For this board, active and contributing committees are needed to move the agency along its own path of development. And for this board, without committees, the priorities of the board will not be met.

A focus on infrastructure will always be salient in a committed and high-performing board. This kind of board becomes concerned about alignment. It wants to ensure that there is a connection between where the agency is going (that is, direction) and the ability of the board to move it in the desired direction (that is, performance). Most discussions of high-performance systems require this kind of alignment. Direction and performance need to be integrated to get somewhere important (O'Toole, 1995). "Moving" a system is indeed a complex undertaking. It gives good reason to a board to create a plan that will accomplish this challenge. The infrastructure plan can be seen as a collection of tactics needed to perform in a manner consistent with the strategy of the community service agency that surfaces when the board is clear about its institutional direction.

A well-executed infrastructure plan will raise the standing of the board in the eyes of internal and external stakeholders. Certainly possessing an institutional direction is critical to board credibility. But people and groups will recognize the serious posture of the board when they see that it intends to perform effectively and executes a plan in a disciplined manner. The creation of board infrastructure communicates that the board is serious about its role. And it is to be taken seriously both inside and outside of the community service agency.

Substantive Outcome Plan

A strong, vital board is able to progress in its development to a point where it can begin to achieve those outcomes that improve agency performance and community service. The Ventures board development plan focuses primarily on infrastructure. This plan is not outcome-based because it does not speak to those outcomes that the board will bring about on the part of the agency. However, the Ventures board did evolve in this direction. Its most current plan speaks to the achievement of specific outcomes on behalf of the people the agency serves. Achievement of these outcomes will enable the agency to make progress toward its vision.

The most recent plan adopted by the Ventures board captures the substantive outcomes the board will produce on behalf of the agency. This is the fourth annual board development plan the board has formulated. The three previous plans focused on infrastructure development. Four years ago the board was small and basically ineffectual. Its own focus was to maintain some sense of legal accountability. The proactive development of the board over the past three years has strengthened its infrastructure substantially and this has resulted in a board that can increasingly take on challenging tasks. This disciplined and sustained work enables the board to now focus on outcome. As revealed by the following segment from its board development plan, Ventures is now ready to address priorities critical to the advancement of agency practice and impact. The board identifies the five principal outcomes or ends that will ensure that the agency achieves and aligns its infrastructure development objectives with these priorities. This then coordinates board development with the improvement ends sought by the agency.

Priority I/Facility Development
Facilities will be developed to serve as the principal corporate, programmatic, and satellite locations of Ventures Employment Services and to accommodate the growth needs of the agency through the end of the next decade.

Priority II/Information Technology
Ventures will be an agency that acquires and uses state of the art information technology in the execution of its mission as an exemplary rehabilitation facility.

Priority III/Human Resource Development
The human resource development system of Ventures becomes an agency asset that is characterized by the use of best practices, the installation of a viable approach to professional development, and competitive staff salaries and benefits.

Priority IV/Employer Development

Ventures will form and sustain relationships, alliances, and collaborative activities with members of the business community that will create substantial employment options relevant to the choices of the people the agency serves.

Priority V/Resource Development

A sustained, multiyear capital campaign will produce the resources needed to fulfill the facility, technology, and human resource development needs of Ventures Employment Services.

To act on these priorities, the Ventures board plans to expand its board size again by adding members who offer substantive expertise in the new priority areas. In particular, the board wants to attract members who understand information technology and its acquisition. The board will augment its membership in the area of capital campaigns and will strengthen the board's training in this key area of performance. The current board development plan also recognizes that these priorities will remain relevant over a three-year period. As a consequence, the board will prepare for succession to ensure that the leadership is in place to sustain these priorities and to ensure that there is continuity in the policy agenda of the board.

The substantive outcome plan is relevant to a board that makes a commitment to achieving specific and valued ends on behalf of a community service organization. It does require ends that are relevant to the agency's situation. Most important, however, it requires a preparation and readiness on the part of the board to make a substantial difference in the performance of the agency itself. Thus, as noted above, it is not unusual for a board to spend sometime focusing on its own development as a system before it progresses on to an outcome plan.

Elements of the Plan

A plan has to be right for a board. Thus, it is important for a community service board to consider the form and substance of the plan at the time the basic decisions are made about its content. This means that some time is devoted at the board development retreat to consider the question of how the actual plan is to be prepared, by whom, and how much detail it will contain. Some boards like brief statements and will opt for a bulleted format that summarizes what the board seeks to achieve in terms of its own development or a list of action steps. Other boards want development plans that spell out all of the details about what the board will achieve, key responsibilities of board members and others, and a timeframe guiding the work of the board. These plans also will outline the projected activities organized under each priority, objective, or achievement. Boards can consider their own styles when making these decisions. What is important, however, is that each board adopts a format it will actually use in practice.

Increasing the specificity of the board development plan requires a formalization and projection of ends and means. A board will want to make statements about what it seeks to achieve and perhaps justify these ends in relationship to where the board is in its development and where it projects its destination by the end of the plan's timeframe. These ends can be linked to the overarching theme of the board development that will coordinate the actual plan. In the first year of one board's work, successfully addressing the theme of "Establishing Our Vision of Involving Youth in Community Service" built a foundation for the following year's theme of "Building an infrastructure of board performance and productivity." The third-year theme was impact oriented, focusing on demonstrating the effectiveness of the agency in helping high-risk youths achieve positive outcomes through community service. The theme of the plan itself can become a metaphor helping board members as individuals and as a group to be mindful of what board development means in any given year.

Other elements of the board development plan have been suggested already:

- Specific aims or goals of board development in a given year
- Specific activities the board will undertake to achieve the ends of board development
- Desired end state or outcome that will be produced
- Roles and responsibilities of board members and committees in completing activities and in producing outcomes
- Supports that are needed by board members and committees to complete their assigned duties and to perform in a productive and effective manner

Using the Board Development Plan

Putting the board development plan to use is a critical aspect of the board development process. Perhaps one of the most important contributions of the plan to the board is that it helps members to achieve a focus on the role and performance of the board. It also helps members to consider the manner in which the board needs to change to serve the community service agency more thoughtfully. The written plan is a reference point for the board that can easily drift away from board development if there is not some kind of statement that members can refer to during the course of the year.

Hopefully, once the board development plan is in place, it captures the imagination of board members concerning what the board can do in advancing community service. The process of board development can have an aesthetic quality. The process itself can generate action spurred on by feelings of excitement, pleasure, and satisfaction for people who come to the leadership of a community service agency because they are most likely stewards. They are people who seek to serve and want, most likely, to obtain some level of personal gratification.

Further understanding of the plan by board members is achieved by using it as a tool to guide board deliberations. Using it regularly to frame dialogue and to guide action infuses the plan itself with value. Putting the plan on the shelf is problematic. This result can deflate even the most vigorous process of board development.

How can the plan be put to use to advance board development? The board needs to monitor all development activity. Thus, a monitoring process is essential. This process incorporates time devoted to board development on the standing agenda of board meetings. It involves regular discussion of progress made and barriers experienced, and it includes written reports offered to the board at milestone periods of the year to highlight the progress (or lack of progress) in the area of board development.

The formalism of the monitoring process is not what counts. It is the energy and focus given to this process that is important. Monitoring board development like other board activities becomes important when leadership takes it seriously. The board chair is one of the most important positions to the monitoring of board development. The more the board chair pays attention to board development during the course of the year, the more the board as a whole will likely attend to board development tasks. A well-respected board chair will command respect for board development. The board as a whole and its members will take cues from the board chair. If the board chair overlooks or ignores board development, the board will likely fail to invest much energy in it. A board chair that uses and attends to the plan will motivate other board members to do likewise.

Remember also that there are other leaders who are important to the successful monitoring of board development. The board development chair must feel a strong sense of responsibility for the execution of the plan. Most likely, it is this chair who will have the principal responsibility for monitoring. It is likely that the chair will assign responsibilities and sustain the momentum of board development. The chair will probably deliver the reports to the board and identify successes and barriers. Like the board chair, the person responsible for board development can push the process on by making it a priority and by investing in it a high level of enthusiasm.

The board must also monitor its success at board development. Considerable change can result from the successful execution of the board development plan (O'Toole, 1995). New faces will appear at board meetings. New members will mean more board education, more mentoring, and more orientation. New structures may emerge requiring changes in agenda, new leadership development, and new reports. The emerging complexity of the board may change the atmosphere of the board and the way it "feels" and is experienced by seasoned board members. These developments can introduce novelty and innovation into the board and spark strong feelings about change (Eadie, 1997). A well-implemented board development plan will mean that a new board is evolving.

Board members will likely have mixed reactions to this change. Some members can be dismayed that the old traditions and ways of doing things give way to new traditions and new norms introduced by newcomers. Other members will have different reactions, hopefully positive ones. Again, this raises the idea of change and it will make visible the resiliency of the board or its lack of resiliency in addressing this change (Eadie, 1997).

The board needs to monitor these developments and devote some time to considering how the board is changing (Shanklin & Ryans, 1985). This real-time reflection can be handled on an informal basis (Jacobs, 1994). Board leaders can reflect on how the membership drive is changing the tone and substance of board members. They can identify how they feel about this and the board can respond by preserving some stability and some traditions in the face of these changes. A small segment of a board meeting can be devoted to these reflections. But such reflection does not have to take place each meeting. Indeed, the rate of change will probably not warrant this. Periodically, the board can plan for these reflections and examine their implications for the modification of the board development plan. The plan is not immutable. It can be modified during the course of the year on the basis of the board's experience with the implementation of the plan.

The monitoring routine or procedures the board establishes should also consider how successes are handled. Another way to deflate board development is to ignore the successes, especially the small ones. The board development committee or task force can identify small but inspiring ways to recognize the accomplishments of the board. For example, one board development chair uses the first meeting of a newly recruited board member as a welcoming event. Board members share a small cake to celebrate the person's membership on the board and the assets the person brings to board service. The celebration recognizes the people who recruited the board member and who oriented the member to the board. The use of food, announcements, and small presents are useful ways to recognize accomplishments. Recognition keeps the monitoring process alive. It also invests the process with energy and helps the board to highlight what has been achieved.

Finally, the board development plan can be used as a framework of board self-evaluation. It becomes an excellent tool to appraise what the board has accomplished during the course of a year. A board committed to a multiyear process of board development will find that the current plan builds on the previous plan. Evaluation of the accomplishments helps board members to understand how much developmental activity they can handle in a given time period. It helps board members to understand the barriers they experience in achieving board development outcomes. And it helps board members to gauge what they need to undertake in subsequent years. This realization can make the board more sensitive and wiser in the important area of board development.

Conclusion

The preparation and use of the board development plan indicates that a community service board is committed to the process of its own development. The process does demand considerable work. It requires the board to initiate this work through reflection on its hopes and aspirations for the agency and for community service. The development plan requires a board to identify how it wants the board to change and to become mindful that this change is based on a direction the board wants to take the agency.

The substance of board development cannot be prescribed by an outsider or by the executive director. The conception of board development, the commitment to it, and the direction it takes emerges within a caring board. A caring board then takes this to the next step: to formulate an actual plan guiding board development.

The board development plan becomes truly an asset to the community service agency when it helps to integrate the board with the organization. The board's conception of development is based on its understanding of where the agency will go in the future, and it links the present situation of the board and agency to forward movement toward a valued and visionary end. Thus, perhaps the most important quality of the board development plan is that it helps board members to become mindful of how the board must change to anticipate future agency success. The plan can become a driving force of governance. And the plan can serve the purposes of stewardship. Changes to the board system are intentionally undertaken in service to the cause of community service the agency embodies.

Questions for Board Discussion

1. Imagine the content of your first board development plan. What is its theme? Why do you choose this particular theme?
2. What kind of board development plan should your board prepare? Should you place emphasis on institutional development, on the development of board infrastructure, on the advancement of board impact on the agency and its vision?
3. How formal do you envision your board's plan to be? Is it highly structured and formal complete with timelines, roles and responsibilities, and action steps? Or is it, rather, unstructured and informal? What style fits your board? What kind of plan with help your board to be effective in the area of self-development?

4. How do you see using your board development plan? How will members incorporate it into the routine of your board work?
5. Who will offer leadership to ensure that the board development plan is used? How will your board ensure that it remains relevant and viable?
6. How will your board sustain its momentum in board development? How will it ensure that the plan is brought to fruition? Are there any special arrangements, events, or reports that the board needs to incorporate to ensure that the plan is implemented successfully?

JOURNEY WITHOUT END

During the course of their work, community service boards will find that board development is a never-ending journey. Because board development is a commitment to ongoing improvement, members of community service boards will find what everyone finds out when they commit themselves to the pursuit of quality. It is a "race without a finish line," to invoke Schmidt and Finnigan's (1992) statement about quality improvement. Some board members will find this observation a burden. Others will assert that board development will lose importance as a community service board puts its house in order. Other board members recognize what the journey is all about. Community service in the United States is characterized by an ever-changing horizon. This horizon goes through a metamorphosis as expectations of what community service means change (sometimes quite dramatically), as conceptions of what community services should achieve change, and as expectations about agency performance change.

Public perceptions and public support are crucial to the establishment of this horizon. And the nature of society and the changes and challenges society faces become instrumental in shaping and forming this horizon (Sklar, 1995). Indeed, community service agencies exist because of change. Social change creates social needs. Change creates the principal markets of community service. Community service agencies perform in dynamic and turbulent environments. The ability to change and the ability to create become core competencies of any successful organization committed to the advancement of community service in whatever form it takes (Eadie, 1997).

These observations may frustrate the members of community service boards. "No one told me that I would need to have a constant vigilance about this stuff," one very well-meaning board member shared with me in a voice punctuated by desperation. "Our executive vice president at the firm told me that community service would be an asset on my record and I would just be involved in several evening meetings during the course of the year." "But this is hard work." Board development is hard work. And it is a journey without an end. However, it does have milestones along the way. The process of board development offers destinations each year that, when they are achieved by the community service board, can produce excitement and satisfaction. Personal and group satisfaction are products of a well-executed plan. A good plan also raises expectations about the next year. And the next year. Shall I go on?

"But you know," another board member pipes in,

> we sure do get a lot done now. I like paying attention to the agency's future. I like contemplating our vision, aspirations, and expectations. I like talking with the executive director about where we are going, why we should go there, and what community service is all about. This kind of work gives me a great deal of pleasure. This is what I enjoy about community service. One time I thought board service was about using my auditing skills to help staff members with the financial system. I gave this up three years ago when the agency achieved an exemplary financial planning system. This success was, in part, a result of board development—of us ensuring that the administrative vision of the agency was achieved. Now, I am no longer an auditor who serves on a board. I think of myself as a citizen who is pushing forward excellence in community service. This is very consistent with who I am—it taps into me as a spiritual being who wants to contribute to the improvement of the world.

Consistent board development may well set the tone of change, preparation, and creation within the agency. Fundamental to board development is the formulation of agency vision, outcomes, and performance expectations. These ends themselves can propel the entire agency along the journey of change and creation. Board development can be a rallying call that the entire agency needs to discover the horizon and enrich the journey to this horizon with meaning and inspiration. Indeed, board development can become a part of the agency's spirit.

Constant change, turbulence, and new social needs and expectations stimulate, if not drive, the spirit of the community service agency. Board development signals that the agency cannot stay in one place. It can rest and repair. But it cannot stop the journey unless the choice of the agency is to become less vital, less important, or simply pass on. Most boards and their members will not choose this option. Most board members know from their own organizational experience that right now, and into the future, change will be constant, and organizational environments will be unstable. As leaders of community service agencies, they face the challenge of change. Board development requires the board to anticipate and prepare for this change. That is the principal message of this volume.

REFERENCES

Ackoff, R. L. (1991). *Creating the corporate future: Plan or be planned for.* New York: John Wiley & Sons.

Ackoff, R. L. (1994). *The democratic corporation.* New York: Oxford University Press.

Adams, F. (1998). *Unearthing seeds of fire: The idea of Highlander.* Winston-Salem, NC: Blair.

Adizes, I. (1988). *Corporate lifecycles.* Englewood Cliffs, NJ: Prentice-Hall.

Argyris, C. (1990). *Overcoming organizational defenses: Facilitating organizational learning.* Boston: Allyn & Bacon.

Bass, B. M. (1981). *Stogdill's handbook of leadership: A survey of theory and research.* New York: Free Press.

Bateson, M. (1994). *Peripheral visions: Learning along the way.* New York: HarperCollins.

Behn, R. D. (1991). *Leadership counts: Lessons for public managers.* Cambridge, MA: Harvard University Press.

Belfiore, E., & Bennett, O. (2008). *The social impact of the arts.* Houndmills, England: Palgrave.

Bennis, W. (1989). *Why leaders can't lead.* San Francisco: Jossey-Bass.

Bennis, W. (1993a). *Beyond bureaucracy: Essays on the development and evolution of human organization.* San Francisco: Jossey-Bass.

Bennis, W. (1993b). *An invented life: Reflections on leadership and change.* Reading, MA: Addison Wesley.

Bennis, W., & Nanus, B. (1985). *Leaders: The strategies for taking charge.* New York: Harper & Row.

Bergquist, W. (1993). *The postmodern organization: Mastering the art of irreversible change.* San Francisco: Jossey-Bass.

Bethanis, S. J. (1995). Language as action: Linking metaphors with organization transformation. In S. Chawla & J. Renesch (Eds.), *Learning organizations: Developing tomorrow's workplace* (pp. 185–197). Portland, OR: Productivity Press.

Bettencourt, B. (1996). Grassroots organizations: Recurrent themes and research approaches. *Journal of Social Issues, 52*(1), 207–220.

Block, P. (1993). *Stewardship: Choosing service over self-interest.* San Francisco: Berrett-Koehler.

Bolman, L. G., & Deal, T. E. (2007). *Reframing organizations: Artistry, choice, and leadership*. San Francisco: Jossey-Bass.

Bonner, J. Tyler (1993). *Life cycles: Reflections of an evolutionary biologist*. Princeton, NJ: Princeton University Press.

Bozeman, B. (1987). *All organizations are public*. San Francisco: Jossey-Bass.

Bridges, W. (1992). *The character of organizations: Using Jungian type in organizational development*. Palo Alto, CA: Consulting Psychologists Press.

Brinckerhoff, P. C. (1994). *Mission-based management: Leading your not-for-profit into the 21st century*. Dillon, CO: Alpine Guild.

Brown, J. (1995). Dialogue: Capacities and stories. In S. Chawla & J. Renesch (Eds.), *Learning organizations: Developing tomorrow's workplace* (pp. 153–164). Portland, OR: Productivity Press.

Brudney, J. L., & Murray, V. (1997). Improving nonprofit boards: What works and what doesn't. *Nonprofit World, 15*(3), 11–17.

Buchholz, S., & Roth, T. (1987). *Creating the high-performance team*. New York: Wiley.

Burton, T. T., & Moran, J. W. (1995). *The future focused organization*. Englewood Cliffs, NJ: Prentice Hall.

Campbell, J. (1972). *Myths to live by*. New York: Penguin.

Carlson, R. V. (1996). *Reframing and reform: Perspectives on organization, leadership, and school change*. White Plains, NY: Longman.

Carroll, A. B., & Hall, J. (1987). Strategic management processes for corporate social policy. In W. R. King & D. I. Cleland (Eds.), *Strategic planning and management handbook* (pp. 129–144). New York: Van Nostrand Reinhold.

Carver, J. (1992). The founding parent syndrome: Governing in the CEO's shadow. *Nonprofit World, 10*(3), 14–16.

Carver, J., & Carver, M. (1997). *Reinventing your board: A step-by-step guide to implementing policy governance*. San Francisco: Jossey-Bass.

Chait, R. P., Holland, T. P., & Taylor, B. E. (1993). *The effective board of trustees*. Phoenix, AZ: Oryx.

Chait, R. P., Holland, T. P., & Taylor, B. E. (1996). The new work of the nonprofit board. *Harvard Business Review, 74*, 36–46.

Champagne, A., & Harpham, E. J. (1984). *The attack on the welfare state*. Prospect Heights, IL: Waveland.

Chandler, R. C. (1987). *Civic virtue in the American republic: Essays on moral philosophy and public administration*. Kalamazoo, MI: New Issues Press.

Chappell, T. (1993). *The soul of a business: Managing for profit and the common good*. New York: Bantam.

Charan, R. (1998). *Boards at work: How corporate boards create competitive advantage*. San Francisco: Jossey-Bass.

Clifton, R. L., & Dahms, A. M. (1993). *Grassroots organizations*. Prospect Heights, IL: Waveland.

Coates, J. (1986). *Issues management*. Mt. Airy, MD: Lomond.

Cohen, S., & Brand, R. (1993). *Total quality management in government*. San Francisco: Jossey-Bass.

Coles, R. (1989). *The call of stories: Teaching and the moral imagination.* Boston: Houghton Mifflin.

Coles, R. (1993). *The call of service.* New York: Houghton Mifflin.

Collins, B., & Huge, E. (1993). *Management by policy: How companies focus their total quality efforts to achieve competitive advantage.* Milwaukee, WI: ASQC Quality Press.

Collins, J. C., & Porras, J. I. (1998). Building your company's vision. In *Harvard Business School on change* (pp. 21–54). Boston: Harvard Business School Press.

Creech, B. (1994). *The five pillars of TQM.* New York: Dutton.

Cunningham, I. (1994). *The wisdom of strategic learning.* New York: McGraw-Hill.

Czarniawska, B. (1997). *Narrating the organization: Dramas of institutional identity.* Chicago: University of Chicago Press.

Denhardt, R. B. (1981). *In the shadow of organization.* Lawrence: University Press of Kansas.

Douglas, M. (1998). *Natural symbols: Explorations in cosmology.* New York: Routledge.

Drucker, P. F. (1990). *Managing the nonprofit organization. Principles and practices.* New York: HarperCollins.

Dubois, B. (1993). *Competency-based performance improvement.* Amherst, MA: HRD Press.

Duca, D. J. (1996). *Nonprofit boards: Roles, responsibilities, and performance.* New York: John Wiley & Sons.

Dybwad, G., & Bersani, H. (Eds.). (1996). *New voices: Self advocacy by people with disabilities.* Cambridge, MA: Brookline.

Dykstra, A. (1995). Outcome management: Achieving outcomes for people with disabilities. New Lenox, IL: High Tide Press.

Eadie, D. (1991). Planning and managing strategically. In R. Edwards & J. Yankey (Eds.), *Skills for effective human services management* (pp. 124–136). Silver Spring, MD: National Association of Social Workers.

Eadie, D. (1997). *Changing by design: A practical approach to leading innovation in nonprofit organizations.* San Francisco: Jossey-Bass.

Egan, G. (1985). *Change agent skills in helping and human service settings.* Monterey, CA: Brooks/Cole.

Egan, G. (1993). *Adding value: A systematic guide to business-driven management and leadership.* San Francisco: Jossey-Bass.

Eisner, E. W. (2002). *The arts and the creation of mind.* New Haven, CT: Yale University Press.

Ezell, M. (2001). *Advocacy in the human services.* Belmont, CA: Brooks/Cole.

Falsey, T. (1989). *Corporate philosophies and mission statements.* New York: Quorum.

Fetterman, D. M. (1996). Empowerment evaluation: An introduction to theory and practice. In D. M. Fetterman, S. Kaftarian, & A. Wandersman (Eds.), *Empowerment evaluation: Knowledge and tools for self-assessment and accountability* (pp. 3–46). Thousand Oaks, CA: Sage Publications.

Fomburn, C. J. (1994). *Leading corporate change.* New York: McGraw-Hill.

Fox, C. J., & Miller, H. T. (1995). *Postmodern public administration.* Thousand Oaks, CA: Sage Publications.

Freedman, K. (2003). *Teaching visual culture: Curriculum, aesthetics, and the social life of art*. New York: Teachers College Press.

Gaillard, F. (1996). *If I were a carpenter: Twenty years of Habitat for Humanity*. Winston-Salem, NC: Blair.

Galbraith, J. R., Lawler, E., & Associates. (1993). *Organizing for the future: The new logic for managing complex organizations*. San Francisco: Jossey-Bass.

Gardner, H. (1993). *Creating minds: An anatomy of creativity*. New York: Free Press.

Gardner, H. (1995). *Leading minds: An anatomy of leadership*. New York: Basic Books.

Gardner, J. (1990). *On leadership*. New York: Free Press.

Garr, R. (1995). *Reinvesting in America: The grassroots movements that are feeding the hungry, housing the homeless, and putting Americans back to work*. Reading, MA: Addison-Wesley.

Gastil, J. (1993). *Democracy in small groups: Participation, decision-making, and communication*. Philadelphia: New Society Publishers.

Gauthier, A. (1995). The challenge of stewardship: Building learning organizations in healthcare. In S. Chawla & J. Renesch (Eds.), *Learning organizations: Developing tomorrow's workplace* (pp. 385–401). Portland, OR: Productivity Press.

Gawthrop, L. C. (1984). *Public sector management, systems, and ethics*. Bloomington: Indiana University Press.

Gilbert, N. (1983). *Capitalism and the welfare state: Dilemmas of social benevolence*. New Haven, CT: Yale University Press.

Gillies, J. (1992). *Boardroom renaissance: Power, morality, and performance in the modern corporation*. Whitby, Ontario, Canada: McGraw-Hill Ryerson.

Gilmore, T. (1988). *Making a leadership change*. San Francisco: Jossey-Bass.

Glassman, B. (1998). *Bearing witness: A Zen master's lessons in making peace*. New York: Bell Tower.

Grace, K. Sprinkel. (1997a). *Beyond fund raising: New strategies for nonprofit innovation and investment*. New York: John Wiley & Sons.

Grace, K. Sprinkel. (1997b). *The nonprofit board's role in strategic planning*. Washington, DC: National Center for Nonprofit Boards.

Gray, S. T., & Associates (1998). *Evaluation with power*. San Francisco: Jossey-Bass.

Guarasci, R., & Cornwell, G. H. (1997). *Democratic education in an age of difference: Redefining citizenship in higher education*. San Francisco: Jossey-Bass.

Gummer, B. (1990). *The politics of social administration: Managing organizational politics in social agencies*. Englewood Cliffs, NJ: Prentice Hall.

Gunther, J., & Hawkins, F. (1996). *Total quality management in human service organizations*. New York: Springer.

Hackman, J. R. (1990). *Groups that work (and those that don't): Creating conditions for effective teamwork*. San Francisco: Jossey-Bass.

Hall, J. (1980). *The competence process: Managing for commitment and creativity*. The Woodlands, TX: Teleometrics.

Hall, R. H. (1987). *Organizations: Structures, processes, and outcomes*. Englewood Cliffs, NJ: Prentice-Hall.

Hamel, G., & Prahalad, C. (1994). *Competing for the future*. Boston: Harvard Business School Press.

Hamilton, L., & Tragert, R. (1998). *100 best nonprofits to work for*. New York: Macmillan.

Handy, C. (1989). *The age of unreason*. Boston: Harvard Business School Press.

Handy, C. (1994). *The age of paradox*. Boston: Harvard Business School Press.

Handy, C. (1995). *Beyond certainty*. Boston: Harvard Business School Press.

Hanna, D. P. (1988). *Designing organizations for high performance*. Reading, MA: Addison-Wesley.

Hardy, R. E., & Schwartz, R. (1996). *The self-defeating organization*. Reading, MA: Addison-Wesley.

Harris, M. (1993). Clarifying the board role: A total activities approach. In D. Young, R. Hollister, & V. Hodgkinson (Eds.), *Governing, leading, and managing nonprofit organizations* (pp. 9 25). San Francisco: Jossey Bass.

Hasenfeld, Y. (1983). *Human service organizations*. Englewood Cliffs, NJ: Prentice-Hall.

Hegelsen, S. (1995). *The web of inclusion*. New York: Doubleday.

Henton, D., Melville, J., & Walesh, K. (1997). *Grassroots leaders for a new economy*. San Francisco: Jossey-Bass.

Herman, R. D., & Heimovics, R. D. (1991). *Executive leadership in nonprofit organizations: New strategies for shaping executive–board dynamics*. San Francisco: Jossey-Bass.

Hick, S. F., & McNutt, J. G. (2002). *Advocacy, activism, and the Internet: Community organization and social policy*. Chicago: Lyceum.

Hinings, C. R., & Greenwood, R. (1988). *The dynamics of strategic change*. New York: Blackwell.

Hirschhorn, L., & Associates. (1983). *Cutting back: Retrenchment and redevelopment in human and community services*. San Francisco: Jossey-Bass.

Hodgkinson, V. A., Lyman, R. W., & Associates. (1989). *The future of the nonprofit sector*. San Francisco: Jossey-Bass.

Holland, T. P., Leslie, D., & Holzhalb, C. (1993). Culture and change in nonprofit boards. *Nonprofit Management and Leadership, 4*, 141–151.

Horton, M. (1998). *The long haul: An autobiography*. New York: Teachers College Press.

Horton, M., & Freire, P. (1990). *We make the road by walking: conversations on education and social change* (B. Bell, J. Gaventa, & J. Peters, Eds.). Philadelphia: Temple University Press.

Hosmer, L. T. (1987). A strategic view of leadership. In W. R. King & D. I. Cleland (Eds.), *Strategic planning and management handbook* (pp. 45–59). New York: Van Nostrand Reinhold.

Houle, C. O. (1989). *Governing boards*. San Francisco: Jossey-Bass.

Houle, C. O. (1997). *Governing boards: Their nature and nuture*. San Francisco: Jossey-Bass.

Howe, F. (1997). *The board member's guide to strategic planning*. San Francisco: Jossey-Bass.

Hult, K. M., & Walcott, C. (1990). *Governing public organizations: Politics, structures, and institutional design*. Pacific Grove, CA: Brooks/Cole.

Jackson, P. (1995). *Sacred hoops: Spiritual lessons of a hardwood warrior.* New York: Hyperion.

Jacobs, R. W. (1994). *Real time strategic change.* San Francisco: Berrett-Koehler.

Jaques, E., & Clement, S. D. (1991). *Executive leadership: A practical guide to managing complexity.* London: Blackwell.

Joyce, W., Nohria, N., & Roberson, B. (2003). *What really works: The 4+2 formula for sustained business success.* New York: HarperBusiness.

Judson, A. S. (1990). *Making strategy happen: Transforming plans into reality.* Cambridge, MA: Blackwell.

Juran, J. M. (1992). *Juran on quality by design.* New York: Free Press.

Katzenbach, J. R., & Smith, D. K. (1993). *The wisdom of teams: Creating the high performance organization.* Boston: Harvard Business School Press.

Kaufman, H. G. (1990). Management techniques for maintaining a competent professional work force. In S. L. Willis & S. S. Dubin (Eds.), *Maintaining professional competence: Approaches to career enhancement, vitality, and success throughout a work life* (pp. 249–261). San Francisco: Jossey-Bass.

Kennedy, L. W. (1991). *Quality management in the nonprofit world.* San Francisco: Jossey-Bass.

Kets de Vries, M. (1989). *Prisoners of leadership.* New York: Wiley.

Kiefer, C. F., & Senge, P. M. (1984). Metanoic organizations. In J. D. Adams (Ed.), *Transforming work* (pp. 69–84). Alexandria, VA: Miles River Press.

King, A. (1980). Self-fulfilling prophecies in training the hard core: Supervisors' expectations and the underprivileged workers' performance. In J. A. Shtogren (Ed.), *Models for management: The structure of competence* (pp. 28–38). The Woodslands, TX: Teleometrics.

Kline, P., & Saunders, B. (1993). *Ten steps to a learning organization.* Arlington, VA: Great Ocean.

Knauft, E., Berger, R., & Gray, S. (1991). *Profiles of excellence: Achieving success in the nonprofit sector.* San Francisco: Jossey-Bass.

Knowles, M. (1990). *The adult learner.* Houston: Gulf Publishing.

Koestenbaum, P. (1991). *Leadership: The inner side of greatness.* San Francisco: Jossey-Bass.

Kofman, F., & Senge, P. (1995). Communities of commitment: The heart of learning organizations. In S. Chawla & J. Renesch (Eds.), *Learning organizations: Developing tomorrow's workplace.* (pp. 15–43). Portland, OR: Productivity Press.

Kotter, J. P. (1998). Leading change: Why transformation efforts fail. In *Harvard Business Review on change* (1–20). Boston: Harvard Business School Press.

Kouzes, J. M., & Posner, B. Z. (1987). *The leadership challenge.* San Francisco: Jossey-Bass.

Kramer, R. M. (1981). *Voluntary agencies in the welfare state.* Berkeley: University of California Press.

LaMarsh, J. (1995). *Changing the way we change: Gaining control of major operational change.* Reading, MA: Addison-Wesley.

Lappe, F., & Du Bois, P. (1994). *The quickening of America: Rebuilding our nation, remaking our lives.* San Francisco: Jossey-Bass.

Larson, C. E., & LaFasto, F. M. J. (1989). *Teamwork: What must go right/what can go wrong.* Thousand Oaks, CA: Sage Publications.

Lauffer, A. (1993). *Strategic marketing for not-for-profit organizations: Program and resource development.* New York: Free Press.

Lawrence, P. R., & Lorsch, J. W. (1986). *Organization and environment.* Boston: Harvard Business School Press.

Lee, J. A. (1989). *Group work with the poor and oppressed.* Binghamton, NY: Haworth Press.

Levitt, T. (2008). *Marketing myopia.* Boston: Harvard Business Press.

Lewis, E. (1980). *Public entrepreneurship: Toward a theory of bureaucratic political power.* Bloomington: Indiana University Press.

Lewis, E. (1991). Social change and citizen action: A philosophical exploration for modern social group work. In A. Vinik & M. Levin (Eds.), *Social action in group work* (pp. 23–34). New York: Haworth.

Light, P. C. (1998). *Sustaining innovation: Creating nonprofit and government organizations that innovate naturally.* San Francisco: Jossey-Bass.

Livingston, J. (1980). Pygmalion in management. In J. A. Shtogren (Ed.), *Models for management: The structure of competence* (pp. 39–53). The Woodlands, TX: Teleometrics.

Markowitz, G., & Rosner, D. (1996). *Children, race, and power: Kenneth and Mamie Clark's Northside Center.* Charlottesville: University of Virginia Press.

Maslow, A. H. (1998). *Maslow on management.* New York: John Wiley & Sons.

McCall, M. W., Lombardo, M. M., & Morrison, A. M. (1988). *The lessons of experience: How successful executives develop on the job.* Lexington, MA: Lexington Books.

McInerney, F., & White, S. (1995). *The total quality corporation.* New York: Truman Talley Books.

McLagan, P., & Nel, C. (1997). *The age of participation: New governance for the workplace and the world.* San Francisco: Berrett-Koehler.

McMaster, M. D. (1996). *The intelligence advantage: Organizing for complexity.* Boston: Butterworth-Heineman.

McNiff, S. (1992). *Art as medicine.* Boston: Shambhala.

Meier, D. (1995). *The power of their ideas: Lessons for America from a small school in Harlem.* Boston: Beacon Press.

Middleton, M. (1987). Nonprofit boards of directors: Beyond the governance function. In W. Powell (Ed.). *The nonprofit sector research handbook.* New Haven, CT: Yale University Press.

Miller, J. (1988). New management concepts in family and children's services. In P. Keys, & L. Ginsberg (Ed.), *New management in human services* (pp. 212–234). Silver Spring, MD: National Association of Social Workers.

Mintzberg, H. (1983). *Power in and around organizations.* Englewood Cliffs, NJ: Prentice-Hall.

Misumi, J. (1985). *The behavioral science of leadership.* Ann Arbor: University of Michigan Press.

Mitroff, I. I. (1989). *Stakeholders of the organizational mind.* San Francisco: Jossey-Bass.

Morris, L. E. (1995). Development strategies for the knowledge era. In S. Chawla & J. Renesch (Eds.), *Learning organizations: Developing tomorrow's workplace* (pp. 323–335). Portland, OR: Productivity Press.

Moxley, D., & Jacobs, D. (1992). Building a clubhouse from the ground up. *Psychosocial Rehabilitation Journal, 16*, 125–139.

Nanus, B. (1992). *Visionary leadership*. San Francisco: Jossey-Bass.

Nelson, L., & Burns, F. (1984). High performance programming: A framework for transforming organizations. In J. D. Adams (Ed.), *Transforming work* (pp. 226–243). Alexandria, VA: Miles River Press.

Neugeboren, B. (1991). *Organization, policy, and practice in the human services*. White Plains, NY: Longman.

Nonaka, I. (1998). The knowledge creating company. In *Harvard Business Review on knowledge management* (pp. 21–46). Boston: Harvard Business School Press.

Nonaka, I., & Takeuchi, H. (1995). *The knowledge-creating company*. New York: Oxford University Press.

Olsen, J. B., & Eadie, D. C. (1982). *The game plan: Governance with foresight*. Washington, DC: Council of State Planning Agencies.

O'Neill, M. (1989). *The third America: The emergence of the nonprofit sector in the United States*. San Francisco: Jossey-Bass.

Osborne, D. (1988). *Laboratories of democracy*. Boston: Harvard Business School Press.

Osborne, D., & Gaebler, T. (1992). *Reinventing government*. Reading, MA: Addison-Wesley.

Ostrom, E., & Davis, G. (1993). Nonprofit organizations as alternatives and complements in a mixed economy. In D. C. Hammack & D. R. Young (Eds.), *Nonprofit organizations in a market economy* (pp. 23–56). San Francisco: Jossey-Bass.

O'Toole, J. (1995). *Leading change*. San Francisco: Jossey-Bass.

Pascarella, P., & Frohman, M. L. (1989). *The purpose-driven organization*. San Francisco: Jossey-Bass.

Perlmutter, F. (Ed.). (1984). *Human services at risk*. Lexington, MA: Lexington Books.

Perlmutter, F. (1988). *Alternative social agencies: Administrative strategies*. Binghamton, NY: Haworth Press.

Pfeffer, J. (1992). *Managing with power: Politics and influence in organizations*. Boston: Harvard Business School Press.

Raskin, M. G. (1986). *The common good: Its politics, policies, and philosophy*. New York: Routledge.

Riesenberg, P. (1992). *Citizenship in the western tradition*. Chapel Hill: University of North Carolina Press.

Rifkin, J. (1995). *The end of work: The decline of the global labor force and the dawn of the post-market era*. New York: Putnam.

Rosenthal, S., & Young, J. (1980). The governance of the social services. In F. Perlmutter & S. Slavin (Eds.), *Leadership in social administration* (pp. 152–167). Philadelphia: Temple University Press.

Rummler, G., & Brache, A. (1991). *Improving performance*. San Francisco: Jossey-Bass.

Ryan, S. (1995). Learning communities: An alternative to the "expert model." In S. Chawla & J. Renesch (Eds.), *Learning organizations: Developing tomorrow's workplace* (pp. 279–291). Portland, OR: Productivity Press.

Salamon, L. M., & Anheier, H. K. (1996). *The emerging nonprofit sector*. New York: Manchester University Press.

SANNO. (1992). *Vision management: Translating strategy into action*. Cambridge, MA: Productivity Press.

Sashkin, M., & Kiser, K. J. (1993). *Putting total quality management to work*. San Francisco: Berrett-Koehler.

Schein, E. H. (1983). The role of the founder in creating organizational culture. *Organizational Dynamics, 12*(1), 13–28.

Schein, E. H. (1992). *Organizational culture and leadership* (2nd ed.). San Francisco: Jossey-Bass.

Schmidt, W. H., & Finnigan, J. P. (1992). *The race without a finish line*. San Francisco: Jossey-Bass.

Schneider, R. L., & Lester, L. (2001). *Social work advocacy*. Belmont, CA: Brooks/Cole.

Schon, D. A. (1971). *Beyond the stable state*. New York: Norton.

Schwartz, D. B. (1997). *Who cares: Rediscovering community*. New York: Westview.

Schwartz, P. (1991). *The art of the long view*. New York: Doubleday.

Scott, R. (1994). Institutional analysis: Variance and process theory approaches. In W. R. Scott & J. W. Meyer (Eds.), *Institutional environments and organizations: Structural complexity and individualism* (pp. 81–99). Thousand Oaks, CA: Sage Publications.

Scott, W. R. (1987). *Organizations: Rational, natural, and open systems*. Englewood Cliffs, NJ: Prentice-Hall.

Selznick, P. (1957). *Leadership in administration: A sociological interpretation*. Berkeley: University of California Press.

Selznick, P. (1992). *The moral commonwealth: Social theory and the promise of community*. Berkeley: University of California Press.

Senge, P. (1990). *The fifth discipline: The art and practice of the learning organization*. New York: Doubleday.

Senge, P., Laur, J., Schley, S., & Smith, B. (2006). *Learning for sustainability*. Cambridge, MA: SoL.

Senge, P., Smith, B., Kruschwitz, N., Laur, J., & Schley, S. (2008). *The necessary revolution*. New York: Doubleday.

Shanklin, W. L., & Ryans, J. K. (1985). *Thinking strategically: Planning for your company's future*. New York: Random House.

Shaw, R. (1996). *The activitist's handbook*. Berkley: University of California Press.

Silberberg, M. (1997). The evolution of assistance to grassroots organizations: The impact of linkage. *Public Productivity and Management Review, 20*, 432–445.

Sklar, H. (1995). *Chaos or community: Seeking solutions not scapegoats for bad economics*. Boston: South End Press.

Smith, D. (1997). The international history of grassroots associations. *International Journal of Comparative Sociology, 38*, 189–216.

Smith, S., & Lipsky, M. (1993). *Nonprofits for hire: The welfare state in the age of contracting*. Cambridge, MA: Harvard University Press.

Sparrow, J. (1998). *Knowledge in organizations: Access to thinking at work.* Thousand Oaks, CA: Sage Publications.

Stacey, R. (1996). *Complexity and creativity in organizations.* San Francisco: Berrett-Koehler.

Stoesz, E., & Raber, C. (1997). *Doing good better! How to be an effective board member of a nonprofit organization.* Intercourse, PA: Good Books.

Stonich, P. J. (1982). *Implementing strategy: Making strategy happen.* Cambridge, MA: Ballinger.

Stringer, E. T. (1996). *Action research: A handbook for practitioners.* Thousand Oaks, CA: Sage Publications.

Taylor, B. (1987). An overview of strategic planning styles. In W. R. King & D. I. Cleland (Eds.), *Strategic planning and management handbook* (pp. 21–35). New York: Van Nostrand Reinhold.

Taylor, S. J., Bogdan, R., & Racino, J. A. (1991). *Life in the community: Case studies of organizations supporting people with disabilities.* Baltimore: Paul H. Brookes.

Thompson, J. W. (1995). The renaissance of learning in business. In S. Chawla & J. Renesch (Eds.), *Learning organizations: Developing tomorrow's workplace.* (pp. 85–99). Portland, OR: Productivity Press.

Tolbert, P. S., & Zucker, L. G. (1996). The institutionalization of institutional theory. In S. Clegg, C. Hardy, & W. Nord (Eds.), *Handbook of organization studies* (pp. 175–190). Thousand Oaks, CA: Sage Publications.

Turnbull, W. (1995). *Lift every voice.* New York: Hyperion.

Tweed, S. C. (1990). *Strategic focus.* Hollywood, FL: Fell.

Vaill, P. B. (1989). *Managing as a performing art: New ideas for a world of chaotic change.* San Francisco: Jossey-Bass.

Vella, J. (1994). *Learning to listen, learning to teach: The power of dialogue in educating adults.* San Francisco: Jossey-Bass.

Ward, R. D. (1997). *21st century corporate board.* New York: John Wiley & Sons.

Wareham, J. (1991). *The anatomy of a great executive.* New York: HarperBusiness.

Waterman, R. H. (1990). *Adhocracy: The power to change.* New York: W. W. Norton.

Weick, K. E. (1995). *Sensemaking in organizations.* Thousand Oaks, CA: Sage Publications.

Weisbord, M. R. (1987). *Productive workplaces: Organizing and managing for dignity, meaning, and community.* San Francisco: Jossey-Bass.

Weissman, H. (1973). *Overcoming mismanagement in the human service professions.* San Francisco: Jossey-Bass.

Wenger, E., McDermott, R., & Snyder, W. M. (2002). *Cultivating communities of practice.* Boston: HBS Press.

West, A. (1992). *Innovation strategy.* New York: Prentice Hall.

Wheatley, M. J. (1992). *Leadership and the new science: Learning about organization from an orderly universe.* San Francisco: Berrett-Koehler.

Whitmont, E. C. (1978). *The symbolic quest.* Princeton, NJ: Princeton University Press.

Wilkins, A. (1989). *Developing corporate character.* San Francisco: Jossey-Bass.

Wilson, J. Q. (1995). *On character.* Washington, DC: AEI Press.

Yukl, G. A. (1989). *Leadership in organizations.* Englewood Cliffs, NJ: Prentice-Hall.

Zander, A. (1985). *The purposes of groups and organizations.* San Francisco: Jossey-Bass.

Zander, A. (1993). *Making boards more effective.* San Francisco: Jossey-Bass.

Index

In this index, *f* stands for figure and *t* stands for table.